ALASKA'S MUSHROOMS

A Wide-Ranging Guide

GARY A. LAURSEN
NEIL McARTHUR

D1518467

ALASKA
NORTHWEST
BOOKS®

Text © 1994, 2016 by Harriette Parker, Gary A. Laursen,
    and Neil McArthur
Photos © 1994, 2016 by Gary A. Laursen and Neil McArthur
    except as noted on p. 221

Library of Congress Cataloging-in-Publication Data

Names: Laursen, Gary A., author. | McArthur, C. Neil, author.
Title: Alaska's mushrooms : a wide-ranging guide / Gary A. Laursen,
    C. Neil McArthur.
Description: Portland, OR : Alaska Northwest Books, [2016] |
    Includes bibliographical references and index.
Identifiers: LCCN 2016006545 (print) | LCCN 2016007330 (e-book)
    | ISBN 9781943328499 (pbk.) | ISBN 9781943328765 (hardbound)
Subjects: LCSH: Mushrooms—Alaska—Identification. |
    Mushrooms—Alaska—Pictorial works.
Classification: LCC QK605.5.A4 L38 2016 (print) | LCC
QK605.5.A4 (ebook) |
    DDC 579.609798—dc23
LC record available at http://lccn.loc.gov/2016006545

Front cover photos: Gary A. Laursen
Back cover illustrations: Maggie Hallam

Editor: Jennifer Newens
Designer: Vicki Knapton
Illustrator: Maggie Hallam
Map: Marge Mueller and Vicki Knapton

Alaska Northwest Books®
An imprint of

GRAPHIC ARTS
BOOKS®
P.O. Box 56118
Portland, OR 97238-6118
(503) 254-5591
www.graphicartsbooks.com

Printed in the United States of America

CONTENTS

MUSHROOM DESCRIPTIONS

HYMENOMYCETE BASIDIOMYCOTA: Organized Hymenium Present

A NOTE OF CAUTION

We take mushroom poisoning seriously and want you to do the same; hence, we have included in this edition a new section covering mushroom toxin groups. It's essential that you do not consume any mushroom without being certain of its identity. If you are unsure, ask a professional mycologist or someone steeped in the art of collecting and eating wild mushrooms. But the caveat still remains: if you've never eaten it, but are sure others do with no ill effect, always begin by eating the mushroom in small amounts and be sure to cook the mushroom well before consuming it, as some toxins are destroyed by heat. That being said, some edible mushrooms can still make people sick if they have an allergic reaction to a component of the mushroom's makeup. It is always better to err on the side of caution. Mushroom authorities recommend that you do not consume alcoholic beverages before, during, or after a meal of mushrooms that you have never tried before. Alcohol acts as an extractor of ipecac-like substances in some fungi, thus having the effect of unwitting gastric evacuation! When you are eating new mushrooms, introduce them one variety at a time.

This symbol is shown when the species has been reported to be fatal or very severely toxic if eaten. Absence of this symbol does NOT mean the mushroom is safe to eat.

DEDICATION

We dedicate this revised edition to two entities, Harriette Parker, in keeping with her vision and legacy, and to you, the users, who have asked repeatedly that we share this information with you, as you have shared with us a wealth of information on Alaska mushrooms we might not have encountered otherwise. Your enthusiasm further drives our work.

ACKNOWLEDGMENTS

In this edition we acknowledge many National Park Service funding sources and grants that supported field and laboratory work and bibliographic resources used in constructing our own compendium on the higher fungi of Alaska. We are particularly indebted to Ms. Maggie Hallam, talented freelance artist for her realistic line drawings; and to the contributors of jpeg images, other than the authors, that were used from image collections of Jozsef Geml, two figures, and one figure each from Ana Aguilar-Islas, Neil Brown, Lisa Jodwalis, Angela Richardson, and Mr. Rogers; and the ever-helpful, patient staff at Alaska Northwest Books: Doug Pfeiffer, Jennifer Newens, Kathy Howard, Vicki Knapton, and Angie Zbornik.

HOW TO USE THIS COMPENDIUM ON ALASKA'S MUSHROOMS

The authors, first and foremost, hope you glean satisfaction in learning more about the mushrooms that are all around us while using guided practice in learning to recognize some of the more common mushrooms in Alaska. We challenge you to visit often Alaska's natural beauty in the forests, riparian stream environs, sand dunes, marshes, and fields found throughout its six large physiographic regions (Fig. 1), every one of which is the size of many "lower 48" states.

We want you to become familiar with the often bizarre and unfamiliar groups into which mushrooms are placed (e.g.,

Agaric, Bolete, Tooth, Polypore, Puffball fungi, etc.). Once you learn just a few of these common named groups, your hunting success will escalate. Your knowledge base will most likely build to include some scientific names of mushrooms to which you've matched your mushroom using our 155 plates (containing 384 figures), or to the 114 fully described and photographed species (enhanced by 125 figures, with 235 additional species noted in our species descriptions); hence, a treatment that presents 349 mushroom species to our readers.

A natural progression is that you will then become familiar with and learn some of the names of "Mushroom Phyla" (i.e., Basidiomycota and Ascomycota, etc.), the four principal "Roles Played by Mushrooms" (saprophytes, parasites, mycorrhizae, and lichens) and how to "Identify Wild Strangers." Beginning this process may ultimately develop into a life-long endeavor and "love affair" with the familiarization of myriad "Mushroom Groups," their scientific names, which often "describe" some important aspect of the mushroom, and about the morphology of "Spore-Producing Surfaces," to say nothing of the "morphology" of mushrooms and all of their many parts. The "Use of Common Names" is not preferred among mycologists, but we know it is for those just beginning to learn about the fascinating world of fungi so we herein present common names along with scientific names.

We present a listing of "Species Included" for the 114 mushrooms herein and then share with you the processes of "Describing and Labeling Treasured Finds," how to make valuable "Fungal Collecting Labels," and even how to critically write "Formal Fungal Descriptions." We share with you the art of "Hunting Mushrooms in the Wild," which provides you with a list of select "tools" to use and then how to further identify them by making "Mushroom Spore Prints," which to the artistically inclined, may conjure up hosts of ideas for make "greeting cards, collages, and decorative art hangings."

What brings many of us to "study" mushrooms is their culinary potential; hence, we share with you the art of "Drying and Preserving Fungi," and how to enjoy "Safe Shrooming" while "Collecting with Care." We even anticipate your "Frequently Asked Questions" and attempt to answer them, but each question will lead to many more. It is then that we notice that you're "hooked" into this amazing journey to learn more about saprophyte, parasite, mycorrhizal, and lichenized mushrooms. It is at this juncture we feel you also need to know the downside of mycophagy so we take you on a walk through the seven "Mushroom Toxin Classifications." Terms and their definitions unfamiliar to you can be found in our "Pictorial Glossary of Terms" of 257 figures or our "Glossary of Terms" with its 368 entries.

Eating edible varieties is an upside to all of this study, too, but we feel it important to know how one would go about "Preparing Wild Mushrooms for Use."

There are several excellent books on preparing mushrooms for your table in which many excellent recipes are shared. Go to the Internet and search "Books on eating mushrooms" and a host of suggested sources will pop up. There are also many books on mushroom identification, and for almost any region of the country you might want to investigate. We identify 156 of these "Mushroom Field and Reference Guides" and other cited works.

Now that you have the basic tools for a meaningful introduction to the wonderful world of mushrooms, go at it with the anticipation we all once felt in the Easter egg hunts of our youth!

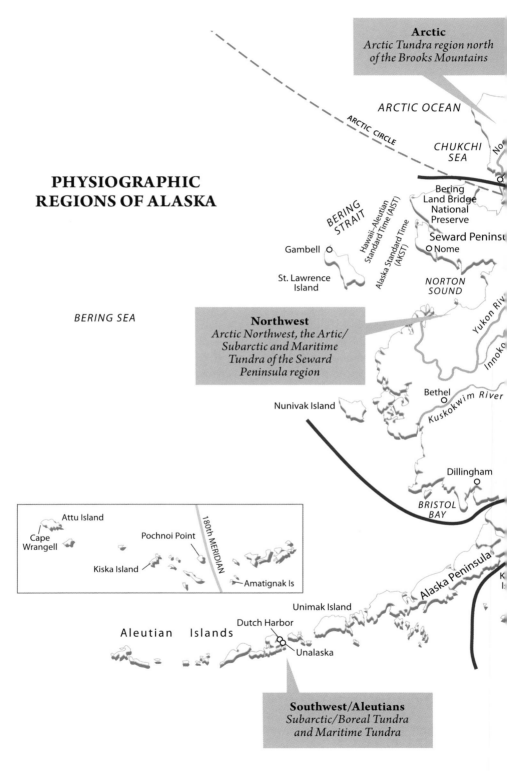

PHYSIOGRAPHIC REGIONS OF ALASKA

Arctic
Arctic Tundra region north of the Brooks Mountains

ARCTIC OCEAN

ARCTIC CIRCLE

CHUKCHI SEA

No

Bering Land Bridge National Preserve

BERING STRAIT

Hawaii-Aleutian Standard Time (AlST)

Alaska Standard Time (AKST)

Gambell O

Seward Peninsu

O Nome

St. Lawrence Island

NORTON SOUND

BERING SEA

Yukon Riv

Innoko

Northwest
Arctic Northwest, the Artic/ Subarctic and Maritime Tundra of the Seward Peninsula region

Bethel O

Kuskokwim River

Nunivak Island

Dillingham O

BRISTOL BAY

Attu Island

Cape Wrangell

Pochnoi Point

180th MERIDIAN

Kiska Island

Amatignak Is

Unimak Island

Alaska Peninsula

K I

Dutch Harbor

Aleutian   Islands

Unalaska

Southwest/Aleutians
Subarctic/Boreal Tundra and Maritime Tundra

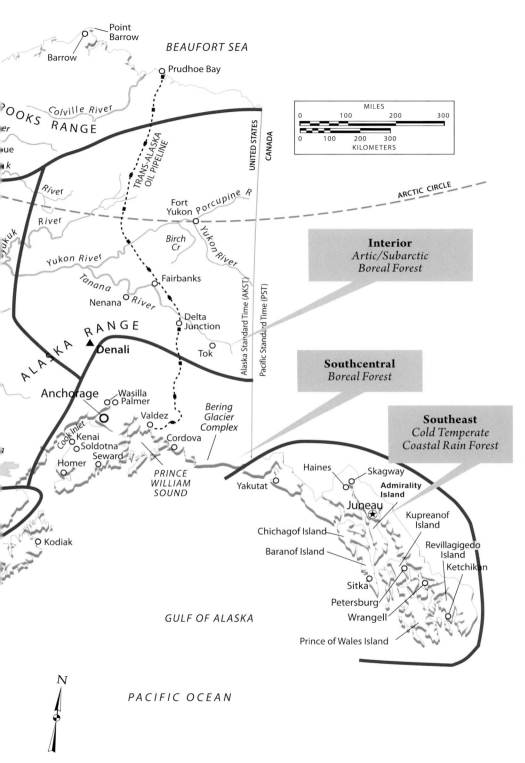

Point
Barrow

BEAUFORT SEA

Barrow

Prudhoe Bay

Colville River

OOKS RANGE

er

ue

k

River

TRANS-ALASKA
OIL PIPELINE

UNITED STATES

CANADA

MILES

| 0 | 100 | 200 | 300 |

| 0 | 100 | 200 | 300 |

KILOMETERS

ARCTIC CIRCLE

River

Fort
Yukon

Porcupine R

yuk

Birch
Cr

Yukon River

Yukon River

Interior
*Artic/Subarctic
Boreal Forest*

Yukon River

Tanana

Fairbanks

River

Nenana

Alaska Standard Time (AKST)

Pacific Standard Time (PST)

ALASKA RANGE

Delta
Junction

▲ Denali

Tok

Southcentral
Boreal Forest

Anchorage

Wasilla
Palmer

Bering
Glacier
Complex

Southeast
*Cold Temperate
Coastal Rain Forest*

Valdez

Cook Inlet

Kenai

Cordova

Soldotna

Seward

Homer

PRINCE
WILLIAM
SOUND

Haines

Skagway

Yakutat

Admiralty
Island

Juneau
⭐

Kupreanof
Island

Kodiak

Chichagof Island

Revillagigedo
Island

Baranof Island

Ketchikan

Sitka

Petersburg

GULF OF ALASKA

Wrangell

Prince of Wales Island

N

PACIFIC OCEAN

MAP   9

Meet the Mushroom

Mushrooms are fungi and there are about 70,000 species worldwide. They persist in myriad forms, sizes, shapes, colors, and often have unique odors, tastes, consistencies, and form interesting relationships with all sorts of organisms, including you! Mushroom is a general term, most often referring to fleshy macrofungi, some being tough, woody, corky, and those you can see with an unaided eye. However, the identification of mushrooms in the field is often greatly enhanced with the 10X loupe, or hand lens, so often worn around the neck. Loupes also come in 5X, 15X, and 20X—even 30X magnification sizes.

Mushroom Phyla

Macrofungi, the mushrooms, primarily represent the latter two of five phyla of fungi; the Chytridiomycota, Zygomycota, Glomeromycota, Ascomycota, and Basidiomycota. So it is that when you pick up a mushroom, you most likely have either a member of the Phylum Ascomycota (the "sac" fungi—because their spores are produced in sacs called asci) or Basidiomycota (the "club" fungi—because their spores are produced on club-shaped basidia).

This presentation deals only with two of the five phyla and one "form Phylum," the Deuteromycota, or sexless fungi.

The Ascomycota constitute almost 75 percent of all fungi, many of which are microfungi, as most folks just don't note them. Ascomycota forms have interesting names, like:

- Dead Man's Fingers
- Disc, Cup or Sac Fungi
- Earth Tongues
- Keratinophiles
- Lichens
- Morels (true and false)
- Powdery Mildews
- Tar Spots
- Truffles (true)

Basidiomycota also have some interesting names, like:
- Agarics (gilled fungi)
- Bird's Nest
- Boletes
- Chanterelles
- Corals
- Earthstars
- Jellies
- Polypores (Bracket, Conch, or Shelf Fungi)
- Puffballs

- Resupinates (form-fitted to their substrates, such as under logs)
- Rusts
- Smuts
- Stinkhorns
- Thelephores
- Tooth
- Truffles (false)

Other macro-mushroom fungi are placed into unique groups with names like:
- Imperfect (sexless fungi often placed into a Form Phylum, the "Deuteromycota")
- Hallucinogens (shrooms)
- Bioluminescent Forms; yes, some forms actually glow in the dark!

Roles Played by Mushrooms

All of these interesting mushroom forms play serious roles in Alaskan micro- and macro-environments. Typically, there are four roles played by fungi, each with a preferred source of absorbed nourishment:
- Those that decompose dead animal and plant tissues (**saprophytes**);
- Those that live on, and generally harm an animal or plant host (**parasites**);
- Those that form comprehensive and valuable, but symbiotic relationships between fungi and plant roots (**mycorrhizae**); and
- Those that form symbioses with green and blue-green algae (**lichens**). (Yes, lichens are fungi and all of which belong to the Ascomycota are called ascolichens. Only a very few species of Basidiomycota form basidiolichens.)

SAPROPHYTES: Live on dead animal and senesced plant tissues

a. Bryicolous/muscicolous .... on bryophytes (mosses and liverworts)
b. Carbonicolous/ pyrophilous........................ (fire loving) on campfire sites and burns
c. Coprophilous .... (animal dung loving)
d. Insectivorous .... on/in insects, mostly dead
e. Keratinophilous................... (on skin, bone, feather, or nail)
f. Lichenicolous ....on lichens (ascolichens)
g. Lignicolous............. on dead/ dying wood
h. Siliceous................ on rocks, glass
i. Terricolous/geophilous .... on soil, ground/earth

PARASITES: live on living animal and plant tissues as epi- and endophytes
a. Antagonists............ capturing and endosymbiotic
b. Interfungal .... necro- and biotrophic (lichenicolous)

MYCORRHIZAE: mutualistic symbioses between fungi and plant roots
a. Endomycorrhizae (within/ inside—internal hyphae)
  1. Vescicular-Arbuscular (VAM) or Sclerotinoid
  2. Orchid
  3. Ericoid
b. Ectendomycorrhizae (thin external mantle and internal hyphae)
  1. Monotropoid
  2. Arbutoid
  3. Pyroloid
c. Ectomycorrhizae (thick mantle, external hyphae with internal Hartig nets)

1. Gymnospermae (cone-bearing naked seed evergreens)
2. Angiospermae (flowering enclosed seed [ovary] plants)

LICHENS: fungus-alga associations
a. Ascolichens
   i. Squamulous.................... small crusty-leafy and with upright podetia....(stalk-like growths)
   ii. Crustose .... crusts on rock, wood, bark, etc.
   iii. Foliose................. leaflike, flattened, often expansive
   iv. Fruticose........... fruit tree-like, much branched
b. Basidiolichens
   i. Agarics .... those lichen fruit bodies with gills
   ii. Corals .... single clubbed coral-like fruit bodies

So it is that Alaska's mushrooms are an endless source of wonder, beauty, and nourishment. Our guide introduces you to some 114 species of mushroom fungi commonly seen in Alaska and intriguing enough to make us wonder, "What mushroom is that?"

Mushrooms are actually the fruit bodies (not a fruit that bears seeds) of fungi, the sexual component that produces and releases millions of microscopic spores that serve to reproduce fungi. Vectored by wind and animals, fungal spores germinate if they land on suitable substrates in appropriate habitats, and produce a mass of microscopic hyphal strands that form a mycelium, the vegetative assimilating body of the fungus.

Fungi can't harness sunshine to make their own food as plants do, or move about to graze or capture food as animals can. They may use light, however, to incite the fruit body phase of the fungus. Instead, mycelia absorb nutrients from externally digesting its surroundings. When conditions become favorable, mycelia form initials, embryonic mushrooms that swell with the absorption of water, into "buttons" and develop further into the mushrooms that are the subject of this book. From these mushrooms, another generation, a fruit body that produces millions of spores for forcible release, continues the mushroom's life cycle.

You can get to know mushrooms personally by becoming familiar with their names and habits (their forms or shapes). It takes only a few simple tools, the help of an up-to-date regional field guide, a knowledgeable local mentor or two, and patience. You can often find these resources by searching out the nearest mycological society and attending their outings and workshops.

Identifying Wild Strangers

Alaska is vast and all too often uncharted when it comes to mushroom collecting in any one of its six geographic provinces; Arctic, Interior, Northwest, Southcentral, Southwestern/Aleutian, and Southeast. There are literally thousands of mushroom species in Alaska and few mushroom collectors. This book contains only a sampling of some of our best-known species and easily identified forms found in more populated areas. Anyone can use this book to become familiar with some of the mushrooms most often encountered and the techniques used to identify them.

From May through September, and even into October in a good year, you will encounter many intriguing mushrooms in Alaska. If you find a mushroom you wish to identify, gather both mature and immature specimens. Note their overall appearance, color, shape, size, and particularly the mushroom's spore-bearing surface, the hymenophore composed of or housing gills, pores, or teeth, usually found on the undersides of caps or on upright coral-like fingers. Use a mature cap to prepare a spore print, an important clue to mushroom identity (see page 24 for more details on spore prints).

Mushroom Groups, Their Common Names, and Spore-Producing Surfaces

Once you've gathered your samples, read the brief introduction to each of the seventeen mushroom groups and find the category that most closely matches your mushroom. You can also browse the photos and fungal descriptions on pages 33-163.

If the mushroom you have found has all the features of one described above, you are probably close to identifying it. We recommend consulting another field guide, several of which are listed on pages 167-174 to help you further identify your mushroom. Any mushroom that you've never seen before and that you intend to eat should be identified in more than one current field guide and verified by a local knowledgeable expert. Only then should you carefully, but fully cook and then consume the mushroom, proceeding with extreme caution.

Herein lies an import caveat. No field guide to mushrooms can be all-inclusive. Ours is intended to be an introduction to the mushrooms that can be found in Alaska, but is not comprehensive. This guide presents 155 plates

containing 384 figures, of which 114 are described and photographed species in 125 figures with another 235 additional species noted in the species discussions for a total of 349 species considered.

Use of Common Names

For the record, most mycologists dislike using common names of mushrooms even though they may know them. This is perhaps perceived to be a weakness in not knowing a Latin binomial of a fungus, or a sense of clearly separating the professionalism they wish to portray in contrast to a more relaxed approach to studying and working with fungi. We have included common names here because this work is written primarily with you, the enthusiastic beginner, in mind. We have pulled our common names from two primary texts, Arora (1986) and Lincoff and Nehring (1984). One thing to note is that a common name to a fungus in the West may not be the common name used for the same or very similar fungus in the East. In essence, common names may end up being confusing, or too similar so as to cause confusion and mycologists emphasize clarity rather than promulgate confusion—or add to it. Take, for example, the name, "Fuzzy False Truffle" for *Geopora cooperi*, a true truffle in reality, or the "Scum Lover" for *Multiclavula mucida,* which I've only seen on relatively dry ground. This is why, in some cases, we show two or three common names for the same fungus. Feel free to choose whatever naming convention you wish to use. It's your day in the field and our goal is that you feel inspired, inquisitive, and empowered, whether you're learning something new or merely refreshing past associations with the world of fungi.

Mushroom Groups, Their Common Names, and Spore-Producing Surfaces

Mushroom Group	Common Name	Hymenium Organization
Agaricoid fungi	Gilled	Lamellae, or "gills"
Boletinoid fungi	Boletes, fleshy pored	Spongy tubes with pores that peel off as a thick mass
Polyporoid fungi	Pored or tubed woody, corky to leathery	Crusts, corky brackets, tubed or pored shelves
Hydnoid fungi	Spine or hedgehog	Pendent teeth under cap
Coralloid fungi	Club	Single to branching, upright clubs
Cantharelloid fungi	Chanterelle	Blunt ridges looking like precursors to gills
Thelephoroid fungi	Vaselike	Smooth, bumpy, or winkled surfaces
Gasteroid fungi	Stomach	Having a dry, powdery, or slimy gleba at maturity
Gasteroid fungi	Puffballs	"Stomach" balls of dry brownish powder when mature
Gasteroid fungi	Bird's nests	Small flattened "eggs" in a vaselike, sessile "bird's nest" on woody substrates
Rust fungi	Plant leaf or needle rust	Brightly colored (yellow-orange) pustules
Jelly fungi	Jelly	Wood-inhabiting, brightly to multicolored gelatinous masses
Cup fungi	Sac	Inner surfaces of tan to brightly colored "cups" that occur close to the substrate
Earth tongues	Sac	Little "spades" sticking up and out of the mosses
Truffles False True	Club and Sac Basidiomycetes Ascomycetes	Underground (hypogeous) to erumpent Club fungi or Sac fungi
Lichens	Lichenized Sac and Club fungi	Fungal (mycobiont)—Algae (photo- or phycobiont) relationships
Ascolichen Sac fungi	Crustose Foliose Fruticose Squamulose	Oddly colored black, orange, yellow to bluish-green crusts Leaflike Tree-like forms attached to a variety of substrates A mixture of foliose and fruticose forms
Basidiolichen Club fungi	Corals Agarics	A lichenized coral-like mushroom A lichenized gilled mushroom

Species Included

Agaricoid fungi

Fig. 003a-c

WHITE or light colored spores

Fly Amanita or Fly Agaric (*Amanita muscaria* var. *muscaria*)

Fly Amanita or Fly Agaric (*Amanita muscaria* var. *flavivolvata*)

Fly Amanita or Fly Agaric (*Amanita muscaria* var. *formosa*)

Fly Amanita or Fly Agaric (*Amanita muscaria* var. *regalis*)

Fly Amanita or Fly Agaric (*Amanita muscaria* var. *persicina*)

Fly Amanita or Fly Agaric (*Amanita muscaria* var. *alba*)

Witch's Hat or Conical Waxy Cap (*Hygrocybe acutoconica*)

Fading Scarlet or Miniature Waxy Cap (*Hygrocybe miniata*)

False Chanterelle (*Hygrophoropsis aurantiaca*)

Slimy-Sheathed Waxy Cap (*Hygrophorus* [*olivaceoalbus*] *persoonii*)

Elm [Birch] Oyster (*Hypsizygus tessulatus*)

Old Man of the Woods, Lackluster, or Common Laccaria (*Laccaria laccata*)

Northern Spruce Milky (*Lactarius deterrimus*)

[Squatty] Pink-Fringed Milky (*Lactarius pubescens* var. *betulae*)

Yellow, Purple-Staining or Northern Bearded Milky (*Lactarius repraesentaneus*)

Red-Hot Milky (*Lactarius rufus*)

[Tall] Pink-Fringed or Bearded Milky (*Lactarius torminosus*)

Cockle-Shell *Lentinellus* (*Lentinellus cochleatus*)

Fried Chicken (*Lyophyllum decastes*)

Late Oyster (*Panellus serotinus*)

Orange Mock Oyster (*Phyllotopsis nidulans*)

Angel Wings (*Pleurocybella porrigens*)

Tacky Green Russula (*Russula aeruginea*)

Short-Stalked White Russula (*Russula brevipes*)

Sickener (*Russula emetica*)

The Yellow Russula (*Russula lutea*)

Shelfish-Scented Russula (*Russula xerampelina*)

Lichen-Agaric Basidiolichen

Agaric Lichen (*Lichenomphalia umbellifera*)

PINK to SALMON colored spores

Deer Mushroom (*Pluteus cervinus*)

YELLOW to ORANGE-BROWN colored spores

Sunny Side Up or Yellow Bolbitius (*Bolbitius vitellinus*)

Golden Pholiota (*Phaeolepiota aurea*)

DULL to CLAY-BROWN colored spores

Poison or Inrolled Pax (*Paxillus involutus*)

DULL, CINNAMON- to RUSTY-BROWN colored spores

Belted Slimy Cort (*Cortinarius* [*collinitus*] *trivialis*)

Red-Gilled Cort (*Cortinarius ominosus*)

Lilac Conifer Cort (*Cortinarius traganus*)

Violet Cort (*Cortinarius violaceus*)

Gypsy (*Rozites caperata*)

DARK to PURPLE-BROWN colored spores

Horse Mushroom (*Agaricus arvensis*)

Prince (*Agaricus augustus*)

Meadow Mushroom, Pink Bottom (*Agaricus campestris*)

Wetland Agaricus (*Agaricus sylvicola/silvicola*)

Hemispheric or Dung Dome Stroph (*Stropharia semiglobata*)

BLACK colored spores

Gray Alcohol Inky Cap, Tippler's Bane (*Coprinus [Coprinopsis] atramentarius*)

Shaggy Mane, Lawyer's Wig, Shaggy Beard, or Maned Agaric (*Coprinus comatus*)

False Truffles

Alder False Truffle or Red Gravel (*Alpova diplophloeus*)

Conifer False Truffle (*Gautireia graveolens*)

Boletinoid fungi

King Bolete, Porcini, Steinpiltz, or Cep (*Boletus edulis*)

Admirable Bolete (*Boletus mirabilis*)

Peppery Bolete (*Chalciporus piperatus*)

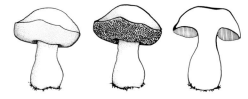

Fig. 004a–c

Common Scaber Stalk (*Leccinum scabrum*)

Birch Bolete (*Leccinum alaskanum*)

Trembling or Quaking Aspen Scaber Stalk (*Leccinum atrostipitatum*)

Red-Orange Capped Scabre Stalk (*Leccinum aurantiacum*)

Quaking Aspen Bolete (*Leccinum testaceoscabrum*)

Short-Stalked Suillus (*Suillus brevipes*)

Hollow-Stalked Larch Suillus (*Suillus cavipes*)

Larch Suillus (*Suillus grevillei*)

Brown and Yellow-Cracked Bolete (*Xerocomus subtomentosus*)

Polyporoid fungi

Sheep Polypore (*Albatrellus ovinus*)

Tinder Polypore (*Fomes fomentarius*)

Red-Belted Polypore (*Fomitopsis pinicola*)

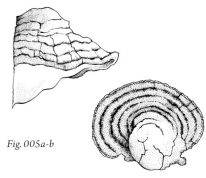

Fig. 005a–b

Artist's Conk (*Ganoderma applanatum*)

Hemlock Varnish Shelf (*Ganoderma tsugae*)

Clinker Polypore (*Inonotus obliquus*)

Hemlock Sulfur Shelf (*Laetiporus conifericola*)

Flecked-Flesh, False Tinder, Birch Polypore, or Conk (*Phellinus igniarius*)

Aspen Polypore or Conk (*Phellinus tremulae*)

Birch Polypore or Conk (*Piptoporus betulinus*)

Turkey Tail or Many-Colored Polypore (*Coriolus [Trametes] versicolor*)

Hydnoid fungi

Hedgehog or Pig's Trotter Mushroom (*Dentinum repandum*)

Comb-Toothed Hericium (*Hericium coralloides*)

Blue-Gray Hydnellum (*Hydnellum caeruleum*)

Strawberries and Cream or Bleeding Hydnellum (*Hydnellum peckii*)

Scaly Tooth Shingled Hedgehog (*Sarcodon imbricatus*)

Fig. 006a–b

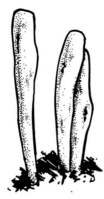

Fig. 007

Coralloid fungi

Hairy-Based Fairy
    Club Strap Coral
    (*Clavariadelphus
    ligula*)
Strap-Like Coral
    (*Clavariadelphus
    sachalinensis*)
Truncate Club Coral
    (*Clavariadelphus
    truncatus*)
Crested or Wrinkled
    Coral (*Clavulina
    [coralloides] cristata*)
Handsome Yellow-Tipped or Pinkish
    Coral (*Ramaria formosa*)
Lichen-Coral Basidiolichen
    Scum Lover (*Multiclavula mucida*)

Cantharelloid fungi

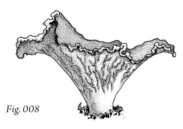

Fig. 008

Golden Chanterelle (*Cantharellus
    [cibarius] formosis*)
Funnel or Winter Chanterelle (*Craterellus
    tubaeformis*)
Pig's Ear (*Gomphus clavatus*)
Blue Chanterelle (*Poloyzellus multiplex*)

Thelephoroid fungi

Common Earth Fan or Fiber Vase
    (*Thelephora terrestris*)

Fig. 009

Gasteroid fungi

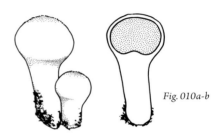

Fig. 010a-b

Puffballs

Tumbling Puffball or Tumble Ball
    (*Bovista plumbea*)
Western Giant Alpine Puffball
    (*Calvatia
    booniana*)
Sessile Earthstar
    (*Geastrum
    saccatum*)
Common or Gemmed
    Puffball
    (*Lycoperdon
    perlatum*)
Pear-Shaped Puffball
    (*Lycoperdon pyriforme*)

Fig. 011

Bird's nests

Cannon Fungus or Sphere Thrower
    (*Sphaerobolus stellatus*)
    Woodchip Loving Bird's Nest
        (*Cyathus olla*)

Fig. 012

Rust fungi

Spruce or Witch's Broom Rust (*Chrysomyxa arctostaphyli*)

Fig. 013a-b

Jelly fungi

Witch's Butter (*Tremella mesenterica*)

Fig. 014

Cupuloid Sac fungi

Yellow Fairy Cup (*Bisporella citrina*)

Common Cudonia (*Cudonia circinans*)

Pixie Cup (*Geopyxis carbonaria*)

Brain False Morel Mushroom (*Gyromitra esculenta*)

Saddle Shaped or Hooded False Morel (*Gyromitra infula*)

Smooth-Stalked Helvella (*Helvella elastica*)

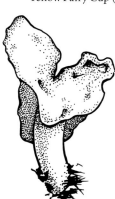

Fig. 015a

Lobster Mushroom (*Hypomyces lactifluorum*)

Black Morel (*Morchella elata*)

Yellow Rabbit Ear (*Otidea leporina*)

No Common Name (*Peziza praetervisa*)

Boring Brown Cup Fungus (*Peziza [silvestris-sylvestris] arvernensis*)

Wrinkled Thimble Cap (*Verpa bohemica*)

Earth tongues

Fig. 015b

Irregular Yellow Earth Tongue (*Neolecta irregularis*)

Yellow Paddle Earth Tongue (*Spathularia flavida*)

True Ascomycete Truffle

"Brain" Truffle (*Hydnotrya tulasnei*)

Fuzzy True Truffle (*Geopora cooperi*)

Marbled Deer Truffle (*Elaphomyces muricatus*)

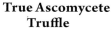

Fig. 016

Lichens-Ascolichens
(99.9 percent of all lichens are members of the Ascomycota)
Crustose

Candy, Spray-Paint, Fairy, or Peppermint Drop Lichen (*Icmadophila ericetorum*)

Fig. 017

Foliose

Studded Vein Lichen (*Peltigera apthosa*)

Fig. 018

Fruticose

Gray or True Caribou and/or Reindeer
Lichen (*Cladina rangiferina*)

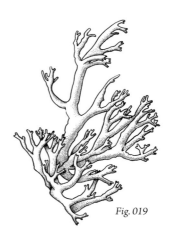

Fig. 019

Describing and Labeling Treasured Finds

The mushrooms described in this book emphasize five factors: The nature of the macroscopic cap (pileus); the stalk (also called a stipe—never a stem); the spore-producing surface (hymenophore), for example the gills (Lamellae); the collection material, which includes the mushroom's habit (form) and habitat (where it lives); and the mushroom's odor and even taste. If you choose to taste the mushroom, you must be very cautious. Chew a very small bit of cap and gill tissue between your front teeth and appressed tongue. NEVER swallow! Once you've determined any variance, remove all bits from your mouth. Other constructive observations and/or discussions of environmental factors such as rainfall, substrate nutrients, or temperature may be noted on the reverse side of a fungal collection label, explained below, or you can write them on 3" X 5" or 5" X 7" note cards.

Fungal Collecting Labels

FUNGI of ALASKA USA

Taxon (name): _____

Coll.#: INTL and # _____ **Date:** mm/dd/yyyy

Substrate (what the fungus is on): _____ **Spore Print:** Y / N

Habitat (general description of surrounding flora): _____

Locality (general named location, i.e., Chena Lakes): _____

Latitude: _____ Deg.Min.Sec. N;

Longitude: _____ Deg.Min.Sec. W

Elevation: _____

Collector(s): _____

Color/dig. Photo: Y / N   **Notes:** Y / N   **Card:** Y / N

Identified by:_____

Annotator: _____

Depending on whether or not you're really into studying mushrooms, you may have a microscope in addition to a loupe (hand lens). If you are using a microscope, you may want to also make and examine slides of the mushroom's cap, stalk, and gill tissues for spores, spore-producing cells (basidia in this case) and other "sterile" cells of note, along with the hyphae inside the gill, stalk, and cap. Macroscopic information constitutes what we call a "Description Card," as they and drawings might be made on 3" X 5" or 5" X 7" cards.

Formal Fungal Descriptions

Genus species Authority *variety*   Figure(s)_____
Synonymy (if appropriate or useful)

MACROSCOPIC DESCRIPTION includes:

Pileus	size, shape, habit, color, texture, moisture, taste, odor, and feel central disc—configuration, color margin—configuration, color cuticle—and pileus context color, texture, thickness
Stipe	length, width, apex vs. base shape, texture, color, context, cuticle (caulopellis)
Lamellae	size (height, thickness, breadth, and width), shape, color, texture, and attachment
Color and Bruising	reactions (atmospheric and chemical)

MICROSCOPIC DESCRIPTION includes:

Spores	length-width range, shape, ornamentation, wall thickness, +/- apical pore, appendages, epicutus, contents, chemical reactions
Basidia	size, shape, sterigmata # and length, chemical reactions, wall, contents
Cystidia	size, shape, type (origin), wall, contents, pres./absence Cheilocystidia on **gill edge** Pleurocystidia on **gill face** Pileocystidia on **cap** (pileus) Caulocystidia on **stalk** (stipe)
Subhymenium	elements
Lamellar trama	cell size, shape, arrangement, wall, contents
Pileus trama	as subhymenium and lamellar trama
Cutis	pilipellis type, thickness, element size, shape, arrangement, walls, contents (same for caulopellis)
Material Examined:	County, State/Country/District (City, Village, Community), Collector Number and Date
Material Examined:	General shape, attachment to substrate, higher and lower plant associates, substrate characters (acid, peaty, woody, etc.), locality and environmental parameter measurements typifying the mycological environment.
Observations and Discussion:	Synopsis of key descriptive and distinguishing taxonomic characters; differences between closely allied species; occurrence (whether new to locality, state, country); suspected importance to community (i.e., decomposer, mycorrhizal, etc.); phenology (date and relative abundance); and synonymy.

Mushrooms are best collected for identification when newly produced spores are mature and ready to be discharged, and when spore prints are more readily made. Very immature or over-mature mushrooms don't produce spores, or they simply make a mess on your paper with maggots and bugs.

Hunting Mushrooms in the Wild

Folks often begin collecting careers by tearing into the woods, yanking up mushrooms with their bare hands, dumping them into grocery bags (mixing them all up), and moving on. If you are planning to collect mushrooms for the table, to study them, or just for fun, you might find some of these items useful.

CLOTHING
- Boots.................................. comfortable hiking/rubber, Gortex
- Rain gear...........................pants, jacket with hood and zippered pockets
- Layers .... warm socks, polypro, wool, fleece
- Hat.........preferably rimmed or billed

CONTAINERS AND
MISCELLANEOUS ITEMS
- Basket .... collection receptacle lessens specimen damage
- Waxed paper ....sheets or bags for separating collections
- Whistle or bell .... for alerting animals of your presence
- Knife...pocket or sheath type
- Grub rake................................... for true and false truffle hunting
- Hatchet or axe... for collecting woody substrate-attached fungi
- Pruning shears....................................... for collecting twigs or small limbs with fungi
- Hand/pruning saw....... for collecting fungi on larger branches
- Soft toothbrush .... removal of soil, debris, and insects
- Collection labels .... numbering, making notes, spore prints

- Paper bags.......................... for assorted large collections
- Spore print cards...............................for capturing spore drops in the field
- Regional field guide .... to identify specimens
- Containers.................................plastic, tin, cardboard for protection
- Bug dope .... Cutter's preferably
- Resealable plastic bags .... only used for mosses, lichens, or DRIED fungi
- EpiPen .... if you are allergic to bees

HI-TECH GEAR:
- Loupe (hand lens) .... 10X to 20X on an around-the-neck lanyard
- Compass .... for trekking in as well as out of the woods
- Digital camera .... with extra digital cards and battery
- GPS .... for collecting coordinate information

FOOD AND DRINK:
- Water .... for drinking/hydration
- Cheese ....for munching
- Pilot crackers ....for munching

CAUTIONS:
- Firearms unless absolutely necessary to protect against megafauna

ENTHUSIASM:
- Lots of it for probing the little known world of the mystical, yet not so magical mushrooms

When you encounter a mushroom, it's important to collect not just the stalk and the cap, but also the stalk base, which is often buried in the soil. The base can be important in identifying the mushroom. For example, cuplike or saclike tissue surrounding a mushroom's base is characteristic of some deadly poisonous *Amanita* species.

Plastic bags aren't good for collecting fungi because they cause mushrooms to sweat and deteriorate quickly. Interestingly, 87.2 percent of fungal "poisonings" happen when eating "edible" fungi that were collected and stored in plastic bags. Separate each kind of mushroom in a waxed paper or paper sandwich bag so it will be easy to identify later. More importantly, keep different species separate to help prevent mixing of poisonous varieties with the ones you plan to eat for dinner.

Mushrooms do tend to show up each year at roughly the same time and place, and good notes can direct you to favorite spots each season. More serious mushroom hunters will keep a notebook to record useful information.

Mushroom Spore Prints

Spore prints reveal the color of a mushroom's spores, providing useful clues for determining the mushroom's identity. Many serious mushroom poisonings could be avoided if collectors would routinely determine the spore color of mushrooms they intend to eat. Though most often useful in identifying gilled mushrooms, spore prints can also be made from boletinoid, hydnoid, and coralloid mushrooms.

To make a spore print, remove the mushroom cap and lay it, with the gills facing down, on a white note card or label. (For non-gilled mushrooms, place the spore-bearing surface down.)

Cover the mushroom cap with a bowl to prevent air currents from disturbing the spore discharge from the gill plates. Minute spores will usually drop and collect over a two- to twelve-hour period by the jet-drop, bubble-burst forcible discharge mechanism. One can never be certain that the fungus is mature enough to discharge its spores, but without knowing the color of the spores (gill color is a pretty good indicator), it may be nearly impossible to identify the fungus. Always use "white" paper onto which spores are discharged, as colored or black paper "absorb" light differentially and does not yield a true spore color, particularly for pastel colored spores.

To see white spores on white paper, look at them at an angle to the light. Black paper is sometimes used, but again it distorts color perception. If mushrooms are too old, too young, or are dry, soggy, or sterile, a print generally won't happen.

Spore prints sometimes occur naturally on a mushroom's stalk, on other mushrooms, or on the ground below the cap. But these spore prints may be misleading. It's best to collect the spore print on white paper.

Caution: Exposure to mushroom spores may cause airway irritability and, in some cases, negative allergenic reactions.

Drying and Preserving Fungi

Proper fungal preservation is paramount to future use, whether it be mycophagy or for research and microscopic study. If preservation is for future consumption, then the fungi must be thoroughly dried. In this state, they can literally be kept for decades!

Drying is best performed by placing the fungi onto drying screens under which a forced air space or Colman fueled catalytic heater is placed. The passing of warm air over the fungi for a four-to-fourteen-hour period of time is needed for sufficient drying. Of course, this does depend on the size and thickness of the fungus. Small fungi (e.g., *Mycena*) will dry out completely in only a few hours. Much larger fungi (e.g., boletes and bracket fungi) may take much longer unless cut into thin sections before drying.

Once thoroughly dried (and labeled if for later research use), the fungi can be placed into glass jars with tight-sealing lids. Collecting boxes or plastic bags are generally used only for temporary transport.

Of course, there are other methods of preserving fungi if the plan is to use them for later microscopic or molecular studies. Besides drying, fungi may be placed into 70 percent ethyl alcohol (ETOH), DNA-Later or RN-Later (preservatives that retain fungal DNA and RNA in good condition for later extractions), or FAA (Formalin-Acetic acid-Alcohol) in 5:5:90 percent proportions. The latter is a caustic mix and should be handled with care.

Safe Shrooming

Perhaps the most often-asked question from mushroom hunters is, "Can I eat it?" The answer—for most people and mushrooms found in Alaska—is "Perhaps." It's a decision to be purposefully made and not made lightly. Following are some important safety guidelines.

- Be certain you've correctly identified a mushroom species before eating it. Consult regional field guides and ask a knowledgeable local collector to examine and identify your collection. When in doubt, throw it out!

- Learn to recognize poisonous look-alikes of species you collect for the table.

- Keep different species in separate containers when you collect mushrooms so that poisonous and edible pieces won't be inadvertently mixed.

- Collect only mature, insect-free mushrooms for the table. Avoid the very young and the very old. Remove obvious dirt, insects, or debris before bagging.

- Collect mushrooms in areas uncontaminated by pollutants (vehicle exhaust, herbicides, lawn care products, and fertilizers, etc.).

- Cook all wild mushrooms thoroughly.

- Sample only a tiny portion (one teaspoon) of any edible wild mushroom that is new to you, and be aware of any symptoms of an allergic reaction or delayed symptoms of poisoning. If no symptoms develop within a couple of days, you are probably not allergic.

- Eat modest servings of edible wild mushrooms, even those familiar to you, to avoid indigestion.

- Avoid drinking alcohol when eating a species for the first time. Alcohol can combine with or extract mushroom toxins, such as with false morels and *Coprinus* species.

- Avoid serving wild mushrooms to young children or to people with impaired immune systems.

- Guard young children by preventing them from eating any mushrooms in the wild.

- Avoid inhaling spores, which may cause respiratory disorders.

- Avoid panic if you become ill after eating mushrooms. Induce vomiting and consult a doctor. Show the doctor an uncooked specimen of the mushroom you ate for identification by experts at Poison Centers.

Collecting with Care

Whether you hunt mushrooms for food or for fun, you can help protect Alaska's mushrooms by keeping the woodlands, fields, and other places where mushrooms grow in your community clean, healthy, and undisturbed.

- Never rake the forest floor to uncover the mycelium (the underground body of the fungus) and hidden "buttons," and never dig up more mushrooms than needed for food or identification purposes. These practices can damage the mycelium and destroy the mushroom patch.

- Collect mushrooms sparingly, only for your personal needs. Leave a few behind to release spores, renew the resource, and delight other mushroom seekers.

Frequently Asked Questions

Where and when do mushrooms grow in Alaska?

Mushrooms grow wherever higher plants are found growing, which means everywhere! The fruiting season (the period of time during which mushroom species put up and out fruit bodies) over most of the state ranges from the spring snowmelt (April through June) until the fall freeze (September through November).

What kinds of mushrooms are the most dangerous?

Potentially fatal mushrooms, often spotted in populated areas, include the Fly Agaric (*Amanita muscaria*), Poison Pax (*Paxillus involutus*), Sulfur Tuft (*Naematoloma fasciculare*), false morels such as the Brain Mushroom (*Gyromitra esculenta*) and the Hooded False Morel (*Gyromitra infula*), *Cortinarius* species, and *Galerina* species. And there are almost surely more out there; Alaska has a huge outdoors with only a handful of people looking for mushrooms. (This book includes photos and descriptions of the Fly Agaric, Poison Pax, Brain Mushroom, Hooded False Morel, and *Cortinarius* species.) To date, there have been no reported fatalities due to mushroom poisoning in Alaska, but many have fallen ill.

Which are the safest mushrooms for beginning mushroom hunters?

Hedgehogs (*Dentinum repandum*) and Shaggy Manes (*Coprinus comatus*), as they're easy to identify and easy to digest for most people.

What kinds of mushrooms are the best eating?

In the spring, Black Morels (*Morchella elata*). In summer, King Boletes (*Boletus edulis*), Shaggy Manes (*Coprinus comatus*), Meadow Mushrooms (*Agaricus campestris*), and the rarely found Prince (*Agaricus augustus*). In fall, Hedgehogs (*Dentinum repandum*) and Combs (*Hericium [ramosum] coralloides*), other Hericium species, and Tumbleballs (*Bovista plumbea*).

What is your favorite mushroom?
For beauty: Golden Pholiota. For fun and the unabashed thrill of the hunt: morels.

Mushroom Toxin Classifications

Traditionally, in the world of fungi, there are seven to eight toxin groups, depending on what the source may be, but generally, they are put into six broad classifications:

Protoplasmic Poisons *(Groups 1 and 5 toxins)*
Neurotoxins *(Groups 2, 3, and 4 toxins)*
Disulfiram-like regurgitates *(Group 6 toxins)*
Gastrointestinal and allergenic reactions *(Group 7 toxins)*
Miscellaneous gastrointestinal and allergenic poisoning *(Group 8 toxins)*
False "Mushroom Poisoning" *(Secondary metabolites of other microbes)*

Protoplasmic Poisons
GROUP 1 Toxins: *Amitoxins* (cyclic octapeptides), *Phallotoxins* (cyclic heptapeptides), *Hydrazines* (MMH/Gyromitrins), and *Orellanines.*
a. *Amatoxins* (cyclic octapeptides), *Phallotoxins* (cyclic heptapeptides),
  1. Serious protoplasmic poisoning of liver and kidney.
  2. Most **deadly** = complex "polypeptides."
  3. Phallotoxins dilate endoplasmic reticulum within 15 minutes.
  4. Amatoxins attack all nuclei.
  5. Ingestion, no revulsion, feeling of well being, mitochondria swell, fat droplets are deposited in cytoplasm, violent abdominal pain, vomiting and diarrhea, causes 95 percent of all mushroom fatalities.
  6. Spp. = *Amanita verna, A. virosa, A. bisporigera, A. phalloides, A. tenuifolia, Galerina marginata, G. veninata, G. automnalis.*
  7. **Antidote**—for PPs = Thioctic acid (α lipoic acid) 300 mg/day Cytochrome, Corticicoides (= steroids); NO ATRAPINE!
  8. α amanitin damages cells of proximal convoluted tubules in the kidneys followed by kidney dysfunction 3 days later. Liver damage in 2 days with negative action on nuclei and nucleoli after 15 minutes. General inhibition of RNA transcription from nuclear DNA and ribosomal RNA (in nucleus) and nuclear RNA.

GROUP 5 Toxins:
b. *Gyromitrin* (MMH, monomethylhydrazine) a rocket fuel.
  1. Affects central nervous system—protoplasmic/hemolytic and gastrointestinal poisoning, helvellic acid thought to be the cause, but they turn out to be only a group of harmless fatty acids.
  2. Kills blood cells—causes jaundice (hepato-nephro-toxin) symptoms—nausea, pain, and vomiting 6-8 hours after ingestion.
  3. **Antidote**—Gastric lavage, electrolyte balance, pyridoxine HCL_{25}.
c. *Orellanines*
  1. Found in some *Cortinarius* spp.

Neurotoxins *(Muscarine, Ibotenic acid, and Muscimol* [Pilzatropines]*, and Psilocybin).*

GROUP 2 Toxins:

a. *Pilzatropines*—muscimol, ibotenic acid + muscazon, tricholomic acid and pantharine, LSD compared.
1. Affects central nervous system ca. 1 hour after ingestion.
2. Symptoms—muscular incoordination, twitching, no pain, indifferent, mood fluctuation, can't concentrate, daydreams, space distortion, reality lacking, time unawareness, and disturbed vision.
3. **Antidote**—none (excretion/urination), treat symptoms.
4. Seldom fatal.
5. Found in *Amanita muscaria, A. strobiliformis, A. pantherina, A. citrina, A. solitaris,* and *A. porferia.*
6. Evidence of fungi hybridization
A. gemmata
no toxin
cap yellow.

A. pantherina
high level of toxin
cap butterscotch brown.

Hybrids show variation in toxin level and cap color.

GROUP 3 Toxins:

b. *Muscarin*
1. Found in
   a. *Clitocybe dealbata, C. cerussata, C. rivulosa, Omphalotus illudens (olerius).*
   b. *Inocybe spp.*
   c. *Amanita muscaria.*
2. Acts on Parasympathetic nervous system + Autonomic nervous system (alcohol-like intoxication with spasms and delirium).
3. Poorly absorbed by intestinal tract.

4. Symptoms—½ -2 hours pupil contraction and blurred vision, **sweating, salivation, tears (PSL),** pulse slows, increased peristalsis, lower BP, asthmatic breathing, lacrymation (tears).
5. **Antidote**—Atropine sulfate, ipecac, chlorpromazine, prochloroperazine, electrolyte supportive care.

GROUP 4 Toxins:

c. *Psilocybin Psilocybin, Psilocin, Baeocystin, Norbaeocystin, and Bufotenin* (the Indoles).
1. Found in 25 species of
   a. *Psilocybe*
   b. *Stropharia*
   c. *Panaeolus*
   d. *Conocybe.*
2. The "Acids"—hallucinogenic with recovery (dysphoric mental states, rise in body temperature).
3. Affects central nervous system.
4. **Antidote**—Chlorpromazine (to stop hallucinogenic); NO ASPIRIN! Symptomatic reassurance, Diazepam (Valium) for convulsions.

Disulfiram-Like Toxicity (regurgitates)

GROUP 6 Toxins:

a. **Coprine** *Coprinus [Coprinopsis] atramentarius.*
b. **Antidote**—None known.

Gastrointestinal Toxicity (allergenic reactions)

GROUP 7 Toxins

a. Affects central nervous system.
b. Catch all group.
c. Many spp.; 1. *Russula emetica,* 2. *Entoloma lividum,* 3. *Coprinus [Coprinopsis] atramentarius* with Disulfiram-like reaction if taken with an alcoholic beverage.

d. Symptoms—vascular system dilation.
e. **Antidote**—Reassurance and "hand holding."

Miscellaneous Poisons
GROUP 8 Toxins
a. *Metabolites* perhaps having some taxonomic significance.
   1. Norcaperatic acid, *Gomphus floccosus*.
   2. Thelephoric acid, *Polyzellus multiplex*.
   3. Terphenylquinones and thelephoric acid, *Hydnellum*.
   4. Hippocratic screening toxin tests using fungal extracts, injection into "clean" rats (non-previously drugged) regularly checked and activities observed.
   b. **Antidote**—Reassurance and "hand holding."

False "Mushroom Poisoning"
Secondary metabolites of other microbes (bacteria).
a. Produced by bacteria that live on other fungi, as in "neatly wrapped" store-bought *Agaricus* spp.
b. Most of these are food poisoning–like inflictions or mild to severe gastrointestinal anomalies (cramps, vomiting, diarrhea, etc.).

Descriptive entries in this book include:
Family name
Common Name
Genus and Species names and Figure #
Striking Field Characters
Macro- and Microdescription
Habitat and Role
Edibility, Taste, and Odor
Look-alikes
Comments

MUSHROOM DESCRIPTIONS

HYMENOMYCETE BASIDIOMYCOTA:
Organized Hymenium Present

Agaric (Gilled) Mushrooms:
The Agaricoid Fungi

When identifying mushrooms, it is necessary to consider the fertile surface (**hymenium**) upon which minute spores are produced. Agaric (from "Agaria," a city in Sarmatia of Ancient Greece) refers to the platelike gills, the spore-bearing structures found hanging beneath the cap and lined by the hymenium (Fig. 134a-d). Gill plates (**lamellae** and **lamellulae**) of varying thickness, length, width, separation distance, color, and texture (especially the knife blade–like edge), make up what is known as the **hymenophore**. It is on those flat gill "faces" that spores are borne and forcibly discharged from the tips of specialized cells called basidia (in contrast to saclike asci in the Ascomycota—the Sac Fungi). The spores develop on specialized, but tiny hornlike basidial protrusions called **sterigmata**. All members of this group possess gills on the underside of their caps (**pileus**). A beautiful spore print can often be made by removing the stalk (**stipe**) from the cap where joined, and placing the cap, gill side down, over a piece of white paper and covered for several hours. A cup or bowl should be put over the cap to retain the moisture needed by the fungus to forcibly discharge its spores—in the millions! In some species of mushrooms there is a "skin" (veil) that covers the entire mushroom when the button is very young. A complete covering is termed "universal" (**universal veil**). Secondarily, mushrooms may not have the universal veil, but may display a skin or cobweb-like tissue that covers only the hymenium (**partial veil**) and may be attached to the stalk and/or to the margin of the cap. This latter tissue may become detached from the cap margin early in development and collapse down around the stalk, where it may even disappear completely in due time. If the partial veil is retained as a membrane-like ring, it is referred to as an **annulus**. Gilled mushrooms are usually found on lignin-rich detritus, soil or older wood, living or decaying. More than 2,000-gilled mushroom species have been reported in North America. They include some choice edibles as well as dangerously poisonous species.

Other literature sources with complete citations are found in our "Literature Citations" section and have been found to be very useful in working with these fungi. They are:

Agarics with WHITE or lightly colored spores

The Hymenomycetes: Fungi having an "organized" hymenium supporting forcible spore discharge

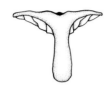  

Amanita Variety	Cap Color	Universal Veil Color	Stipe Color
muscaria	red	white	white
flavivolvata	orange-red	tan-yellow	white
formosa	orange-yellow	yellow-tan	yellow-tan
regalis	brown	tan-yellow	tan-yellow
persicina	melon	tan-yellow	tan-yellow
alba	white–buff	white-tan	white-tan

FAMILY: Amanitaceae
COMMON NAME: Fly Amanita, Fly Agaric (or the RED *Amanita muscaria*)
GENUS AND SPECIES: *Amanita muscaria* var. *muscaria* (L.) Lam. 1783

STRIKING FIELD CHARACTERS:
The deep red *Amanita muscaria*, but often fading to orange or yellow, smooth and tacky, with white pyramidal warts (remains of a broken universal veil); white free gills; thick white stalk with a membranous ring and a bulbous base, with the upper portion of the latter breaking up into concentric rings.

MACRO- & MICRODESCRIPTION:
Cap 2.5-23.0 cm broad, narrowly convex (oval or derby-shaped), expanding to convex, broadly convex to plane in age; moist, sticky to viscid; deep red (mostly), to red-orange, orange, orange-yellow to

Fig. 020

yellow; with white pyramidal warts not easily rubbed off, dense near margin and becoming widely-spaced over disc; context (flesh) white, firm, thick; margin inrolled slightly at first, becoming straight with age. **Gills** crowded, moderately thick, broad and with fuzzy edges (especially near margin), free from stalk. **Stalk** 5-20 cm long, 15-20 mm thick; expanding or straight toward a bulbous base; white; almost smooth to flocculent (tufted cottony) with a broad white, persistent skirting, hanging, membranous (partial) veil; top of bulbous base with universal veil remnants broken up into 3 to 5 concentric rings. **Basidiospores** 9-13 X 6.5-9 µm white in deposit, broadly elliptical, smooth, non-amyloid.

HABITAT AND ROLE:

This is an ectomycorrhizal associate (terrestrial, but connected to the root system of its host) with paper birch and quaking aspen and probably several other plant species. The fungus can be found singly to scattered and quite abundantly some years and comes in no-less-than six varieties.

EDIBILITY, TASTE, AND ODOR:

Amanita muscaria is toxic and contains a suite of different toxins. It has been used recreationally for its one psychoactive component, but also may cause 12 hours of frightening toxicity for which mycologists have been called to the hospital bedsides of very sick consumers. Death has been known, but rarely to occur, from eating this fungus. Taste is mild, and odor is pleasant. However, one should just simply never eat any *Amanita*!

LOOK-ALIKES:

Remember, these come in white, melon, brown, orange-yellow, orange-red, and all red forms that resemble a lot of other mushroom species like some large *Lepiota* (however, only two species of *Lepiota* have been found in Alaska to date) and *Agaricus* species.

COMMENTS:

Poisonous and hallucinogenic. Eating any of the six varieties (Geml et al. 2006 2008 2010) of this mushroom can produce varying unpredictable physical reactions from mild giddiness, alcohol-like intoxication, headache, deep sleep to delirium, intense gastrointestinal discomfort, and convulsions. Occasional death may occur in susceptible adults or young children. Because the genus *Amanita* can be difficult to identify and/or can be confused with several other species that contain the deadly amatoxins, I advise admiring them all, as you would the stark scarlet presence of baneberries on your path or the volcanic plume over Cook Inlet from Mount Augustine. Nod respect for their beauty and move on.

Agaric (Gilled) Mushrooms

FAMILY: Amanitaceae
COMMON NAME: Fly Amanita, Fly Agaric, The Orange–Red Colored *Amanita Muscaria*
GENUS AND SPECIES: *Amanita muscaria* var. *flavivolvata* (Singer) D.T. Jenkins 1977

STRIKING FIELD CHARACTERS:
Orange- to brownish-red cap; margin paler; context white to pale yellowish to reddish; buff to yellowish universal remains; volva rings of warts or powdery, deep yellow, orange- to buff-yellow; margin with flocculent velar remains.

MACRO- & MICRODESCRIPTION:
Cap 5-17 cm; convex to plane, ± depressed; subviscid, glabrous; orange–red, universal veil remains tan–yellowish; margin ± flocculent. **Gills** free, white to pale cream, crowded. **Stalk** 7-13 X 1-2 cm; white, bruising buff; tapering to apex; tightly stuffed; fibrous to fibrous-scaly; bulb ovoid, white to buff; annulus superior, sub-membranous, creamy, evanescent; volva yellowish to buffy ascending rings, warts or powder. **Basidiospores** 10-12 X 7-8.5 μm; broadly elliptic to long-elliptic, white in deposit. Very similar in stature to *A. muscaria* v. *muscaria*.

HABITAT AND ROLE:
An ectomycorrhizal associate with birch predominately in upland mixed forests.

EDIBILITY, TASTE, AND ODOR:
☠ Inedible; mild; fungoid.

LOOK-ALIKES:
In its youth, it may look a lot like *A. muscaria* v. *muscaria*, but look for hints of yellow especially just under the cap cutis.

COMMENTS:
Adore, but do not store! This particular variety of *A. muscaria* in Alaska is the cause of most of our serious gastrointestinal upsets and hospitalizations.

Agaric (Gilled) Mushrooms

Fig. 021

FAMILY: Amanitaceae

COMMON NAME: The Fly Amanita, Fly Agaric

GENUS AND SPECIES: *Amanita muscaria* var. *formosa* Pers. 1800

STRIKING FIELD CHARACTERS:

Cap 4.5-17 cm; convex to plane; striate to tuberculate-striate; ± viscid; glabrous; pale- to orange-yellow; context white to yellowish; universal veil yellow-tan, floccose patches to warts; margin ± flocculent. **Gills** free, crowded, white to pale yellow. **Stalk** -15 X 0.5-3 cm; ± tapering to apex; white, cream to yellow-tan; stuffed; ± fibrillose; bruising yellowish; bulb subglobose to sub-radicate, white to pallid; superior creamy- to yellow-white; annulus, ± evanescent; volva remnants pale-yellow to buff rings. **Basidiospores** 8.5-13 X 6.5-8 μm; elliptic to broadly so, white in deposit.

MACRO- & MICRODESCRIPTION:

Very similar in stature to *A. muscaria* v. *muscaria*.

HABITAT AND ROLE:

An ectomycorrhizal associate with birches primarily.

EDIBILITY, TASTE, AND ODOR:

 Poisonous and should never be eaten.

LOOK-ALIKES:

Old faded specimens of *A. muscaria* v. *flavivolvata*.

COMMENTS:

Adore, but do not store!

Fig. 022

FAMILY: Amanitaceae
COMMON NAME: Fly Amanita, Fly Agaric, Panther, Panther Cap, False Blusher
GENUS AND SPECIES: *Amanita muscaria* var. *regalis* (Fr.) Sacc. 1887

STRIKING FIELD CHARACTERS:
Appearing less robust; cap pale tan, gray-tan to tawny brown (no yellow, orange, or red tints); universal veil is tan-yellow, more slender tan-yellow stalk with "stretch mark" patches on the stalk near its bulbous and collared base.

MACRO- & MICRODESCRIPTION:
Cap 1.5-7.5 cm broad; pale tan, grayish-tan, tan to tawny-brown; subviscid (sticky to tacky); convex, broadly convex in age; ivory-colored pyramidal universal veil remnants over cap, but thicker toward the faintly striate margin; context (inside) flesh fairly firm, ivory (just under cap) to white, thick. **Gills** free, close together, edges finely floccose (cottony or fluffy), white, and broad. **Stalk** 1.5-10 cm long, 7-15 mm wide, white and smooth near apex, surface breaking up into fibrils below annulus and appearing "stretched" (lacerate) and expanding slightly toward the bulbous, but collared base. **Basidiospores** 10-13 X 6.5-11 μm; white in deposit; broadly elliptical, smooth, non-amyloid. Very similar in stature to *A. muscaria* v. *muscaria*.

HABITAT AND ROLE:
This stately mushroom is terrestrial, solitary to gregarious, and it too is a mycorrhizal associate with aspen, birch, and white spruce.

EDIBILITY, TASTE, AND ODOR:
☠ Poisonous, this mushroom should never be eaten. The taste is mild, and the odor is pleasant, but it reminds one of what something bitter tasting would smell like. Once again, **never** eat this or any other *Amanita*.

LOOK-ALIKES:
Amanita aspera.

COMMENTS:
Adore, but do not store!

Fig. 023

Fig. 024

FAMILY: Amanitaceae
COMMON NAME: The Melon-Colored Fly Amanita, Fly Agaric *Amanita muscaria*
GENUS AND SPECIES: *Amanita muscaria* var. *persicina* Dave T. Jenkins 1977

STRIKING FIELD CHARACTERS:
Light orange to melon cap with yellow to buff warts; pale pink-tinted gills; stalk cream to yellowish, darker where bruised; volva powdery to ± ringed.

MACRO- & MICRODESCRIPTION:
Cap 4-21 cm; convex to plane; striate; subviscid; glabrous; light orange to melon, margin lighter; context white, yellowish to pinkish; universal veil thin floccose-fibrillose patches or irregular warts, yellow to tan in age. **Gills** free, crowded, creamy with pale pinkish tints. **Stalk** 8-26 X 1-3 cm; ± tapering toward apex; densely stuffed; fibrillose above to fibrous-lacerate below annulus; whitish to tannish-yellow; bruising yellowish; bulb ovoid, subglobose to sub-radicate; annulus superior, ± evanescent, sub-membranous, whitish to cream-buff; volva remnants thin, powdery, yellowish-buff to tannish, rarely as ascending rings. **Basidiospores** 9.5-12.5 X 7-8.5 µm; broadly to long elliptic, white in deposit; very similar in stature to *A. muscaria* v. *muscaria*.

HABITAT AND ROLE:
An ectomycorrhizal associate with birches and spruce in mixed forest.

EDIBILITY, TASTE, AND ODOR:
 Poisonous and should never be eaten.

LOOK-ALIKES:
Amanita aspera.

COMMENTS:
Adore, but do not store!

FAMILY: Amanitaceae
COMMON NAME: The White Fly
Amanita, Fly Agaric *Amanita
muscaria*
GENUS AND SPECIES: *Amanita
muscaria* var. *alba* Peck 1897

STRIKING FIELD CHARACTERS:
Cap white to pallid, buffy warts, stalk white to yellowish staining, volva ascending rings of warts or patches.

MACRO- & MICRODESCRIPTION:
Cap 4-21 cm; convex to plane; margin ± striate; subviscid, glabrous; white to silvery-white, light buff-white in age; context white to yellowish; white to buff-white universal veil remains thin, floccose, patchy, angular to pyramidal warts; annulus pendant, collapsing against stalk, pale cream to yellowish. **Gills** free to deeply notched, crowded, white to pale cream. **Stalk** 5-14 X 0.5-2 cm; ± tapering to apex; stuffed; fibrous above and below annulus; bruising ± yellow, otherwise white; base bulbous, ovoid, subglobose to sub-radicate; with floccose rings ascending onto lower stalk. **Basidiospores** 8-14 X 6-9.5 µm; broadly elliptic; white in deposit. Otherwise, very similar to *A. muscaria* v. *muscaria*.

HABITAT AND ROLE:
An ectomycorrhizal associate with willow, cottonwood, and white spruce.

EDIBILITY, TASTE, AND ODOR:
 Poisonous and should never be eaten.

LOOK-ALIKES:
Might be easily confused with other WHITE to whitish, but deadly poisonous *Amanita* spp. such as *A. bisporigera, A. phalloides, A. verna, and A. virosa.*

COMMENTS:
Adore, but do not store!

Fig. 025

Fig. 026

FAMILY: Hygrophoraceae
COMMON NAME: Cone-Shaped or Conic Hygrocybe (Hygrophorus), Witch's Hat
GENUS AND SPECIES: *Hygrocybe acutoconica* (Clem.) Singer 1951

STRIKING FIELD CHARACTERS:

Bright yellow, orange-yellow, orange to orange-red, conic cap; candy-cane (twisted) stalk with yellow-green tints but not bruising black; sticky cap; hollow stipe.

MACRO- & MICRODESCRIPTION:

Cap 10–35 mm broad, conic with blunt to rounded apex, broadly expanding to form an umbo; tacky to viscid; smooth yellow with ± orange to reddish-orange fibrils, blue-gray stipe base and context under cap apex; flesh yellowish to yellow-orange, thin. **Gills** are close to subdistant (somewhat separated), thick, narrow, yellow in youth becoming the same color as but lighter than cap and blackening when bruised, waxy if rubbed vigorously between fingers. Gill trama is parallel (regular). **Stalk** 2.5–7.5 cm long, 3–8 mm broad, smooth, moist, candy-cane twisted with longitudinal lines, orange-yellow (olive); base is the first part of the fruiting body to show signs of bruising black; hollow. **Basidiospores** 9–13 x 5–7 μm, white in deposit, elliptical, smooth.

HABITAT AND ROLE:

Scattered to gregarious in grassy to mossy disturbed sites (old paths, runway edges, roadsides, and stream bank terraces), terrestrial.

EDIBILITY, TASTE, AND ODOR:

The edibility of this fungus is questionable. It is reported as being edible or non-poisonous, yet is thought to be responsible for at least four deaths in China and may possibly be hallucinogenic. While the taste is mild and odor is pleasant, you should simply not risk eating this fungus.

LOOK-ALIKES:

H. conica (with a more orange to red cap), *H. persistens* (perhaps a synonym of a European species).

COMMENTS:

This fungus is common throughout Alaska and found in high grassy meadows, alpine and Arctic tundra. It's often spectacular when first seen amongst its graminoid cover, but with further searching you may find it to be abundant in these areas.

Fig. 027

FAMILY: Hygrophoraceae
COMMON NAME: Witch's Hat, Conical or Miniature Waxy Cap
GENUS AND SPECIES: *Hygrocybe miniata* (Fr.) P. Kumm. 1871

STRIKING FIELD CHARACTERS:
Small bright red, scarlet red to reddish-orange cap and lighter colored and distant gills.

MACRO- & MICRODESCRIPTION:
Cap 0.5-3 cm, convex to sub-plane, even depressed in age; minutely scaly, moist; color red to scarlet-red in youth, fading to orange-red or deep yellow-orange; context thin, concolorous with cap, but generally more toward the yellow-orange side. **Gills** shallowly notched, broadly attached to ± decurrent; waxy, thick, spaced, reddish-orange. **Stalk** (1-) 1.5-2.5 cm X 2-4 mm; concolorous with cap.

Basidiospores 6-10 X 4-6 µm; smooth, elliptic and white in deposit.

HABITAT AND ROLE:
Scattered and dispersed in graminoids (grasses and sedges) over peaty soil.

EDIBILITY, TASTE, AND ODOR:
Reported to be edible, but you'll need to search for a long while to get enough to savor.

LOOK-ALIKES:
H. subminiata, H. turunda.

COMMENTS:
We find this little mushroom on wet lignin-rich peaty soil, but never on wood as reported by others, and almost always associated with graminoids with dwarf birch and willow often in close proximity.

FAMILY: Hygrophoropsidaceae
COMMON NAME: False Chanterelle
GENUS AND SPECIES: *Hygrophoropsis aurantiaca* (Wulfen) Maire 1921

STRIKING FIELD CHARACTERS:

Small stature, orange to yellow-orange cap, stipe, and gills, forking (1-4X) gills, inrolled cap margins and found on woody substrates.

MACRO- & MICRODESCRIPTION:

Cap 2-4 (-5) cm, broadly convex to plane, disc depressed in age; color is burnt orange to orange to orange-yellow, particularly at the margins. **Gills** thin, blunt, short decurrent, forking 1-4X; lighter than cap color. **Stalk** 1.5-4 cm X 2-5 mm; ± central, and equal, often compressed, dry. **Basidiospores** 5-8 X 2.5-4.5 μm, white in deposit, elliptic, and smooth.

HABITAT AND ROLE:

Conifer forest as a decomposer of lignin-rich substrates.

EDIBILITY, TASTE, AND ODOR:

Mild, fungoid. There are no reports of folks in Alaska eating this fungus, even though some (Arora 1986) have eaten it. I think it may be best left to the slugs.

LOOK-ALIKES:

Small fruit bodies of *Cantharellus cibarius*, but nothing else in Alaska except for possibly *H. citrinopallida*, which is much yellower, fading to yellowish-white and quite viscid when fresh.

COMMENTS:

This fairly common, strikingly beautiful and symmetrically formed mushroom has been moved around within gilled mushroom families (having been placed into the Tricholomataceae, but it lacked white spores; then into the Hygrophoraceae, but it had forking gills; then into the Cantharellaceae because of its chanterelle-like appearance, thick and blunt-edged gills; then into the Paxillaceae because of its dull to brightly colored clay-brown to brown spores; and finally into its own family). We find this mushroom growing on lignin-rich substrates, as found in ovuliferous cone scale bracts of white spruce that the squirrels have deposited into large middens at their tree bases, or in wood chip pathways.

Fig. 028

Fig. 029

FAMILY: Hygrophoraceae
COMMON NAME: Slimy-Sheathed Waxy Cap, Olive Hygrophorus
GENUS AND SPECIES: *Hygrophorus (olivaceoalbus) persoonii* sensu Lange

STRIKING FIELD CHARACTERS:
Smoky gray, streaked, and slippery cap; stalk annulate, white above gray-brown to black below and with white, distant, and decurrent gills.

MACRO- & MICRODESCRIPTION:
Cap 2.5-5.0 cm broad, convex, expanding to flat and finally with a depressed disc; smooth slimy in wet weather; smoky-gray to almost black and with streaking fibers, darker and solid over disc, ashen (grayish-brown) over inrolled margin. **Gills** subdistant, white, thickened, waxy, decurrent, and fairly broad. Gill trama divergent (irregular). **Stalk** 5.0-7.5 cm long, 4-7 mm wide, pure white above annulus-like ring, broadly streaked, gray below; thin blackened veil, smooth. **Basidiospores**

9-12 X 5-6 μm, white in deposit, elliptical, smooth.

HABITAT AND ROLE:
This fungus fruits under white spruce, but it is suspected to be forming mycorrhizae with ericaceous understory plants such as lingonberry and crowberry. Fruiting bodies occur singly to scattered on moss covered soils.

EDIBILITY, TASTE, AND ODOR:
Hygrophorus is described as being edible "with caution" by some, but unless a profuse fruiting is found, it probably would not be worth the trouble to cook up only a few fruiting bodies. Taste and odor are mild. This fungus is very recognizable and not easily confused with any others we've seen.

LOOK-ALIKES:
Gray, gray-brown to brown *H. inocybiformis*, but no other Alaskan species.

COMMENTS:
This is a late (wet) summer to fall fruiter in Alaska.

Agaric (Gilled) Mushrooms

FAMILY: Lyophyllaceae
COMMON NAME: Elm [Birch] Oyster
GENUS AND SPECIES: *Hypsizygus tessulatus* (Bull.) Singer 1947 = *Pleurotus ulmarius* sensu A.A. Pearson (1938)

STRIKING FIELD CHARACTERS:
Large robust whitish fungus growing high up on living birch predominantly with large eccentric and curving stipe.

MACRO- & MICRODESCRIPTION:
Cap 12-16 X 3-5 cm, broadly convex; acentric, smooth, dry; color buff to light tan to cream; margin straight to undulating with white flocculent remains; disc rimulose, ± raised, darker tan to light brown and not smooth; tough pliant. **Gills** adnexed to almost seceding; uneven, lamellulae tiered, thick, crowded, fleshy and tough; edges tan to light-brown in age, otherwise white in youth becoming cream in age. **Stalk** 20-30 (-36) X 11-18 mm; ± flattened, eccentric with dry sheen, tapering to apex; apex downy-flocculent, and chalky-white; longitudinally rimose and long-fibrillose; fibrils white in youth to straw-yellow to tan in age; context white, solid, and unchanging. **Basidiospores** 5-7 X 5-7 µm; white in deposit.

HABITAT AND ROLE:
This fungus decomposes heartwoods of birches. We have not found it on spruce, alder, or aspen, but on some ornamental hardwoods in Interior Alaska like elm and chokecherry.

EDIBILITY, TASTE, AND ODOR:
Reportedly edible, but tough.

LOOK-ALIKES:
Pleurotus ostreatus.

COMMENTS:
This fungus is fairly common at our higher latitudes on white-barked birch, *Betula neoalaskana*. To my knowledge, it has not been found on *Betula keniaca*, the darker barked birch of Interior and Southcentral Alaska.

Fig. 030

Fig. 031

FAMILY: Hydnangiaceae
COMMON NAME: Old Man of the Woods, Common or Waxy Laccaria
GENUS AND SPECIES: *Laccaria laccata* (Scop.) Fr. 1884

STRIKING FIELD CHARACTERS:
Pinkish brown cap, stipe and rosy flesh pink gills; long flexuous and longitudinally fibrillose stalk; cap and stalk smooth to scurfy (unevenly roughened) fibrillose.

MACRO- & MICRODESCRIPTION:
Cap 1.0-6.5 cm broad, convex to broadly convex, but never flat; moist, smooth to minutely scurfy (roughened) or rimose (cracked); margin faintly striate, wavy with a thin sterile margin (gills not reaching to edge) earthy to pinkish brown, sometimes with faint violaceous tints; flesh thin, same color as stalk. **Gills** broadly attached (adnate) to sub-decurrent, rose to flesh pink, spaced, fleshy, narrow and tiered. **Stalk** 3.5-10.0 cm long, 6-12 mm broad, moist, smooth to scaly, unequal and flexuous, longitudinally striate, same color as cap to lighter. **Basidiospores** 7-10 X 6-9 μm; white in deposit, ± globose, spiny.

HABITAT AND ROLE:
This is a known ectomycorrhizal fungus found chiefly in white spruce forests on moss-covered soil.

EDIBILITY, TASTE, AND ODOR:
This is reported as being a good edible, but with caution. No known toxins have been reported, but then that's not necessarily saying much, given one's own body chemistry and allergenic reaction potentials.

LOOK-ALIKES:
Several other *Laccaria* species, albeit smaller in most cases, like *L. altaica*, *L. montana*, *L. proxima*, *L. striatula*, and *L. tortilis*. The latter three are particularly common in Arctic tundra environs.

COMMENTS:
This is perhaps the most ubiquitous mushroom you will find in our northern boreal forests, and it can fool you with its many differing morphologies and colors. The distant rosy gills and white spore deposit should be dead giveaways.

Fig. 032

FAMILY: Russulaceae
COMMON NAME: Northern Spruce Milky, Orange-Latex Lactarius
GENUS AND SPECIES: *Lactarius deterrimus* (Gröger) Hesler and A.H. Sm. 1979

STRIKING FIELD CHARACTERS:
Large, convex to expanded, later depressed, carrot orange, zoned cap and green discolorations or staining, tacky, orange latex, with a lighter carrot-orange stalk and mild taste.

MACRO- & MICRODESCRIPTION:
Cap 2.5-10 cm convex to broadly so; smooth; disc depressed and deeply so with age; frosted whitish to pinkish orange at first becoming bright orange with multiple zones and dull orange with increased green staining with age; tacky to slippery in wet weather; flesh pale light orange to flesh-orange, staining dull greenish-orange in age; margins inrolled at first, expanding in age. **Gills** thick, spaced, broad, broadly attached to very shortly decurrent; orange, more orange than cap, and staining green on edges and where bruised. **Stalk** 3.0-10 cm long, 2-3 cm broad, thick, short, and subequal, expanding a bit at apex and base in youth, the longer it is, the more equal it becomes with a narrow blunt base in age; light pinkish orange, staining green; smooth and dry to moist, but never slimy. **Basidiospores** 7.5-9 X 6-7 μm; pale buff in deposit, broadly elliptical, reticulate.

HABITAT AND ROLE:
This fungus is terrestrial, scattered to gregarious in deep moss carpets under mixed white spruce, paper birch (*B. neoalaskana*), and quaking aspen in upland forests and is a suspected mycorrhizal symbiont with understory ericoids and white spruce.

EDIBILITY, TASTE, AND ODOR:
This is one of our best edibles, easily identified, and when fruiting, is abundant enough for a good meal. Its taste is mild to that of weak radishes with age. Cut your morsels for the table in half to make sure the flies haven't chosen your mushrooms for the same reasons you have, lest you get a bit more protein than planned!

LOOK-ALIKES:
It is most often confused with *L. deliciosus* var. *areolatus* A.H. Sm. (1960) in our high latitude boreal forests. Also, the red rather than green staining *L. thinos* in bogs, which I have never seen, recognized or collected, possibly *L. pseudodeliciosus* with yellow-orange to reddish-orange latex, which I have also not seen in Alaska. This does not mean they don't occur here. I suspect they do if their plant associates do, and *L. rubrilacteus*, which again, I've not seen in Alaska.

COMMENTS:
This fungus, most likely not even *L. deterrimus* genetically, has been confused with *L. deliciosus* in Alaska for years and eaten predicated on that identification. Fortunately, it is a delicious edible and simply cannot be mistaken for any other *Lactarius*, given its bright orange latex and green staining over the cap and stalk, much like *L. deliciosus*.

Agaric (Gilled) Mushrooms

FAMILY: Russulaceae
COMMON NAME: [Squatty] Pink-Fringed Milky
GENUS AND SPECIES: *Lactarius pubescens* var. *betulae* Smith 1960

STRIKING FIELD CHARACTERS:
Small, squatty, whitish-pink, inrolled and bearded margin and white and unchanging latex.

MACRO- & MICRODESCRIPTION:
Cap 3-8 cm; convex-depressed; margin incurved, coarsely bearded; color pale cinnamon-pink; subviscid to dry; densely appressed tomentum; context pinkish-white; latex white, changing to yellow. **Gills** broadly attached (adnate) to sub-decurrent, white to yellowish-buff, close to crowded, fleshy, narrow, and tiered. **Stalk** 3-5 X 1-1.5 cm; pinker than cap; sub-fibrillose, unpolished, dry, hollow. **Basidiospores** 6.5-8 X 5.5-6.5 μm; elliptical; reticulate-ridges; white to yellow-white in deposit.

HABITAT AND ROLE:
Abundant under birch in our mixed aspen-birch-spruce upland forests.

EDIBILITY, TASTE, AND ODOR:
Taste is slowly acrid to nondistinctive, but this fungus should be avoided.

LOOK-ALIKES:
Small and lighter colored than *L. torminosus*, having larger spores.

COMMENTS:
This fungus looks a lot like *L. torminosus*, but has a much squattier stipe and lighter color.

Fig. 033

Agaric (Gilled) Mushrooms

Fig. 034

FAMILY: Russulaceae

COMMON NAME: Yellow, Purple-Staining or Northern Bearded Milky Lactarius

GENUS AND SPECIES: *Lactarius repraesentaneus* Britzelm. 1885

STRIKING FIELD CHARACTERS:

Large, dull to bright yellow, yellow-orange, densely bearded cap and margin; margin tacky to shiny, subzonate; white latex stains tissues lilac; in white spruce forests; with nutmeg odor and acrid (bitter) taste.

MACRO- & MICRODESCRIPTION:

Cap 2-13 cm broad, convex, convex-depressed and may become deeply depressed in age; tacky in dry weather to very slimy or gooey in wet weather; ± zoned with honey to butterscotch, coarse fibrils that are abundant over the heavily bearded margin; fibrous margin white at first becoming yellow to dull yellow to yellow-orange; disc often smooth; flesh white, staining lilac when exposed to air, white milk unchanging or turning lightly wheylike (watery-white); flesh firm to brittle. **Gills** 5-8 mm broad, close to sub-distant, broadly attached to slightly decurrent; often contorted from convex cap; light cream yellow to paler buff-yellow, spotted (especially edges) by latex when fresh. **Stalk** 2.5-9 cm long, 1.5-4.0 cm broad, relatively short, stocky, equal to irregular, hollow, dry to shiny, white glistening dots at apex, yellow to yellow-buff, pitted; flesh white, staining same as gills and cap tissues. **Basidiospores** 8-12 X 6.5-9 μm; whitish to yellowish; broadly elliptical, warted and ridged. Latex white to creamy-white, staining tissues lilac to dull purple.

HABITAT AND ROLE:

We find this fungus almost always in white spruce to mixed white spruce, paper birch, and quaking aspen forests, projecting from the soil through thick moss carpets. *Lactarius repraesentaneus* is most probably a mycorrhizal associate of the spruce and/or understory ericaceous

Agaric (Gilled) Mushrooms

shrubs. Most often scattered to occasionally gregarious, the tissues of this fungus stain lilac quickly in wet weather when copious white milky juice is present.

EDIBILITY, TASTE, AND ODOR:
The large size, fragrant (nutmeg) odor, and mild to acrid (peppery) taste of this fungus might suggest something good to eat, but **DON'T!** Several authors report that no *Lactarius* that stains lilac or violaceous should be eaten. They can cause mild to severe gastrointestinal upset. This complex of fungi has two or three closely related species in our northern forests that need substantial work. So why take the chance of ruining a good hike?

LOOK-ALIKES:
L. alnicola, *L resimus*, and *L. scrobiculatus*, which are inedible, tend to be smaller, not as glutinous in wet weather, and whose latex stains brightly yellow or gill tissues ± yellow.

COMMENTS:
This fungus is almost exclusively restricted to fruiting in association with our white spruce amongst the green moss carpet; hence easily seen with its bright yellow color. Once again, one should never eat these acrid-tasting *Lactarii*.

Agaric (Gilled) Mushrooms

FAMILY: Russulaceae
COMMON NAME: Brick-Red,
  Red-Hot Milky Lactarius
GENUS AND SPECIES: *Lactarius rufus* (Scop.) Fr. 1838

STRIKING FIELD CHARACTERS:

A reddish-brown dry cap, cream to pinkish buff, short decurrent gills, a very strong acrid (radish) bite to the flesh; latex that is first white, unchanging and becoming wheylike (watery).

MACRO- & MICRODESCRIPTION:

Cap 2.5-22 cm broad, convex to convex-depressed, + umbonate; dry, reddish-orange to red brown, darker over disc and often paler pinkish red over ribbed (striate) and wavy margin; margin inrolled and silky flocculose in youth, expanding to straight and becoming lacerate (broken up) with age; flesh moderately thick, to 10 mm, light flesh tan; latex white, very acrid (peppery or bitter) and unchanging in color. **Gills** broadly attached to very short decurrent, close, 2-4 mm broad, pallid (pale), dirty cream to pinkish tan; latex white, unchanging, and not discoloring tissues. **Stalk** 2.5-13 cm long, 5-14 mm broad, brittle, equal to slightly (hairless), smooth; pinkish flesh to rose tinted above, otherwise the same color as the gills; stuffed to hollow. **Basidiospores** 7.5-11 X 5-7.5 µm; cream to pale-yellow, elliptical, amyloid warts and ridges.

HABITAT AND ROLE:

This fungus is almost always found on sites that are at slightly higher elevations than the surrounding landscape, which often occurs in association with dwarf birch on rocky outcrops or prominences called granite tors or on hillsides having fairly well drained soils.

Fig. 035

EDIBILITY, TASTE, AND ODOR:

Described by several authors as poisonous (gastrointestinal upsetting), this mushroom has a very biting (acrid) taste, but a fairly mild odor.

LOOK-ALIKES:

L. rufulus, L. subflammans, and *L. subviscidus.*

COMMENTS:

In reality, with the richness (26+ spp.) of *Lactarii* (Geml et al, 2008, 2009 and 2009) in high latitude Alaska, it wouldn't surprise us that *Lactarius rufus* represents a rather large group of very similar and closely related species, none of which should be eaten.

FAMILY: Russulaceae
COMMON NAME: [Tall] Pink-
Fringed or Bearded Milky
GENUS AND SPECIES: *Lactarius
torminosus* (Schaeff.) Gray 1821

STRIKING FIELD CHARACTERS:
Medium sized, acrid tasting, pinkish
radiating fibrillose cap with an inturned
and bearded margin, white and unchanging latex.

MACRO- & MICRODESCRIPTION:
Cap 3-10 cm, convex, depressed disc,
inrolled bearded margin, ± viscid in wet
weather, pinkish-buff, depressed disc
often darker rose-pink; context white,
brittle (as in all of the Russulaceae members). **Gills** white to yellowish-buff,
crowded, thin, broadly attached to ±
decurrent; latex thin, white, unchanging.
Stalk 3-10 X 0.5-1 cm; ± equal (sub-
knobby), brittle-firm, hollowing; concolorous with or a bit lighter than cap.
Basidiospores 7-10 X 6-8 μm; ivory- to
creamy-white in deposit.

HABITAT AND ROLE:
Abundant under our northern birches,
but also found with spruce. Rarely found
with aspen.

EDIBILITY, TASTE, AND ODOR:
Not considered edible, albeit some use
portions of it for seasoning when dried.
Very acrid!

LOOK-ALIKES:
The poisonous *Paxillus involutus*, which
is an olive-yellow brown and with clay-
brown spores in deposit; and *L. pubescens*, which is lighter colored and much
shorter stalked.

COMMENTS:
This medium-sized fungus is often a
stumper at first, but one of the most common *Lactarii* found in Alaska. I must
admit, *Lactarius torminosus*, like *Mycena
pura*, is so variable that I really have to
stop and think about its binomial when
finding it in the field.

Fig. 036

Fig. 037

FAMILY: Auriscalpiaceae
COMMON NAME: Cockle-Shell Lentinellus
GENUS AND SPECIES: *Lentinellus cochleatus* (Pers.) P. Karst. 1879

STRIKING FIELD CHARACTERS:
Flesh-tan, depressed to infundibuliform, smooth, moist cap, white, spaced, saw-toothed edged gills, and white spores.

MACRO- & MICRODESCRIPTION:
Cap 2-6 cm; irregularly funnel-shaped; flesh-pink to buffy yellow-tan; with upraised hairs. **Gills** white; spaced, saw-toothed; broadly attached to ± decurrent; inrolled in youth expanding with minutely scalloped margin. **Stalk** 2-5 X 1-1.5 cm; ± central; darker to dull yellow- or olive-brown; ovoid to flattened. **Basidiospores** 4.5-5 X 3.5-4 μm; subglobose, white in deposit.

HABITAT AND ROLE:
Tufted at base of alders.

EDIBILITY, TASTE, AND ODOR:
Edible; mild; fungoid.

LOOK-ALIKES:
Nothing else we've seen in Alaska.

COMMENTS:
This is a rather inconspicuous fungus growing in individual or fused groups in mosses at the bases of hardwoods.

Agaric (Gilled) Mushrooms

FAMILY: Lyophyllaceae
COMMON NAME: Fried Chicken
GENUS AND SPECIES: *Lyophyllum decastes* (Fr.) Singer 1951

STRIKING FIELD CHARACTERS:
A dense, meaty, grayish-brown cluster (caespitose) of fruit bodies of varying maturation levels makes this mushroom fairly recognizable.

MACRO- & MICRODESCRIPTION:
Cap 3-14 cm broadly convex to plano-convex, smooth, moist, but not viscid; context white; color variable, but dirty tan to brown generally. **Gills** broadly attached to ± short decurrent, broad, close, white to buff in age. **Stalk** 5-20 X 1-2.5 cm; solid, ± equal, smooth, dry, white. **Basidiospores** 4-6 μm, globose to subglobose, smooth, white in deposit.

HABITAT AND ROLE:
A decomposer of grass and lignin-rich soils, often found in disturbed localities.

EDIBILITY, TASTE, AND ODOR:
Edible; mild; pleasant.

LOOK-ALIKES:
There are several *Clitocybe* (e.g., C. *polygonarum*, an Arctic edible of significant

Fig. 038

size and stature forming rings around polygonal patterned ground), *Lepista* and other *Lyophyllum* species that look very much like this mushroom. If pure white, as in *Clitocybe dealbata*, one should only sense, but never savor, as this mushroom is quite poisonous.

COMMENTS:
There are many other look-alikes, but most do not occur in Alaska. Look around the margins of gravel parking lots for this clumpy, dirty-brown, and white-spored fungus.

Agaric (Gilled) Mushrooms

Fig. 039

FAMILY: Mycenaceae
COMMON NAME: Late Oyster
GENUS AND SPECIES: *Panellus serotinus* (Pers.) Kühner 1950

STRIKING FIELD CHARACTERS:

Fuzzy greenish to greenish-yellow cap and orange gills, on deadwood logs.

MACRO- & MICRODESCRIPTION:

Cap 2-8 cm; fanlike; colored green, yellow-green, yellow-tan, brown, or with a violet flush; smooth; oyster-shaped. Context white, thick and firm. **Gills** yellowish-orange, broadly attached to decurrent, close, pale orange, orange-buff to pale yellowish. **Stalk** when present, lateral, short, yellowish, velvety to hairy. **Basidiospores** 4-6 X 1-2 µm, cream-colored in deposit.

HABITAT AND ROLE:

Grows scattered or in overlapping clusters, usually on dead or dying hardwoods (alder, birch, or willow), sometimes on conifers. Reported from Southcentral and Interior Alaska.

EDIBILITY, TASTE, AND ODOR:

Too bitter to bother, perhaps, mediocre at best, and may cause gastrointestinal upset in some.

LOOK-ALIKES:

Other *Panellus, Panus,* and *Crepidotus* species.

COMMENTS:

A late summer, early fall fruiter, this fungus is an exciting find later in the mushroom season, but its appearance signals the near end of it.

FAMILY: Tricholomataceae
COMMON NAME: Orange Mock Oyster, Nestcap Mushroom
GENUS AND SPECIES: *Phyllotopsis nidulans* (Pers.) Singer 1936

STRIKING FIELD CHARACTERS:

This is a relatively small, striking, orange, dry, fuzzy-velvety shelf or bracket fungus with yellow-orange gills, no stalk, and white spores in deposit.

MACRO- & MICRODESCRIPTION:

Cap 2.5-8.0 cm broad, semicircular, broadly convex to plane, densely hairy upper surface; buff to orange-yellow to yellowish-orange; margin inrolled, scalloped; flesh paler than cap; dry. **Gills** attached to hairy white base, close to crowded, narrow to moderately broad; yellowish buff, orange-yellow to burnt-orange in age. **Stalk** absent. **Basidiospores** 5-8 X 2-4µm, pale pinkish to pinkish-brown in deposit; sausage-shaped, smooth.

HABITAT AND ROLE:

Single to overlapping clusters can be found on alder and white spruce, which it decomposes.

EDIBILITY, TASTE, AND ODOR:

Not known to be poisonous or its edibility reportedly unknown, *Phyllotopsis nidulans* is perhaps best left alone as its odor is strong or disagreeable, like hydrogen sulfide gas (rotten eggs-like), to mild. The taste is unknown to us.

LOOK-ALIKES:

Paxillus panuoides looks similar, but has clay-brown, not white, spores; *Panellus* species with white spore will be light tan, yellowish-tan, brown, or cinnamon, lacking the orange hue.

COMMENTS:

Once seen, this fungus is hard to confuse with other wood-inhabiting shelf fungi.

Fig. 040

Agaric (Gilled) Mushrooms

FAMILY: Marasmiaceae
COMMON NAME: Angel Wings
GENUS AND SPECIES: *Pleurocybella porrigens* (Pers.) Singer 1947

STRIKING FIELD CHARACTERS:
A beautifully thin, pliant, white, shelving fungus found on the rotted stumps or butt ends of downed hemlock and spruce logs.

MACRO- & MICRODESCRIPTION:
Cap 2-8 X 2-4 cm; white, delicate fans with a shelflike habit; context white, thin, pliant. **Gills** white, entire, narrow and crowded. **Stalk** stubby or absent. **Basidiospores** 6-7 X 5-6 μm; globose to subglobose, smooth and white in deposit.

HABITAT AND ROLE:
Scattered or in densely overlapping clusters on very decayed spruce stumps or logs, often growing out through moss. Reported only from Southcentral and Southeast Alaska.

EDIBILITY, TASTE, AND ODOR:
Edible; mild; fungoid.

LOOK-ALIKES:
P. lignatilis (narrow, crowded gills and more prominent stalk) and *Pleurotus ostreatus*, which appears on alder, aspen, birch, and willow, not conifers.

COMMENTS:
This is a thin, pliant, beautiful fungus found generally on spruce and hemlock logs in deep forest settings that are overgrown with moss.

Fig. 041

Agaric (Gilled) Mushrooms

Fig. 042a

FAMILY: Russulaceae
COMMON NAME: Tacky Green Russula
GENUS AND SPECIES: *Russula aeruginea* Lindbl. ex Fr. 1863

STRIKING FIELD CHARACTERS:

Medium sized, smooth, grayish green cap, white stalk, peeling cap cuticle, brittle to crumbly cap and stipe tissues, subdistant (more or less separated), even, white to cream-colored gills.

MACRO- & MICRODESCRIPTION:

Cap 3.5-10 cm; convex to convex depressed in age; smooth, moist, tacky to viscid (sticky) in wet weather; grayish green, darker and brighter over recessed disc, becoming lighter, washed out, light olive to greenish white over expanding substrate; undulating to wavy and often with split margin in age; cap tissue white, fragile to brittle and crumbly, thin; cuticle peels from cap. **Gills** attached, notched, close to spaced, broad, white becoming cream white, brown-spotted, even. **Stalk** 3.5-6.5 X 0.7-2.0 cm; smooth, dull white to greenish-white, uneven to even, sub-clavate with fluted apex and slightly expanded base. **Basidiospores** 6-9 X 5-7 µm; pale, creamy to dull deep yellow in deposit, subglobose, amyloid warts and ridges.

HABITAT AND ROLE:

On ground and most often projecting through thick moss carpets in mixed white spruce-aspen forests.

EDIBILITY, TASTE, AND ODOR:

This fairly easily recognized fungus is edible, as reported by several authors.

LOOK-ALIKES:

R. grisea (dull grayer-green with brown) and *R. parazurea* (dull, matte-appearing, white spores).

COMMENTS:

There are about 12 species of green to gray-green capped Russulas, so one really has to use microscopy or genetic sequencing to clearly delineate them.

Fig. 042b

Agaric (Gilled) Mushrooms

Fig. 043

FAMILY: Russulaceae
COMMON NAME: Short-Stalked White Russula
GENUS AND SPECIES: *Russula brevipes* Peck 1890

STRIKING FIELD CHARACTERS:
Large, dull-white, deeply depressed, centered, inrolled margin and tough mushroom with a massive and short stalk.

MACRO- & MICRODESCRIPTION:
Cap 5-20 cm; broadly convex-deeply depressed; margin inrolled; dry, dull white and dirt-streaked and/or with yellow to yellow-brown staining; context white, thick, brittle. **Gills** white, broad, thin, close to crowded, broadly attached to decurrent; ± brown staining in age. **Stalk** 2-10 (-15) X 2-6 cm; short, stout, hard to rigid, dry and concolorous with cap. **Basidiospores** 8-11 X 6-9 µm; elliptic, warted, white in deposit.

HABITAT AND ROLE:
Scattered, often half buried.

EDIBILITY, TASTE, AND ODOR:
Edible, mild to ± acrid, and mild smelling.

LOOK-ALIKES:
R. cascadensis and possibly *R. delica*, if found in the US or Alaska. We have seen neither in Alaska, but again, that certainly doesn't mean they're not here!

COMMENTS:
In a mixed birch-spruce upland, look for leaf mounds under which you are apt to find these often massive and tough fruit bodies pushing up through the duff. We have seen them push up mounds of sand in the desertlike dunes in Kobuk Valley National Park just north of the Arctic Circle.

FAMILY: Russulaceae
COMMON NAME: The Sickener, Emetic Russula
GENUS AND SPECIES: *Russula emetica* (Schaeff.) Pers. 1796

STRIKING FIELD CHARACTERS:
Medium to small, deep forest floor associate of mixed white spruce-aspen forests; smooth tacky; purple-red, red to reddish-white cap, white gills and white stalk; and acrid tasting; i.e., with a strong radish flavor.

MACRO- & MICRODESCRIPTION:
Cap 2-6 cm broad, convex, plane to irregularly depressed; deep purplish-red, red to bright red, fading in age to yellowish buff (ochraceous) red to almost reddish-tinted buff over glabrous and smooth peeling cuticle and pellucid-striate margin; context white, thin, brittle to crumbly. **Gills** narrow (2-4 mm), close, even, white to yellowish-white and attached, but notched. **Stalk** 2.5-5.0 cm long, 6-14 mm broad, sub-clavate, smooth, dry to grayish-white to same color as the gills. **Basidiospores** 7-11 X 6.5-9 μm; elliptical, amyloid warts and ridges, white in deposit.

HABITAT AND ROLE:
Terrestrial, single to gregarious, this is another suspected mycorrhizal fungus. This common species is found on moist to wet rich humus soil of mixed conifer-hardwood forests during summer (mid to late July) and is usually associated with understory shrubs, mostly lingonberry and *Sphagnum* mosses. Of the nearly 620 species of mosses in Alaska, 57 are species of *Sphagnum* (USDA-FS 2008).

EDIBILITY, TASTE, AND ODOR:
This is a mild smelling, very acrid tasting mushroom; *Russula emetica* should not be eaten.

LOOK-ALIKES:
There are so many "red Russulas." Of 37 Russulas we've seen in Alaska, nearly one-third of them are some shade of red! The other two-thirds are orange, green, yellow, white, and even black.

COMMENTS:
This fungus is closely related to many other red to pinkish-red capped and white stalked *Russula* with an acrid flavor, none of which should be prepared for the table, as they may induce mild to severe vomiting (as in an emetic). Our fungus is closely related to *R. montana* Shaffer and *R. mairei* Sing. Even though our species is not directly associated with *Sphagnum* moss (as is often the case for *R. emetica*), we still think it is closer to *R. emetica* than to either of the other species. Only genetic investigation will more clearly define this large group of Alaskan Russulas.

Fig. 044

Agaric (Gilled) Mushrooms

Fig. 045

FAMILY: Russulaceae
COMMON NAME: Yellow Russula
GENUS AND SPECIES: *Russula lutea* (Huds.) Gray 1821

STRIKING FIELD CHARACTERS:
Yellow, peeling, non-gray staining, in mixed birch-aspen uplands.

MACRO- & MICRODESCRIPTION:
Cap 2-7 cm; convex, to depressed plane; smooth, viscid; margin striate; color golden- to egg-yolk yellow, apricot, peach, flesh to coral; context white. **Gills** light yellow to deep saffron; ± forked. **Stalk** 2-6 X 0.5-1.5 cm; white; cylindrical to subclavate, fragile to brittle. **Basidiospores** 7.5-9 X 6-8 μm; subglobose to short elliptic; warted; ochre in deposit; reported as white by Miller and Miller (2006).

HABITAT AND ROLE:
Ectomycorrhizal with birch (*B. neoalaskana*).

EDIBILITY, TASTE, AND ODOR:
Edible; mildly peppery; sweet.

LOOK-ALIKES:
R. claroflava (stains gray), *R. flava* (stains gray), *R. flavida* (unchanging), *R. ochroleuca* (stains gray), and *R. ochroleucoides* (unchanging).

COMMENTS:
As stated earlier, this is a group of Russulas that needs further and wide-spreading attention.

FAMILY: Russulaceae
COMMON NAME: Shellfish-Scented Russula
GENUS AND SPECIES: *Russula xerampelina* (Schaeff.) Fr. 1838

STRIKING FIELD CHARACTERS:
A dry, unpolished, sturdy, variable colored (purple-red, maroon, red, yellowish-pink, to buff mottling; pinkish stalk and shellfish odor distinctly separate this from other similarly colored Russulas.

MACRO- & MICRODESCRIPTION:
Cap 4-10 cm; convex to wavy-plane; disc depressed in age; smooth, ± viscid in wet weather; color variably deep purplish-red, olive-red, pinkish-brown, tan to buff streaked; context white to ivory, brittle, bruising brown. **Gills** notched to broadly attached; white to creamy in age, stain brown where bruised. **Stalk** 2-10 X 1-2 cm; ± equal; minutely ridged longitudinally; dry; white with pink, coral to rosy flushes; context stuffed. **Basidiospores** 8-11 X 6-9 µm; globose, subglobose to short elliptic; warted; cream-yellow in deposit.

HABITAT AND ROLE:
We find this in close association with dwarf birch and willow in the Arctic, well above the Arctic Circle and in deep moss under spruce in Interior Alaska.

EDIBILITY, TASTE, AND ODOR:
Edible, and good, as claimed by many; mild; mild at first then increasingly shellfish-like (shrimp) becoming almost fetid with age.

Fig. 046

LOOK-ALIKES:
In Alaska there are many red-hued Russulas, we find no other quite like the sturdy *Russula xerampelina* with its combination of easily recognizable characters. Those close to it in other climes, like *R. cyanoxantha*, we have not yet found in Alaska.

COMMENTS:
Some are averse to the shellfish odor that emanates from this mushroom, which becomes stronger to almost obnoxious with age. Unfortunate, claim many, as it is such a good edible mushroom.

Agaric (Gilled) Mushrooms

Lichen-Agaric Basidiolichen

Fig. 047

FAMILY: Hygrophoraceae
COMMON NAME: Agaric Lichen
GENUS AND SPECIES: *Lichenomphalia umbellifera* (L.) Redhead, Lutzoni, Moncalvo and Vilgalys 2002

STRIKING FIELD CHARACTERS:

Small, straw-yellow to yellowish-tan cap and slightly darker stalk, omphalinoid mushroom at the base of which can be found very small egg-shaped blue-green spheres, which are the lichen thallus, once given its own name of *Botrydina vulgare*. Most frequently associated with mosses, *Sphagnum* being most popular.

MACRO- & MICRODESCRIPTION:

Cap 1-2.5 (-3) cm; plane to ± depressed in age; margin inrolled, striate; smooth, moist; drab yellow-tan to straw-yellow in age; context thin, concolorous with cap; pliant. **Gills** decurrent, spaced, lighter yellow-tan. **Stalk** 1.5-3 X 0.2-0.5 cm; smooth, pliant, ± equal with a swollen base/attachment; concolorous with or darker that cap, particularly at the apex. **Basidiospores** 7-9 X 4-6 μm; smooth, elliptical; white in deposit.

HABITAT AND ROLE:

A lichen; hence, a mutualistic and symbiotic association between a fungus (the mycobiont) and an alga (the photo- or phycobiont).

EDIBILITY, TASTE, AND ODOR:

Edible, but generally too tiny to attempt gathering for a meal.

LOOK-ALIKES:

L. hudsoniana with its yellow cap and straw-yellow to buff stalk on rotting conifer wood; *L. alpina* (= *L. luteovitellina*) with its yellow cap and stalk on exposed, lignin-rich peaty substrates.

COMMENTS:

What is really interesting to us is this and five other close relatives constitute the less than 0.1 percent of all lichenized fungi as Basidiolichens, and we have all five in Alaska, three agaric forms (*L. alpina*, *L. hudsoniana*, and *L. umbellifera*) and two coral forms (*Multiclavula muscida* and *M. vernalis*). All other lichens are members of the Ascomycota.

Agarics with PINK to SALMON colored spores

FAMILY: Pluteaceae (=Volvaria-ceae) or Entolomataceae
COMMON NAME: Deer Mushroom, Fawn-Colored Pluteus
GENUS AND SPECIES: *Pluteus cervinus* (Schaeff.) P. Kumm. 1871

STRIKING FIELD CHARACTERS:
Whitish to pinkish tan, light grayish-tan to dull brown cap, broadly convex, pinkish-flesh colored, with free gills, and typically fruiting from downed birch logs.

MACRO- & MICRODESCRIPTION:
Cap 3.5-11.5 cm, broadly convex; smooth, moist to somewhat sticky; often with oppressed fibrils over disc; margin becoming recurved and split; context (flesh) moderately thick, ivory, becoming dirty white. **Gills** free, fairly close, broad, brittle, and easily damaged; whitish-tan becoming flesh-pink at maturity. **Stalk** 3.5-7.5 cm long, 5-10 mm broad, longitudinally fibrous and slightly "candy cane" twisted; firm, pliant, solid, smooth and whitish-tan or ivory. **Basidiospores** 5-8 X 4-6 µm; flesh to pinkish-brown in deposit; elliptical and smooth.

HABITAT AND ROLE:
In the interior of Alaska, this fungus is fairly common. It seemingly always occurs on hardwoods, including birch logs well on their way to decomposition and delignification. *Pluteus cervinus* is a saprobe and, we suspect, a cellulose decomposer, given the spongy condition hardwood logs are in when we see this fungus fruiting on them. Rarely do we find more than two on any one rotting log, and most often only a single fruiting body is present.

Fig. 048

EDIBILITY, TASTE, AND ODOR:
Pluteus cervinus is reported to be edible. We've never eaten this fungus, as it has never been found in great abundance, and when found is often too mature or soggy for the frying pan. Taste is mild to faintly metallic when fresh. Odor is pleasant. This fungus, given its fruiting locality, pinkish flesh-colored gills, and candy cane twist to its stalk, can be clearly separated from other mushrooms found on similar woody substrates.

LOOK-ALIKES:
Entoloma spp. Typically on the ground and with attached gills.

COMMENTS:
At first, you may think you've found a *Tricholoma* (on wood), but the lack of white spores (pink instead) and attached gills (free here), you'll realize you have a member of the Pluteaceae and not the Tricholomataceae.

Agarics with YELLOW to ORANGE-BROWN colored spores

FAMILY: Bolbitiaceae
COMMON NAME: Sunny Side Up or Yellow Bolbitius
GENUS AND SPECIES: *Bolbitius vitellinus* (Pers.) Fr. 1838

STRIKING FIELD CHARACTERS:
This small, fragile mushroom can be distinguished from others in similar habitats with its viscid to slimy, bright yellow-brown to yellow-green disc, yellow conical cap with whitish striate margins, a slimy whitish stalk, and bright orange-brown spores.

MACRO- & MICRODESCRIPTION:
Cap 1-4 cm; viscid to slimy; bright yellow-brown to yellow-green; disc, yellow conical cap; whitish striate margins. **Gills** deeply notched (almost free); buff-yellow to yellow in youth, darkening to greenish-yellow, finally dirty yellow-brown to brown. **Stalk** 4-15 cm X 2-6 mm; ± equal with a swollen base, hollow, very fragile, white to light yellow.

Basidiospores 10-16 X 6-9 µm; smooth, elliptical, and truncated; bright orange-brown in deposit.

HABITAT AND ROLE:
Gregarious to clustered on lignin-rich substrates (wood chips, horse manure, and dead grassy paths); its role is that of a decomposer.

EDIBILITY, TASTE, AND ODOR:
Reported to be edible, but perhaps not desirable thanks to the sliminess, fragility, and small size.

LOOK-ALIKES:
B. coprophilus (pinkish) and *B. lacteus* (whitish) are both found on nitrogen and lignin-rich substrates such as manures, but we have yet to see these kin in Alaska.

COMMENTS:
This bright, fragile, small fungus has only been found on wood chip lined walkways and horse manure piles here in Alaska.

Fig. 049

Fig. 050

FAMILY: Agaricaceae
COMMON NAME: Golden Pholiota
GENUS AND SPECIES: *Phaeolepiota aurea* (Matt.) Maire 1928

STRIKING FIELD CHARACTERS:
Large, robust, dull butterscotch color, *Cystoderma*-like looking mushroom of disturbed sites.

MACRO- & MICRODESCRIPTION:
Cap 7-20 (-30) cm, button convex to sub-ovate becoming broadly campanulate, broadly convex to almost plane in age; orange-buff to orange-ochraceous in youth, paler in age; dry, dull to unpolished, floccose-granulose, easily removed; pile-pellis thick, peeling in part; trama thick, whitish, unchanging. **Gills** pallid, whitish in youth becoming concolorous with cap in age; adnexed, toothed, broad, close, entire. **Stalk** 10-15 (-25) cm X (1.5-) 3-5 (-6) cm broad, sub-clavate, concolorous with cap, apex often darker, dry, glabrous above pronounced annulus, floccose-granulose below; context concolorous with cap, often with yellow streaking; stuffed to hollowing in age; basil white mycelium. **Basidiospores** 10.5-12.5 (-14) X 5-6 μm, elliptic to short fusoid, thin, smooth to verruculose-like wall, light yellow-brown to orange-buff in deposit and non-amyloid. Hyphae clamped.

HABITAT AND ROLE:
Abundant, gregarious to caespitose, disturbed sites, possibly an alder associate; fruits mid-September to mid-October in Southcentral Alaska.

EDIBILITY, TASTE, AND ODOR:
Reported by many to be edible, but caution anyone who has never eaten this mushroom, as it is reported to be gatrointestinally upsetting for some (Wells and Kempton 1965). Mild fungoid odor; mild to lightly tangy taste.

LOOK-ALIKES:
Cystoderma fallax, with white spores and much smaller and yellow to flocculose orange-ochraceous.

COMMENTS:
This is a meaty mushroom and is very tempting for the table, but caution is advised, as your body chemistry may not be compatible to what this beauty offers.

Agarics with DULL- to CLAY-BROWN colored spores

Fig. 051

FAMILY: Paxillaceae
COMMON NAME: Poison Paxillus, Inrolled or Involute Paxillus
GENUS AND SPECIES: *Paxillus involutus* (Batsch) Fr. 1838

STRIKING FIELD CHARACTERS:

Drab orange, dry, feltlike to shiny cap with inrolled hairy margin; stalk off-center, short; gills dull yellowish-orange.

MACRO- & MICRODESCRIPTION:

Cap 3.5-12.5 cm broad, broadly convex to flat and becoming depressed early; slimy capped in wet weather, otherwise dry matted felty (fibrillose); dull yellowish-brown, often spotted; splitting (rimose) near persistently inrolled and fuzzy margin. **Gills** narrow, short decurrent, crowded, forked once, yellow-tan to yellow-orange, bruising reddish-orange to brown. **Stalk** 12-25 mm long, 10-13 mm broad (short-stocky), dry, concolorous with cap to slightly lighter. **Basidiospores** 7-10 X 4-6 µm; smooth, elliptical; yellow-brown to brown in deposit.

HABITAT AND ROLE:

Terrestrial (on soil), solitary, scattered to gregarious on rich humus of alpine tundra peat or mixed white spruce-paper birch forests, and a suspected mycorrhizal associate, if not with paper birch, then with ericaceous understory plants such as crowberry. We have collected this from the low ericaceous shrub-willow-dwarf birch-dominated tundra of high alpine sites near large granite tors north of Coldfoot on the Dalton Highway, clearly some distance from any forests, as we generally think of them.

EDIBILITY, TASTE, AND ODOR:

The mild flavor and fungoid odor of *Paxillus involutus* may deceive, as this fungus is generally regarded as a gastrointestinal irritant and a liver destroyer and should never be eaten. In Europe and parts of North America it has been reported as being edible and is enjoyed by some, even though liver toxicity (red blood cell autoimmune breakdown) is documented. Do not partake of this mushroom.

LOOK-ALIKES:

It will sort of remind you of a dirty greenish-yellow to yellow-brown *Lactarius*, but the noticeably striate margin on an inrolled and bearded margin makes you question your identification. Then you make a spore print, and voila! It's not white, but orange-brown.

COMMENTS:

If you are going to photograph this photogenic mushroom, be very careful to select sturdy specimens with a bit of substrate, otherwise you may break the stalk of this fragile little agaric. Here is another poisonous species that should never be eaten.

Agarics with DULL- to CLAY-BROWN colored spores

Agarics with DULL, CINNAMON- to RUSTY-BROWN colored spores

FAMILY: Cortinariaceae
COMMON NAME: Belted Slimy Cort (Subgenus Myxacium)
GENUS AND SPECIES: *Cortinarius [collinitus] trivialis* J.E. Lange 1940

STRIKING FIELD CHARACTERS:
Netlike veil remnant on stalk, bluish tinged gills and stalk, reddish-, olivaceous- to yellowish-brown, and slimy cap and stalk.

MACRO- & MICRODESCRIPTION:
Cap 3-10 cm; hemispherical to conical, finally plano-convex, ± umbonate; viscid to sub-glutinous; yellow-tan to yellow-brown to reddish-brown. **Gills** crowded, bluish-gray to grayish-brown. **Stalk** 4-10 X 1-2 cm; cylindrical to tapering below, brown base; veil whitish, glutinous; context grayish-white becoming brown. **Basidiospores** 10-12 X 6-7.5 µm; amygdaliform, verrucose; rusty-brown in deposit.

HABITAT AND ROLE:
Ectomycorrhizal with white and black spruce forest in lowlands, but with dwarf birch, willow, and aspen at higher elevations.

EDIBILITY, TASTE, AND ODOR:
Best left for the slugs and bugs; mild; indistinct.

LOOK-ALIKES:
C. crocolitus (slimy cap, but dry stalk—subgen. *Phlegmacium*), *C. elatior* (the aspen associate), *C. mucifluus* (perhaps a form of *C. trivialis*), and *C. pallidifolius* (anther conifer associate).

COMMENTS:
A variable fungus with varying moisture, and a number of forms have been described (Brandrud et al 1994). Arora (1986) refers and describes this fungus as *C. collinitus*. It is important to note that this genus has the largest number of species representing it than any other genus of mushroom in Alaska.

Fig. 052

FAMILY: Cortinariaceae
COMMON NAME: Red-Gilled Cort (Subgenus Dermocybe)
GENUS AND SPECIES: *Cortinarius ominosus* (Fr.) Gillet 1876

STRIKING FIELD CHARACTERS:
Yellow stalk, olive brown cap, and blood-red gills.

Fig. 053a

MACRO- & MICRODESCRIPTION:
Cap 2-5 cm; convex to sub-plane; low umbonate; smooth, dry, minutely fibrillose; yellow to orange-yellow to olive-brown; context whitish-buff. **Gills** broadly attached, crowded, blood red. **Stalk** 3-6 X 0.5-0.75 cm; equal, yellow, fibrillose, slender, yellow; hairy, collapsed partial veil—spore-colored. **Basidiospores** 5-8 X 3-5 μm; elliptic, rugulose.

HABITAT AND ROLE:
Ectomycorrhizal with black spruce in Interior Alaska.

EDIBILITY, TASTE, AND ODOR:
This subgenus is reportedly the worst for edibility due to toxins found in many specimens. It is, therefore, best left to its photogenic properties.

LOOK-ALIKES:
C. cinnabarinus (hardwood favoring, cinnabar-red to rusty-red basidiome), *C. phoeniceus* (maroon-red to reddish-brown cap), *C. puniceus* (yellow- to golden-brown cortina and dark- to purple-red color with hardwood preferences), *C. neosanguineus* (no yellow in cap or stalk).

COMMENTS:
These are beautifully colored fungi and of the 1000+ *Cortinarius* species in North America, they are relatively easy to identify by comparison to other *Cortinarii*. Note, however, this is an extremely dangerous/poisonous group of fungi and should never be eaten.

Fig. 053b

Fig. 054

FAMILY: Cortinariaceae
COMMON NAME: Lilac Conifer Cort (Subgenus Telamonia)
GENUS AND SPECIES: *Cortinarius traganus* (Fr.) Fr. 1838

STRIKING FIELD CHARACTERS:

Lavender, lilac to violaceous with a fine whitish to vinaceous fibrillose sheen, rusty staining cap and stalk, and tawny-brown flesh.

MACRO- & MICRODESCRIPTION:

Cap 4-13 cm; obtuse, convex to plane; smooth, dry, fibrillose to ± scaly; violet to lilac, rusty to orange-brown stains; margin with veil remnants; context rusty- to tawny- or yellow-brown. **Gills** pale cinnamon to yellowish-buff, finally cinnamon- to rusty-brown; spaced, notched to broadly attached. **Stalk** 5-10 X 1-2.5 (-4) cm; solid, dry, fibrillose, lilac to purplish. **Basidiospores** 7-10 X 5-6 μm; elliptic, verrucose.

HABITAT AND ROLE:

Ectomycorrhizal with our many conifers.

EDIBILITY, TASTE, AND ODOR:

Gastrointestinally upsetting; mild; sweetish.

LOOK-ALIKES:

C. amethystinus (much darker violet hues, as name suggests), *C. camphoratus* (badly smelling and lavender to whitish-lilac cap), *C. caesiifolius* (buff-brown cap and bluish gills), *C. fragrans* (odor of pears), and *C. olympianus* (viscid cap).

COMMENTS:

This is a beautiful, photogenic, and easily recognizable *Cortinarius*.

Fig. 055

FAMILY: Cortinariaceae
COMMON NAME: Violet Cort
(Subgenus Cortinarius)
GENUS AND SPECIES: *Cortinarius violaceus* (L.) Gray 1821

STRIKING FIELD CHARACTERS:
This dark bluish- to purplish-black scaly capped fungus is very easily recognized.

MACRO- & MICRODESCRIPTION:
Cap 3-10 (-13) cm; fibrillose scaly; convex; margin inrolled; color dark violet to bluish- or purplish-black; context violaceous. **Gills** dark violet to purplish-brown. **Stalk** 6-10 (-12) X 1-2 cm; base bulbous; woolly fibrous; dark, dull purplish gray. **Basidiospores** 12-15 X 7-8 µm; elliptic, roughened, rusty-brown in deposit.

HABITAT AND ROLE:
Ectomycorrhizal with conifers.

EDIBILITY, TASTE, AND ODOR:
Edible; mild; fungoid.

LOOK-ALIKES:
None other than perhaps *C. hercynicus* with short-elliptic spores.

COMMENTS:
We find this primarily in Southcentral and Southeast Alaska. It is often used by wool, yarn, and knitting enthusiasts for dying their wools.

FAMILY: Cortinariaceae
COMMON NAME: Gypsy, Goat, or Wrinkled Cort
GENUS AND SPECIES: *Rozites caperatus* (Pers.) P. Karst. 1879

STRIKING FIELD CHARACTERS:
Cap light yellowish tan to orange-tan, wrinkled toward margin and "frosted," or with a white dustlike surface in youth, with white annulus on stalk.

Fig. 056

MACRO- & MICRODESCRIPTION:
Cap 3.5-10 cm broad, oval in youth and expanding to convex, becoming broadly convex, broadly knobbed over disc (center), dry, finally wrinkled to margin and with a dusting or frosted appearance that disappears in age. Margins are turned in when young, becoming straight with expansion. Flesh thick, firm, white to buff, pleasant smelling. **Gills** notched, narrowly to broadly attached, close; dull leather-tan, becoming dull rusty-cinnamon with age. **Stalk** 0.6-2.0 cm wide, 5-15 cm long, tapering and longitudinally fibrous from a swollen (sub-bulbous) base to the apex; smooth, dry; white to dull buff to light tan. Annulus is membranous, whitish, and thin. **Basidiospores** 11-15 X 7-10 μm; red-brown, elliptical, roughly warted.

HABITAT AND ROLE:
This mushroom is a suspected mycorrhizal symbiont with our dwarf birch (*Betula nana* subsp. *exilis* and *B. glandulosa*) and white spruce at or near tree line. Here it is found singly to numerous and down in amongst the ground cover in late July to mid-August, where it can be seen in quantity in some years.

EDIBILITY, TASTE, AND ODOR:
This mushroom is considered edible and good, often slightly bitter when eaten raw, but delicately flavored when sautéed. The taste is mild to nutty and the odor is very pleasant. Since this is a close relative to members of the genus *Cortinarius*, make sure the veil is membranous and persistent rather than being cobweb-like, as is typical for many *Cortinarii* that may cause serious gastrointestinal problems.

LOOK-ALIKES:
Close look-alikes to *Rozites caperata* are some *Agaricus* species that have pink flesh to dark chocolate brown gills that are **not** attached to the stalk. For us, this is a rather distinctive mushroom. What may be confusing, however, is the spore color determination—to dull rusty-brown from such light-colored gills. It does look something like a very large stalked *Agrocybe praecox*, but the habitat should give it away.

COMMENTS:
It's always a joy to come across this mushroom, as it is edible for most, remembering the caveat that what's edible to many does not mean it is edible for you. One does not usually associate this with other members of its family, the Cortinariaceae, because its distinguishing characteristics of a "wrinkled" cap margin, a membranous partial veil, and long smooth stalk having a rounded and slightly swollen base just separates it from other *Cortinarii*.

Agarics with DULL, CINNAMON- to RUSTY-BROWN colored spores

Agarics with DARK to PURPLE-BROWN colored spores

FAMILY: Agaricaceae
COMMON NAME: Horse Mushroom
GENUS AND SPECIES: *Agaricus arvensis* Schaeff. 1774

STRIKING FIELD CHARACTERS:
Large, white to buffy, yellow staining, smooth, dry cap, large annulus, and often expanding stipe base.

MACRO- & MICRODESCRIPTION:
Cap 7-20 cm; convex to plane; dry, smooth, ± areolate, bruising yellow; margin ± appendiculate with velar remnants; context thick, white, becoming fetid smelling in age. **Gills** free, close, broad; color pallid, grayish-tan, brown, finally dark to chocolate brown. **Stalk** 5-10 (-15) X 1-2.5 cm; equal to tapering, stuffed to ± hollow, smooth. **Basidiospores** 7-8.5 X 5-6 μm; smooth, elliptic; chocolate or purple-brown in deposit.

HABITAT AND ROLE:
A transitional *Agaricus* species, we find this between *A. campestris* (on lawns), *A. augustus* (forest margins), and *A. silvicola* [*sylvicola*] of our forests.

EDIBILITY, TASTE, AND ODOR:
Edible—if you can get to it before the mycetophilous flies lay their eggs, which hatch into rather large maggots! The odor is anise-like when young.

LOOK-ALIKES:
The smaller *A. silvicola*.

COMMENTS:
This is the largest *Agaricus* and perhaps the most commonly seen species in Alaska, but distinguishable from its close cousin, *A. silvicola*.

Fig. 057

Fig. 058

FAMILY: Agaricaceae
COMMON NAME: Prince
GENUS AND SPECIES: *Agaricus augustus* Fr. 1838

STRIKING FIELD CHARACTERS:
Medium size, dome-shape, brown scales over buff background; almond odor, staining yellow slowly, large annulus.

MACRO- & MICRODESCRIPTION:
Cap 5-10 cm; bluntly ovoid to convex; color yellowish-buff ground with darker brown fibrils scales; context thick, white, flushing to pinkish with time. **Gills** free, close, white to dark-brown in age; bruising light yellow with time. **Stalk** 5-8 X1-1.5 cm; whitish, ± scaly below white annulus. **Basidiospores** 7-10 X 4.5-5.5 μm; elliptical, dark to purple-brown in deposit.

HABITAT AND ROLE:
A decomposer in mixed conifer-deciduous woodlands, especially marginally so.

EDIBILITY, TASTE, AND ODOR:
Edible, mild, and mildly sweet, but those rascal maggots love them, too.

LOOK-ALIKES:
A. smithii.

COMMENTS:
This is a fairly easily recognized fungus in Alaska with no other looking quite like it, although *A. smithii* looks similar.

Fig. 059

FAMILY: Agaricaceae
COMMON NAME: Meadow Mushroom, Pink Bottom
GENUS AND SPECIES: *Agaricus campestris* L. 1753

STRIKING FIELD CHARACTERS:
Small stature, silky-dry, clean white cap and stalk, a thin, fragile membranous annulus, sometimes with brownish fibrils, a margin extending beyond its gills and often with velar remains. Gills are flesh-pink to pinkish-gray in youth; hence, "pink bottom."

MACRO- & MICRODESCRIPTION:
Cap white, dry, silky. Flesh white, thick, doesn't change color when rubbed or broken. **Gills** bright pink, aging to blackish brown; crowded; free from stalk. **Veil** covers gills at first, sometimes leaving a fragile ring on stalk. **Stalk** straight, white, short, thick; usually tapered toward base. Stalk base (bottom) is not swollen, not enclosed in a cup- or saclike tissue, not circled with coarse scales, and does not turn yellow when bruised. **Basidiospores** 6.5-8.5 X 4-5.5 μm; dark chocolate brown in deposit.

HABITAT AND ROLE:
This wildly popular mushroom is a decomposer of plant detritus.

EDIBILITY, TASTE, AND ODOR:
Edible with caution. Almost everyone recognizes the Meadow Mushroom at a glance as the glorified kin of the familiar grocery-store mushroom. However, even edible *Agaricus* mushrooms (including the grocery-store variety) cause mild to severe stomach distress in a good number of consumers, and wild *Agaricus* can be tricky to identify. Heeding cautions can provide a safe start to your future with Pink Bottom mushrooms.

LOOK-ALIKES:
Other *Amanita, Lepiota,* and other *Agaricus* species.

COMMENTS:
Also known as *Psalliota campestris*, Field or Meadow Mushroom, or Champignon, It can found growing in groups, in the grass of pastures, lawns, and meadows (not in forests). It is reported from South-central and Interior Alaska.

FAMILY: Agaricaceae
COMMON NAME: Wetland Agaricus
GENUS AND SPECIES: *Agaricus silvicola/sylvicola* (Vittad.) Peck 1872

STRIKING FIELD CHARACTERS:
White cap and stalk, habitat, lightly staining yellowish with time, licorice odor, prominent skirt-like annulus, and chocolate- to purple-brown spores.

MACRO- & MICRODESCRIPTION:
Cap 5-10 (-15) cm; convex; cream colored; dry, smooth; bruising yellow-brown to yellow; context white. **Gills** close, broad, free, flesh, grayish-pink, brown to chocolate-brown in age. **Stalk** 5-8 (-12) X 1-1.5 cm; concolorous with cap; membranous annulus; base ± bulbous. **Basidiospores** 5-6 X 3-4 µm; elliptic; purple-brown in deposit.

HABITAT AND ROLE:
A decomposer woodland species in our mixed conifer-deciduous forests.

EDIBILITY, TASTE, AND ODOR:
Edible; fungoid; anise.

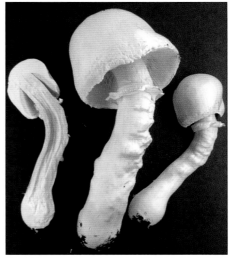

Fig. 060

LOOK-ALIKES:
None except perhaps a large *A. campestris* associated with scattered conifers on golf courses and expansive lawns.

COMMENTS:
One of our most common *Agaricus* species.

Fig. 061

FAMILY: Strophariaceae
COMMON NAME: Hemispheric, Dung Dome, Roundhead Stropharia
GENUS AND SPECIES: *Stropharia semiglobata* (Batsch) Quél. 1872

STRIKING FIELD CHARACTERS:
Straw yellow to buff-tan, sticky to slimy, rounded cap; long slender and annulated stalk; light purplish-gray gills.

MACRO- & MICRODESCRIPTION:
Cap 2-4 cm broad, conic, parabolic (bell-shaped but narrowed at basal margin), pulvinate (cushion-shaped), convex to almost plane; color pale cream, straw, yellowish-buff to buff-tan to light yellowish-brown; smooth, sticky; margin lighter; flesh whitish buff. **Gills** notched to broadly attached and sometimes slightly decurrent and breaking away from the stalk (seceding); color gray-buff when young and then becoming lavender, more or less mottled, to a light purplish-gray to purple-brown and finally to purple-black; uneven, crowded at margin, much less so (subdistant) at stalk; thin and fairly narrow. **Stalk** 6-20 cm long, 3-8 mm broad; long and slender, tapering gently toward apex to equal and enlarging toward base; sticky to slimy glutinous; buff to yellow-tan and lighter than cap disc, often same color as the cap margin. Veil (partial) delicate to fragile, membranous to fibrillose, collapsing about stalk and often blackened from spore deposits on upper surface. **Basidiospores** 15-19 X 7.5-10 μm; smooth, elliptical, dark purple-brown in deposit.

HABITAT AND ROLE:
This fungus has been found as solitary or scattered to rarely gregarious fruitings in mixed aspen-birch-white spruce forests, emanating from what looks like old bear scat and/or badly degraded moose nuggets located under deep moist moss carpets.

EDIBILITY, TASTE, AND ODOR:
This fungus is reported by some to be poisonous, by others as nonpoisonous, or even edible, but mediocre by various sources and is probably of little or no interest due to its relatively small size. At best, it is highly questionable, and for that reason we suggest you leave this one for the squirrels, caribou, and bears. Its taste has been recorded as mildly bitter. Our specimens taste nutty with a slightly bitter aftertaste. The odor is mild to non-distinct.

LOOK-ALIKES:

S. coronilla with a more prominent annular ring; *S. stercoraria* with its ± viscid stalk and flatter capped in age; *S. siccipes* with its dry stalk and radicating stalk base; *S. umbonata* with its cap umbo and dry stalk; and *S. ambigua*, the second Alaskan species, with its shaggy stalk and evanescent annulus. The former four species have yet to be found in Alaska, but are highly suspected to dwell within.

COMMENTS:

This stately, slimy, viscid to dry conical capped mushroom with its long, bulbous-based, and annulated slimy stalk growing on dung is easy to identify. Its substrate, more than anything, gives it away. Horse manure and moose dung are favorite haunts.

Agarics with BLACK colored spores

FAMILY: Psathyrellaceae
COMMON NAME: Gray Alcohol
Inky Cap, Tippler's Bane, or Dark
Flaky Inky Cap
GENUS AND SPECIES: *Coprinus
[Coprinopsis] atramentarius* (Bull.)
Fr. 1838

STRIKING FIELD CHARACTERS:
Thick, fleshy, light grayish tan, radially
lined and often splitting cap; hollow
white stalk with a flaring basal ring from
which the cap margin detaches in time.

MACRO- & MICRODESCRIPTION:
Cap 1.5-5.0 cm broad, ovoid, conic, bell-
shaped to convex; dry, smooth, striate to
furrowed; gray, gray-brown, gray-tan to
light brown (dark tan); margin striate to
furrowed to wrinkled; silky and sometimes with flattened scales; flesh thin,
off-whitish gray. **Gills** white, pinkish-
gray to black; crowded, thin, broad,
nearly free, deliquescing (turning to inky
juice in time). **Stalk** 2.5-7.5 cm long,
6-12 mm broad, tapering from basal ring
toward apex and again toward base; color
white and smooth above ring, whitish
and fibrillose below ring; hollow, brittle;
partial veil leaving basal ring on stipe.
Basidiospores 7-12 X 4-6 µm; smooth,
elliptical, black in deposit.

HABITAT AND ROLES:
A terrestrial saprobic decomposer, this
fungus is rarely solitary, but more commonly occurs in clusters on lignin-rich
humus within mixed white spruce-aspen
forests.

EDIBILITY, TASTE, AND ODOR:
Coprinus [Coprinopsis] atramentarius has
been described as edible, choice, or edible with caution. Do not consume alcohol for at least 36 hours before or after
eating this species.

LOOK-ALIKES:
Nothing in Alaska that we have found!

COMMENTS:
C. [Coprinopsis] atramentarius is edible
when young (when non-deliquescing)
and fairly good, but is reported to contain
a disulfiram-like compound (coprine)
that causes ipecac-like (vomiting) symptoms if consumed along with an alcoholic
beverage. Coprine reportedly reacts with
alcohol and may produce reddening of the
ears and nose, a metallic taste in the
mouth, lightheadedness, tachycardia
(rapid heartbeats), throbbing sensations,
nausea, and vomiting.

Fig. 062

FAMILY: Agaricaceae
COMMON NAME: Shaggy Mane, Inky Cap, Horsetail, Inky Eggs, Lawyer's Wig, Shaggy Beard, or Maned Agaric
GENUS AND SPECIES: *Coprinus comatus* (O.F. Müll.) Pers. 1797

STRIKING FIELD CHARACTERS:

Long ovoid to tall, straight cylinder-shaped; light tan to darker brown-scaled tips; large, stately, and found on compact, but disturbed (roadside, gravelly) soil.

MACRO- & MICRODESCRIPTION:

Cap 5-30 cm tall, barrel-shaped in youth to cylindrical in age, 2.5 to 6.3 cm broad and becoming bell-shaped in age, white with tan to brown apex and covered with tiers of shaggy, fibrous, recurved or reflexed (upturned) scales. Flesh soft, white, and thin. Margin slightly incurved and with a fibrous veil in youth becoming turned out, shaggy to dissolving into an inky juice (liquefaction or deliquescence) with age. **Gills** narrowly attached (notched) to stalk, white, becoming pinkish to smoky and finally black and then dripping away into a black watery juice, densely crowded and thin. Spores black in deposit. **Stalk** 5-36 cm long, 6-23 mm broad, cylindrical, equal to tapering slightly toward apex; dry, white, with an expanded to sub-bulbous base, ringed. Look for a white frilly central "cord" that attaches to the cap, but runs almost to the base within the hollow stipe. **Basidiospores** 10-16 (-18) X 7-9 μm; smooth, elliptical, with a germ pore.

HABITAT AND ROLE:

These mushrooms are solitary, scattered, gregarious to densely clustered in compact groups on hard ground and grassy areas. They are known to be saprophytic (digesting dead organic litter or detritus) and are quite common during mid to late summer (July). This mushroom has been seen pushing up hard-packed gravel roads and even asphalt with relative ease.

EDIBILITY, TASTE, AND ODOR:

These fungi are edible and very good, more so when young. You won't find them to be particularly palatable when they begin the liquefaction stages of development. The enzymes that cause

Fig. 063

their deliquescence are quite active at or near refrigerator temperatures (2-4°C, 35-37°F), so don't wrap them neatly in waxed paper or paper bags and expect to find anything but black dripping ooze all

Agarics with BLACK colored spores

over the inside of your refrigerator the next morning. Freezing works if the specimens are young. As stated above, this fungus is not easily mistaken for any other. The taste is mild but very good and the odor is very pleasant, fresh, and clean smelling.

LOOK-ALIKES:

C. colosseus (1.5-2 feet tall!), and several much smaller forms in *C. alnivorus* (on wood), *C. palmeranus* (on ground), *C. spadiceisporus* (on dung), *C. sterquillinus*, and *C. umbrinus* (on dung or compost) (Arora 1986), in addition to several *Coprinus comatus* varieties (Phillips 1981). At present, we can only assume that some of these may, in fact, be found in Alaska. Another mushroom the untrained eye might confuse with the shaggy mane during certain stages of development is *Coprinus [Coprinopsis] atramentarius*. Even through shorter, stouter, grayish in color, without scales and more bell-shaped, *C. [Coprinopsis] atramentarius* should never be eaten if any alcohol is to be consumed.

COMMENTS:

This fungus hydrologically expands with such pressure as to literally push up through asphalted driveways, my own included, or up through very hard, compacted dirt roads like the Alaska Haul Road from Livengood to Prudhoe Bay, where the fungi were 12-14 inches tall.

FAMILY: Paxillaceae
COMMON NAME: Alder False Truffle or Red Gravel
GENUS AND SPECIES: *Alpova diplophloeus* (Zeller and C.W. Dodge) Trappe and A.H. Sm. 1975

STRIKING FIELD CHARACTERS:
Dull reddish-orange subglobose balls at or near the surface under alder trees; having a chambered gelatinous gleba in youth, becoming dry in age.

Fig. 064

MACRO- & MICRODESCRIPTION:
Basidiome 1-5 cm; sub-hypogeous to epigeous, scattered, irregularly globose, cinnamon-rufous. **Peridium** one-layered, 180–300 μm thick. **Gleba** chambered, 0.8–2.4 mm wide, filled with gelatinous material cinnamon but darkening at maturity, embedded in meandering off-white stroma, producing a marbled appearance, the contents darkening when exposed and drying dark brown to black, hard, and waxy when dry. **Basidiospores** 5-6 X 2-2.5 μm; oblong to broadly allantoid, thick walled, smooth; yellowish en masse.

HABITAT AND ROLE:
Found only in mycorrhizal association with *Alnus crispa*.

EDIBILITY, TASTE, AND ODOR:
Inedible; squirrels love them, but unfortunately that doesn't mean we can eat them. Odor is reported as fruity by Arora (1986).

LOOK-ALIKES:
A. alpestris.

COMMENTS:
Alpova diplophloeus (Boletales, Paxillaceae) is currently the only recognized North American *Alpova* with a brownish peridium, large glebal chambers, and forming ectomycorrhizae with *Alnus* (Hayward, et al. 2014).

Agarics with BLACK colored spores

Fig. 065

FAMILY: Gomphaceae
COMMON NAME: Conifer False Truffle
GENUS AND SPECIES: *Gautieria graveolens* Vittad. 1831

STRIKING FIELD CHARACTERS:
Obovate to spherical, ± lumpy, smooth to mostly pitted

MACRO- & MICRODESCRIPTION:
Fruit body 1-3 (-4) cm; color yellowish-buff to dull grayish-brown; peridium thin; gleba dull yellow- to cinnamon-brown; cavities irregular, small. **Collumella** "gristly looking" and ramifying throughout. **Stalk** substrate attaching, a fragile rhizomorph to 1 cm X 1-1.5 mm. **Basidiospores** 18-19 X 11-12 µm; yellow-brown.

HABITAT AND ROLE:
Ectomycorrhizal with conifers (spruce).

EDIBILITY, TASTE, AND ODOR:
Supposedly edible, but we have never tried them; hence, the taste is also unknown. If bagged however, you can clearly get a strong hint of the acetylene-like sour milk odor that attracts squirrels to them as they mature.

LOOK-ALIKES:
G. otthii (pitted, with no outer covering) and *G. monticola* (with a thin peridial skin covering the fruit body), and *G. morchelliformis* with hardwoods; however, we've not seen the latter species in Alaska.

COMMENTS:
These false truffle fungi, false because they belong to the Basidiomycota, not Ascomycota, occur below ground (hypogeous), and often burst erumpent from surface soils under our spruce.

Spongy Poroid Bolete Mushrooms:
The Boletinoid Fungi

The bolete fungi include some of the largest mushrooms likely to be encountered. All have a fleshy hymenophore consisting of many tubes with pore openings. This pore-filled hymenium (or sponge) is found on the underside of the cap, as in the agaric fungi. Boletes are fleshy, often brightly colored, and become riddled with the brownish entry holes of fly larvae, which are easily seen if you peel the hymenium away from the cap. All boletes found in Alaska are members of a two families, the Boletaceae and Suillaceae, and the majority of those we see belong to four genera, *Boletus*, *Leccinum*, *Suillus*, and *Xerocomus*, or five genera if one accepts *Fuscobolitinus*.

All Alaskan boletes herein described, except for *L. aurantiacum*, *L. insigne*, *L. testaceo-scabrum*, and *L. versipelli*, are considered edible by many, although may not be palatable. They may become slimy when cooked, ill-textured for the palate, or ill-colored to the eye, or may simply not meet your taste expectations. Avoid those infected by insect larvae or fruiting bodies too old to consume safely. Also, avoid alcohol before, during, or after consuming bolete fungi. Bacteria and their metabolic waste products can also make one far sicker than the original mushroom tissue itself. Be selective! Prepare for your camp table only with bolete fungi that are young and freshly picked, and ALWAYS cook them.

FAMILY: Boletaceae
COMMON NAME: King Bolete, Porcini, Steinpiltz, or Cep
GENUS AND SPECIES: *Boletus edulis* Bull. 1782

STRIKING FIELD CHARACTERS:
Light to dark brown, ± reddish, bumpy to almost greasy looking cap; reticulate over pale buff stalk apex, bulbous base; firm flesh; pores white to yellowish-green.

MACRO- & MICRODESCRIPTION:
Cap 4-30 cm broad, hemispherical, convex to broadly so and then tabletop flattened in extreme age; white at margin otherwise biscuit-colored to yellow, cinnamon- to reddish- brown; surface mostly dry, but in wet weather it can be sticky; bumpy to pitted to cracked in dry weather; flesh is thick, firm, white, not bluing when exposed or bruised. **Pores** white to whitish-yellow at first and then becoming yellow, olive-yellow, or tan in extreme age; small, circular, long tubular and can be coerced to peel away from the cap. **Stalk** 4-10 cm long, 2-6 cm broad, bulbous, and less so when expanded or extended upward; firm, solid, white, pallid to buff-colored, covered by a netlike white reticulum most easily seen at the apex. **Basidiospores** 13-19 X 4-7 μm; smooth, spindle-shaped to elliptic, olive-brown in deposit.

HABITAT AND ROLE:
This fungus serves a very important fungus-plant root (mycorrhizal) relationship with our deciduous trees, especially birch and aspen, where you are most likely to find it growing singly to scattered, rarely in groups or troops, over the forest floor.

EDIBILITY, TASTE, AND ODOR:
This fungus can be seen and sold dried in specialty and health food stores. It is a

Fig. 066

delicious edible and reconstitutes nicely in hot water after being dried. It has a pleasant, nutty taste and fresh, pleasant odor. Look for this one. Sautéed over the campfire with butter and a little salt and garlic, *Boletus edulis* makes a great appetizer or topping for a thick juicy steak. One can dry this mushroom by cutting it into thin longitudinal sections and then placing them onto screened racks (like window screens) over a forced air space heater on low heat. (See page 24 for detailed instructions on preserving fungi.) Once dried, they can be put into canning jars, sealed tightly, and stored indefinitely for later use.

LOOK-ALIKES:
B. barrowsii, looking like a fat stalked *Tylopilus* sp., which we have none of in Alaska.

COMMENTS:
The King is a favorite of any mushroom collector and during certain years is abundant, along with its thin-stalked look-alike cousin species.

FAMILY: Boletaceae
COMMON NAME: Admirable
  Bolete
GENUS AND SPECIES: *Boletus
  mirabilis* Murrill 1912

STRIKING FIELD CHARACTERS:
This stately, velvety brownish- to maroon-red cap with concolorous to striped stipe and olive-yellow to olive-brown pore mouths really stands apart from other boletes you're apt to find.

MACRO- & MICRODESCRIPTION:
Cap 5-15 (20) cm; convex to plane in age; dry, granulose to velveteen; dark chocolate-brown, reddish-brown to purple-brown; margin may be fringed to appendiculate in youth; context dirty white to dirty pinkish, not generally bluing where bruised. **Pores** relatively large and up to 2 mm in diameter. **Stalk** 7-20 X 1-4 cm; clavate, dark brown, reddish- to purple-brown, often streaked and roughened; apex is reticulate. **Basidiospores** 18-24 X 7-9 µm; smooth, elliptic to spindle-like, olive-brown in deposit.

HABITAT AND ROLE:
Boletus mirabilis is a conifer lover, especially western lowland hemlock, *Tsuga heterophylla*; hence, it is only in South-central to Southeast Alaska.

EDIBILITY, TASTE, AND ODOR:
It is reported to be deliciously edible, with a hint of lemon.

LOOK-ALIKES:
In our country, there is no look-alike.

COMMENTS:
This fungus, like many of its cousins, may be attacked by an ascomycete, *Hypomyces chrysospermum*, which is white at first, becoming yellow to yellow-orange with age.

Fig. 067

Fig. 068

FAMILY: Boletaceae
COMMON NAME: Peppery Bolete
GENUS AND SPECIES: *Chalciporus (Boletus) piperatus* Bull. 1790

STRIKING FIELD CHARACTERS:
Deep dusky orange, concolorous stalk with a distinctly yellow base (like *Gomphidius glutinosus*) and very peppery taste.

MACRO- & MICRODESCRIPTION:
Cap 2-5 (-8) cm; obtuse to convexed to nearly plane; margin ± recurved in age, entire, incurved in youth; dry, subviscid, unpolished, ± glabrous to areolate in age; color yellow-brown to orange-cinnamon; context thin yellow-buff to pinkish-buff, rose to vinaceous above tubes. **Pores** 3-10 mm deep, ± depressed; ochraceous to reddish in age. **Stalk** (2-) 4-8 (-10) cm X 4-10 mm; context solid, lemon-yellow; surface reddish-cinnamon pruina to yellowish below; base bright yellow. **Basidiospores** 9-12 X4-5 µm; fusiform; smooth; dull cinnamon in deposit.

HABITAT AND ROLE:
Scattered amongst white spruce in the Interior and Sitka spruce in Southeast Alaska; ectomycorrhizal with conifers.

EDIBILITY, TASTE, AND ODOR:
Probably less palatable than edible due to its very sharp-peppery (acrid) taste and nondistinctive odor. Some are reported to dry, grind, and place this fungus powder into a pepper shaker—much like crushed peppers—and use it to season food.

LOOK-ALIKES:
Nothing else in Alaska looks like this small but easily recognized bolete.

COMMENTS:
This is an amazing fungus in its striking burnt-orange cap and stalk color, its yellowish pore/tube mouths, and citron yellow stalk base. It is mild to strongly acidic (peppery) to the taste, which may come on slowly.

FAMILY: Boletaceae
COMMON NAME: Common Scaber Stalk, Birch Bolete
GENUS AND SPECIES: *Leccinum scabrum* (Bull.) Gray 1821

STRIKING FIELD CHARACTERS:
Tan to dull brown cap, dry, tacky when wet, no marginal tissue flaps, flesh white and unchanging or faint pink tints in stalk, found with paper birch or the dwarf birches.

Fig. 069

MACRO- & MICRODESCRIPTION:
Cap 3-8 (-10) cm broad, convex to broadly so and becoming nearly plane in extreme age with a depressed disc; smooth, dry to tacky in wet weather, whitish buff at margin to tan, dingy yellow-brown to dull brown; margin without tissue flaps; flesh tissue white, not staining or only very slight pinkish tone in stem tissue. **Pores** dull white, whitish-brown and becoming brown in age and upon drying; no bluing stains but light tan to brown stains may result from handling. **Stalk** 6-10 cm long, 0.5-2.0 cm broad, tapering toward apex and sunken pores; white, buff, ochre to tan with same colored scabers that darken with age; staining green at or near base. **Basidiospores** 14-20 X 5-7 µm; smooth, spindle-shaped to long elliptical, brown in deposit.

HABITAT AND ROLE:
Here is another mycorrhizal fungus, but this time found with paper and dwarf birch. This is a variable fungus and can be almost sooty brown in youth. It is quite common and occurs as solitary to gregarious (rarely in clumps) fruitings in deciduous forests, mixed forests, or upland shrub tree-line tundra.

EDIBILITY, TASTE, AND ODOR:
Taste and odor are mild. This is a good edible in the north, but once again, the bugs will compete and usually win. It is hard to find good, firm, young specimens for the table that the maggots haven't already discovered.

LOOK-ALIKES:
Several, but best left to the microscope to untangle those too close for field IDs. *L. alaskanum, L. holopus,* and *L. rotundifoliae* are close seconds.

COMMENTS:
Perhaps for us in Alaska, this is one of the most perplexing groups of boletes. When in the field, I can only sort it out by eliminating characters diagnostic of other species. The whole group needs serious attention given to it by DNA studies. It is associated with birch, but then so are many others—and they are all referred to as "birch boletes" when, in fact, they may not be.

The Boletinoid Fungi

Fig. 070

FAMILY: Boletaceae
COMMON NAME: Birch Bolete
GENUS AND SPECIES: *Leccinum alaskanum* V.L. Wells and Kempton 1975

STRIKING FIELD CHARACTERS:

Birch association, small to moderate size (for a bolete), and variegated tan to dark chocolate brown cap, sunken tube mouths around stipe, and with a white to tan hymenophore.

MACRO- & MICRODESCRIPTION:

Cap (3.5-) 6-14 (-18) cm, convex, broadly so to sub-plane; margin without sterile extended cuticular flap or very reduced; variegated dark sooty brown with interspersed light brown to dull whitish-tan streaks; dry, ± glabrous, chammy leather-like; context white, slowly oxidizing to pink to light vinaceous-pink, up to 15 mm thick at apex, firm. **Pores** 7-18 mm long, 1-3 per mm, round to subangular, whitish becoming buff to dull brown in age or where bruised. **Stalk** (8-) 10-16 cm X 9-20 (-30) mm, base broader, 20-35 (-40) mm, clavate, dry, white to tan base color, scabers white in youth becoming tan, grayish-brown, to dark brown in age. **Basidiospores** (14.5-) 15-18 (-20.5) X (5-) 5.5-6.5 (-7) μm; smooth, fusoid; light brown in deposit.

HABITAT AND ROLE:

Solitary to gregarious under *Betula neoalaskana.*

EDIBILITY, TASTE, AND ODOR:

Not distinctive.

LOOK-ALIKES:

This stately fungus is rather distinctive in its small to moderate size (for a bolete) and variegated tan to dark chocolate brown cap. It has the stature of *L. scabrum.*

COMMENTS:

For us in Alaska, this is pretty much a standalone mushroom.

The Boletinoid Fungi

FAMILY: Boletaceae
COMMON NAME: Trembling or Quaking Aspen Scaber Stalk
GENUS AND SPECIES: *Leccinum atrostipitatum* A.H. Sm., Thiers and Watling 1966

STRIKING FIELD CHARACTERS:

A *Leccinum aurantiacum* look-alike; dry orange, rusty-orange, reddish-orange, orange-brown to cinnamon-brown, with appendiculate marginal tissue flaps staining lilac to lilac-gray, purplish-gray to smoky gray (fuscous) with time, with brown to blackish-brown scabers and greenish-blue stalk base.

MACRO- & MICRODESCRIPTION:

Cap 3-12 cm broad, round to convex, becoming broadly so to nearly plane; dry to tacky when wet, smooth to fibrillose, with the fibers separating with expansion; color from light to dark orange, rusty-orange, reddish-orange, cinnamon-brown to ferruginous-red; marginal tissue flaps often gone in age; robust; context white but staining lilac to lilac-gray to purple-gray to smoky-gray. **Pores** dull white, greenish-buff, gray to dull yellowish-buff in age, not or slow staining to lavender or purplish-red (vinaceous). **Stalk** 4-10 cm long, 1-2 cm broad, + equal, dry, solid, off-white, scabers initially whitish-brown, then light reddish-orange to brown and finally dark chocolate-brown to almost blackish-brown in age; base often staining a greenish-blue. **Basidiospores** 13-17 X 4-5 μm; smooth, sub-fusoid, yellow-brown to brown in deposit.

HABITAT AND ROLE:

This mycorrhizal fungus is associated with aspen like *L. aurantiacum*, but its staining reactions and other subtle microscopic characters separate the two species. Fruiting bodies of *Leccinum atrostipitatum* occur scattered to gregarious, and are fairly common to often abundant during July.

Fig. 071

EDIBILITY, TASTE, AND ODOR:

These stately boletes are edible by some and considered good, BUT take every precaution: Cook them thoroughly, never eat them raw, and consume no alcohol before, during, or after your meal for up to three days! They cook up "dirty" (that is, stain gray-black) and may look less than edible. The taste and odor are fairly mild, but don't let that stop you from using your favorite seasonings. See more in the Comments section.

LOOK-ALIKES:

L. aurantiacum, L. insigne, L. testaceo-scabrum, and *L. versipelli.*

COMMENTS:

This fungus, if eaten raw, poorly cooked, or consumed with alcohol at a meal, will send you to the hospital. I've sat with those who did in our local hospital at their bedside for hours as they were thinking they might die, as the symptoms were so severe.

Fig. 072

FAMILY: Boletaceae
COMMON NAME: Red-Orange Capped Scaber Stalk, Quaking Aspen Bolete
GENUS AND SPECIES: *Leccinum aurantiacum* (Bull.) Gray 1821

STRIKING FIELD CHARACTERS:

Association with our northern quaking aspen and having an indistinctly appendiculate margin; orange-red, rusty-orange, to orange-brown or brown cap; stalk with short white, reddish, red-brown scabers that will darken in age to blackish-brown; pores white to off-white (pallid) to yellow-tinted; flesh turning burgundy-red, lilac, lilac-gray then slowly to smoky- to bluish-black, and finally to purplish-black.

MACRO- & MICRODESCRIPTION:

Cap 2-15 cm broad, convex to broadly so, nearly plane in age and ± slightly depressed in age (water will puddle), dry to tacky when wet, bright orange to rusty-red to reddish-brown; margin with remnant patches of marginal veil tissue; flesh dull off-whitish, firm, stains wine reddish to lilac with gray tints and then slowly blackens. **Pores** fairly deep (1.0-1.5 cm deep), round openings, small. **Stalk** 5-15 cm long, 1.5-3.5 cm broad, equal to enlarging toward base, ground tissue white, but overlying scabers white at first, then brown, dark brown to almost black. **Basidiospores** 12-15 X 3.5-5 μm; smooth, spindle-shaped to elongate-elliptic; yellow-brown to brown in deposit.

HABITAT AND ROLE:

This stately mushroom is mycorrhizal with its host, the quaking or trembling aspen, which is relatively common and particularly so in areas of recent (within 25-50 years) forest fires. When found, it will be single, scattered to gregarious, depending on the season and fruiting pattern. It can certainly be abundant some years!

EDIBILITY, TASTE, AND ODOR:

Both the taste and odor are mild, but pleasing, as also reported by several authors. In the Lower 48, and because of its staining reaction, some who do not know this fungus comfortably may feel less inclined to consume it. Don't hesitate, but just remember, our northern flies love them too.

LOOK-ALIKES:

This one has many look-alikes and one needs to exercise significant caution, as they all are difficult to distinguish without a microscope. Some authors suggest that all are evidently edible, but we know of a few serious gastrointestinal cases where individuals ended up in the hospital with 12-18 hours of stressful symptoms. Other close cousins are *L. insigne* (bright rust-orange, reddish-orange to reddish brown, but perhaps only discernible from *Leccinum aurantiacum* when dry!), *L. discolor* (dull brown to cinnamon-colored), *L. atrostipitatum* (birch associated with black dense stipe scabers), *L. testaceoscabrum* (also birch associated with more brightly colored cap than *L. atrostipitatum*), and others like *L. fallax* and *L. subalpinum*, which may not be in Alaska. The genus *Leccinum* in Alaska needs to have serious molecular genetic studies conducted.

COMMENTS:

Following are some important precautions. 1) Never eat these raw; 2) Cook them well to aid digestion; 3) Never consume any alcoholic beverage before, during, or after your meal and then for 2-3 days afterward. This is particularly true for *L. atrostipitatum*.

FAMILY: Boletaceae
COMMON NAME: Quaking Aspen Bolete
GENUS AND SPECIES: *Leccinum testaceoscabrum* Secr. ex Singer 1947

STRIKING FIELD CHARACTERS:

Cap context stains reddish, to avellaneous, finally fuscous; strongly appendiculate cap margin and patchy orange to burnt-orange cap colors.

MACRO- & MICRODESCRIPTION:

Cap 4-10 cm X 5-20 mm; convex to broadly so; color variable from tannish-orange to deep orange with a rose tint, patchy-appearing in age; dry, chammy-like, subviscid in wet weather, often cracking in dry weather; margin appendiculate in youth; context white, staining vinaceous (wine), to avellaneous (grayish, dirty purplish), final fuscous (smoky-

Fig. 073a

Fig. 073b

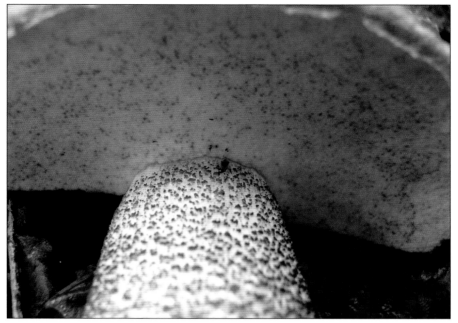

Fig. 073c

violet). **Pores** 1.5 cm, depressed around stipe, whitish in youth, dirty buff, olive to tan in age. **Stalk** 5-10 cm X 1-1.5 cm; short, stout in youth, equal to elongating with broadening base, constricting and flaring at apex; base white to pallid; scabers reddish-black; fuscous staining. **Basidiospores** (12-) 13-16 X 3.5-4.5 μm; smooth, sub-fusoid to elongate-sub-elliptical, dull olive-brown in deposit.

HABITAT AND ROLE:
Scattered to gregarious in mixed birch-aspen-conifer wood margins along road cuts and disturbed, root-exposed sites.

EDIBILITY, TASTE, AND ODOR:
Mild, not distinctive.

LOOK-ALIKES:
L. atrostipitatum, L. aurantiacum, L. insigne, and *L. versipelle.*

COMMENTS:
Almost indistinguishable from *L. atrostipitatum,* except for the lack of orange to more tan to dull tan in the latter. Stipe scabers also are lighter colored in age and the cap margin is conspicuously appendiculate. This species may only be separable for those look-alikes microscopically.

FAMILY: Suillaceae
COMMON NAME: Short-Stalked Slippery Jack
GENUS AND SPECIES: *Suillus brevipes* (Peck) Kuntze 1898

STRIKING FIELD CHARACTERS:

No prominent glandular dotting on stipe apex; no partial veil; smooth dry to slimy, dark reddish-brown; short stipe.

MACRO- & MICRODESCRIPTION:

Cap 5-13 cm, convex to plane; smooth, shiny when dry, viscid to sub-glutinous (slimy) in wet weather; dark reddish-brown (vinaceous) to dark brown in youth, fading becoming reddish-brown, cinnamon to light brown (tan) in age; context thick, white becoming yellowish in age and not staining blue. **Pores** pale in youth becoming dingy- to olive-yellow in age; not bluing. **Stalk** 2-7 cm X 1-2 (-3) cm; ± tapering upward, firm, solid, white becoming yellowish in age; veil absent. **Basidiospores** 7-10 X 3-4 µm; smooth, elliptic to spindle-shaped; dull cinnamon to brown in deposit.

HABITAT AND ROLE:

Scattered under spruce or lodgepole pine.

EDIBILITY, TASTE, AND ODOR:

Reported as an excellent edible, but be sure to peel off the slimy pellicle before cooking!

LOOK-ALIKES:

S. granulatus (having abundant glandular dots on stipe apex), *S. pallidiceps* (of the Rocky Mountains, with its much lighter cap color), which could be in Alaska.

COMMENTS:

As lodgepole pine continues to move more abundantly into the Interior of Alaska, look for this familiar slimy *Suillus*.

Fig. 074

The Boletinoid Fungi

FAMILY: Suillaceae
COMMON NAME: Hollow Foot, Hollow-Stalked Larch Bolete, or Mock Oyster
GENUS AND SPECIES: *Suillus cavipes* (Opat.) A.H. Sm. and Thiers 1964

STRIKING FIELD CHARACTERS:
Fruiting only in muskeg bogs with larch (*Larix laricina*) and black spruce (*Picea marianna*); dry, hairy, reddish-brown, streaked cap, bright yellow-orange and large pores; hollow annulate (ringed) stalk.

MACRO- & MICRODESCRIPTION:
Cap 3-10 cm broad, convex to broadly so, ± umbonate, expanding to plane, uplifted and ± depressed with raised disc; surface dry (not tacky when wet) red fibrils and densely fibrillose, ± leathery texture, margin often lighter, white fibrillose in youth, yellowish-, tawny orange-red, to red-brown in age and uplifted; flesh tissue white to yellow-orange where damaged but not staining green, blue, violet, purple, or gray when bruised. **Pores** ± radially arranged, large, angular to elongated; pale yellow to greenish-yellow, finally golden-yellow and with reddish-orange highlights; not bruising green, blue, violet, purple or gray, and tubes decurrent at least in youth, less so in age. **Stalk** 3-8 cm long, 0.5-2.0 cm broad, swollen toward base in youth, ± equal in age; dry; white to greenish-yellow above red ring, same color as the cap below to a white base; hollow to base; flesh tissue not staining green or blue. Veil fibrillose; white cottony on margin, forming a thin ring, the latter white to pink on the stalk. **Basidiospores** 7-10 X 3.5-4 µm; smooth, elliptical to spindle-shaped; dark olive-brown in deposit.

Fig. 075

HABITAT AND ROLE:
Suillus cavipes is found single to scattered around muskeg hummocks in moss under larch and black spruce in July. This species is a mycorrhizal associate of larch.

EDIBILITY, TASTE, AND ODOR:
The taste and odor of *Suillus cavipes* are mild. It is an edible mushroom, but cooks up to a soft, almost mushy to slimy texture (removing the tube layer helps, but hey, that's where the nutrients are); hence, the name "Mock Oyster" because it slides right down the gullet!

LOOK-ALIKES:
Nothing else in our country, but others like *S. aeruginascens, S. ochraceoroseus,* and *S. grevillei* may be mistaken cousins.

COMMENTS:
This orange-red to red-brown bolete with its olive-yellow stipe in the presence of larch is easily distinguishable.

Fig. 076

FAMILY: Suillaceae
COMMON NAME: Larch Suillus or Tamarack Jack
GENUS AND SPECIES: *Suillus grevillei* (Klotzsch) Singer 1945

STRIKING FIELD CHARACTERS:
Deep golden-yellow to reddish-brown, non-hairy cap; partial veil; no glandular dots; associated with larch (*Larix laricina*); yellow cap context tissue staining pink to red.

MACRO- & MICRODESCRIPTION:
Cap 3-15 cm; convex to ± plane; smooth, viscid to slimy in wet weather, shiny when dry; red to reddish-brown, golden-yellow, yellow with rusty-red disc; margin appendiculate; context thick, yellow and pink to red staining. Context straw- to amber-yellow to salmon-buff. **Pores** 1-2 per mm, 10-15 mm deep, broadly attached to decurrent, sulfur-yellow to olive-yellow in age. **Stalk** 4-10 X 1-3 cm; equal to clavate, solid, fibrous, and yellow; veil present, floccose annulus. **Basidiospores** 8-10 X 3-3.5 µm; oblong, smooth; pale-tan to light olive-brown in deposit.

HABITAT AND ROLE:
With our northern "bog" larch as an important ectomycorrhizal species.

EDIBILITY, TASTE, AND ODOR:
Reported as being edible, but again, as in other *Suillus* species, you have to deal with that slimy cap tissue; mild to slightly astringent to bitter, ± metallic odor.

LOOK-ALIKES:
S. cavipes (hairy and dry), otherwise no other.

COMMENTS:
Another larch baby, but easily discernible from *S. cavipes* with which it is frequently found growing.

FAMILY: Boletaceae
COMMON NAME: Brown and Yellow-Cracked Bolete
GENUS AND SPECIES: *Xerocomus subtomentosus* (L.) Quél. 1888

STRIKING FIELD CHARACTERS:

Dry, olive-yellow to dark olive-brown, and velvety-tomentose (soft, short, hairy surface) cap, generally without cracks, bright golden-yellow pores and a buff- to creamy-tan stalk of fairly equal proportions throughout.

MACRO- & MICRODESCRIPTION:

Cap 4-10 cm broad, broadly convex to plane; dry and minutely velvety (subtomentose) cap that in age may look and feel smooth; yellow-brown to drab olive-brown to dull brown to cinnamon-brown; flesh white, off-white (pallid) cream to straw-yellow. **Pores** are large (1-3 mm), dull to bright chrome-yellow, staining blue-green, but weakly so. **Stalk** 4-10 cm long, 1-2 cm wide; when short, clavate but with extension ± equal to and tapering toward apex; smooth to scurfy, but reticulations are present at the apex; flesh firm and same color as cap flesh; outer surface off-white, buff, or tan with orange tinges. **Basidiospores** 10-16 X 3.5-5 μm; smooth, spindle-shaped to elliptic; olive-brown in deposit.

HABITAT AND ROLE:

This mushroom can be found singly to widely scattered, but closely associated with dwarf birch and shrub tundra members of the Ericaceae (evergreen shrubs and ground cover). It most certainly is a mycorrhizal associate of these plants.

EDIBILITY, TASTE, AND ODOR:

Albeit edible, for those with a delicate palate, this fungus is reported as not being particularly good. Try it and decide for yourself. If you prefer bland food, this may just be the one. The odor is pleasant, certainly not obnoxious, but again, sort of bland.

LOOK-ALIKES:

Boletus huronensis, B. sphaerocystis, and *B. subglabripes.*

COMMENTS:

Our *"Xerocomus subtomentosus"* may well be something other than the real *Xerocomus subtomentosus.* According to Andy Taylor, *"Xerocomus subtomentosus"* is close to *B. impolitus* and *B. depilatus,* which supposedly does not occur in the US. It is, however, also close to the *Boletus huronensis* Smith and Thiers collected by Joe Ammirati in Michigan. Our Alaskan material is perhaps closest to *B. subglabripes,* as so named in the field on occasion, but best fits the description of *B. sphaerocystis.* Only spore sizes will tell with *B. sphaerocystis* having substantially larger spores than are found in *B. subglabripes.* The bottom line, as so often with our Alaskan material, is that it just may be a new species and needs to be described.

Fig. 077

Leathery, Corky, to Woody Bracket, or Conk Mushrooms: Polyporoid Fungi

With very few exceptions, the polypore fungi are tough, leathery, corky, or woody, and some persist (even though they may not be actively growing) for several years. These fungi are found on wood (living trees, dead snags, fallen logs, stumps, or buried wood) that is in some state of decomposition (rotting away), by these and other fungi and bacteria. In Alaska, it is only some members of this group that are truly perennial in their growth habit.

Like the boletes, polypores may have stalks (*Albotrellus*, *Coltricia*, and some *Polyporus* spp.), although this is uncommon. Most members of this group form brackets or shelves that are perpendicular to the substrate on an upright tree, snag, stump, or downed log. The hymenium, like that of the boletes, is composed of many, but generally much smaller, pores. This pore surface (the hymenophore) is, with only a few exceptions, tough and not fleshy, as are the boletes. As a result, it really shouldn't be too difficult to separate the wood rotting polypore fungi from the stalked and fleshy boletes.

None of the polypore fungi except *Laetiporous conifericola* are considered edible. They're not necessarily poisonous, but are simply not palatable, as they are just too tough to chew.

FAMILY: Albatrellaceae
COMMON NAME: Sheep Polypore
GENUS AND SPECIES: *Albatrellus ovinus* (Schaeff.) Kotl. and Pouzar 1957

STRIKING FIELD CHARACTERS:
This fungus is distinguished from the species of boletes, which it resembles, by pores that extend down the stalk and that are not separable from the rest of the tissue of the stalk or cap; hence, leathery, rather than fleshy.

MACRO- & MICRODESCRIPTION:
Fruit bodies 3-15 (-18) cm; annual, irregularly convex, plane to even depressed in age; usually single to almost caespitose in their crowded to clumped habit; cream to pale brown colored. **Pores** pale yellow, circular near the margin, angular toward the stem, 3-5 per

Fig. 078

mm, flesh cream colored to pinkish-cream, fleshy, with a dark layer above the tubes. **Stalk** central to lateral; slightly velvety, circular to sub-circular, upper surface cream colored to tan, smooth, later with cracks of pale yellow coloration. **Basidiospores** 3-5 X 3-3.5 μm; smooth, ovoid, subglobose to short-elliptic, ± thick walled; white in deposit.

HABITAT AND ROLE:

This species is a mycorrhizal associate (terrestrial) of spruce. As such, it occurs on the forest floor in a disturbed area, like trail sides, rather than on wood. It attaches to the spruce roots below the soil's surface. It is not a wood rot fungus.

EDIBILITY, TASTE, AND ODOR:

This species is not to be considered edible because of its dense tough texture, but some do eat it if it is cooked well.

LOOK-ALIKES:

A. avellaneus, which we also have in Alaska with its purplish-gray cap; *A. confluens* is another, having a light burnt orange-brown cap, but I have never seen it in Alaska.

COMMENTS:

Albatrellus ovinus stalked polypore can get rather large in Alaska. It is a beautiful, clean-looking polypore and always fun to find.

Leathery, Corky, to Woody Bracket, or Conk Mushrooms: Polyporoid Fungi

FAMILY: Polyporaceae
COMMON NAME: Tinder Polypore
GENUS AND SPECIES: *Fomes fomentarius* (L.) Fr. 1849

STRIKING FIELD CHARACTERS:

Gray conk, brown pore surface; a white, mottled heart rot of deciduous trees and usually found on birch.

MACRO- & MICRODESCRIPTION:

Fruit bodies perennial, sessile, hoof-shaped, woody, upper surface hard, with a smooth crust, older areas gray, margin light brown, rolled over edge. **Pore** surface pale brown, pores 4-5 per mm; flesh yellowish brown with several tube layers comprising most of the interior. **Basidiospores** 12-18 X 4-7 µm; smooth, cylindrical; brown in deposit.

HABITAT AND ROLE:

This species is commonly found on living and dead birch, aspen, and alder.

EDIBILITY, TASTE, AND ODOR:

The fruiting bodies of *Fomes fomentarius* are very hard, and thus inedible.

LOOK-ALIKES:

Thin specimens of *Phellinus igniarius* and *Phellinus tremulae* (with cracked, unpolished, and blackened upper surface and brown lower hymenophore surface), and non-sporulating *Ganoderma applanatum* (in which the cap becomes rusty brown when it is sporulating). *Fomes fomentarius* has brown, but not rusty cinnamon-brown spores, and a very white hymenophore, which does not stain brown when scratched.

COMMENTS:

This is one of our ubiquitous fungi seen on almost every outing. It is perennial, as are its look-alikes, likes similar habitats, but differs in many other ways.

Fig. 079

Leathery, Corky, to Woody Bracket, or Conk Mushrooms: Polyporoid Fungi

FAMILY: Fomitopsidaceae
COMMON NAME: Red-Belted Polypore
GENUS AND SPECIES: *Fomitopsis pinicola* (Sw.) P. Karst. 1881

STRIKING FIELD CHARACTERS:
Narrow shelf with red to orange margin, found on spruce.

MACRO- & MICRODESCRIPTION:
Fruit bodies perennial, usually sessile, woody, flat, smooth; upper surface of young caps with a sticky reddish-brown surface, older parts gray to black. **Pore** surface cream colored, pores circular, 5-6 per mm; interior cream to buff, rubbery to woody, tubes in layers. **Basidiospores** 6-9 X 3.5-4.5 µm; smooth, cylindric-ellipsoid; yellow-brown to brown in deposit.

HABITAT AND ROLE:
Fomitopsis pinicola occurs in both living and dead conifers, but fruits abundantly on dead spruce and causes a brown cubical rot of many conifers. It is a saprotrophic fungus found primarily on decaying logs throughout temperate regions of the Northern Hemisphere and is abundant throughout Alaska.

EDIBILITY, TASTE, AND ODOR:
This fungus is tough and rubbery, and thus, inedible. It also possesses a rather strong pungent/acidic odor that is not particularly appealing.

LOOK-ALIKES:
Fomitopsis ochracea, and much less so than *Fomes fomentarius*, *Ganoderma* spp., and *Heterobasidion annosum*.

COMMENTS:
As determined by Haight et al. (in press), *Fomitopsis pinicola* is a widespread clade (group of organisms with a common ancestor) of bracket fungi, one of three clades found only in North America, and represents the recently described *Fomitopsis ochracea*. The remaining two North American clades represent previously undescribed species.

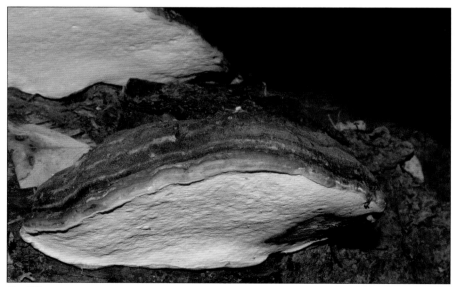

Fig. 080

Leathery, Corky, to Woody Bracket, or Conk Mushrooms: Polyporoid Fungi

Fig. 081a

FAMILY: Ganodermataceae
COMMON NAME: Artist's Conk
GENUS AND SPECIES: *Gano-derma applanatum* (Pers.) Pat. 1887

STRIKING FIELD CHARACTERS:
Dark gray (cinnamon brown when spore covered) conk, white pore surface that easily bruises brown.

Fig. 081b

MACRO- & MICRODESCRIPTION:
Fruit bodies perennial, sessile, woody, flattened to quite irregular in shape; upper or outer surface gray to black, often with layer of brown dust (spores) present; margin narrow, white. **Pore** surface white, bruising brown when touched, darker in age, pores circular, 4-6 per mm, tubes layered; interior tissues purple-brown. **Basidiospores** (8-) 9-12 X 6.5-8 µm; broad elliptic, ovoid, truncate, thick walled, ± spiny; brown to dull red-brown in deposit.

HABITAT AND ROLE:
This species occurs on dead or living hardwoods. It is particularly common on living aspen, where it causes a white mottled root and butt rot, but may occasionally be found on conifers.

EDIBILITY, TASTE, AND ODOR:
Ganoderma applanatum is too hard to be edible.

LOOK-ALIKES:
Some thin *Fomitopsis pinicola* and *G. tsuga*, on hemlock in Southeast Alaska, which differs in its shellacked cap and lateral stalk.

COMMENTS:
This is the true Artist's Conk or Bracket. Sketching the fresh white to buff hymenophore results in brown tracings that will last indefinitely once the basidiome is dried.

FAMILY: Polyporaceae
COMMON NAME: Hemlock Varnish Shelf
GENUS AND SPECIES: *Ganoderma tsugae* Murrill 1902

STRIKING FIELD CHARACTERS:
The highly shellacked, reddish to mahogany-brown "paddle on a stalk" emanating up from its host.

MACRO- & MICRODESCRIPTION:
Fruit body 20-30 X 7 cm; applanate, annual, sessile to laterally stipitate,

Fig. 082a

9 X 5 cm; reddish-brown, varnished, crusted, smooth to rugulose. **Pores** 5-6 per mm; circular to angular; cream, yellowish to light brown in age; context dirty white. **Basidiospores** 13-15 X 7.5-8.5 µm; ellipsoid, truncate, pale- to rusty-brown in deposit.

HABITAT AND ROLE:
White butt rot of conifer, especially of hemlock and spruce.

EDIBILITY, TASTE, AND ODOR:
Inedible, but like so many wood rotting polypore fungi, a medicinal tea can be produced by infusion.

LOOK-ALIKES:
G. lucidum with yellow-brown to dark brown context on hardwoods; and *G. oregonense*, which also occurs on conifers, but much larger.

COMMENTS:
We only see this fungus, with its bright shellacked surface, in Southeast Alaska.

Fig. 082b

FAMILY: Hymenochaetaceae
COMMON NAME: Chaga, Birch Cinder Conk, Clinker Polypore
GENUS AND SPECIES: *Inonotus obliquus* (Ach. ex Pers.) Pilát 1942

STRIKING FIELD CHARACTERS:

An amorphous, blackened, cracked, canker-like growth emanating from older and larger birch.

MACRO- & MICRODESCRIPTION:

Fruit body 25-40 cm, annual, erumpent from beneath bark forming a large cankerous, irregularly cracked, hard, brittle, pitted sclerotium having a fertile margin with sharp protrusions; dark reddish-brown to black outside, cinnamon- to reddish- to yellow-brown interior. **Pores** small, round, 6-8 per mm. **Basidiospores** 9-10 X 5.5-6.5 µm; globose to subglobose; pale brown in deposit.

HABITAT AND ROLE:

Cankerous on living birch, *Betula neoalaskana*, and quaking aspen, *Populus tremuloides*.

EDIBILITY, TASTE, AND ODOR:

This fungus is too difficult to chew or taste. Mild odor, like that of fresh rain on a hot sidewalk.

LOOK-ALIKES:

Nothing else we know of in Alaska comes close to looking like *Inonotus obliquus*, except, perhaps, an old, large, deeply cracked and broken *Phellinus igniarius* with a blackened hymenophore.

COMMENTS:

An infusion (tea) can be brewed from this white rot "sterile conk" or bracket fungus from Alaskan living birch and aspen trees and consumed for its presumed medicinal properties.

Fig. 083

FAMILY: Fomitopsidaceae
COMMON NAME: Hemlock
  Sulfur Shelf
GENUS AND SPECIES: *Laetiporus conifericola* Burds. and Banik 2001

STRIKING FIELD CHARACTERS:
Multiple shelving bright orange caps (when seen in dark woods) with a citron-yellow pore surface, lemony odor, and often exuding moisture droplets when fresh.

MACRO- & MICRODESCRIPTION:
Fruit body up to 25 cm wide, 15 cm deep and 3 cm thick; attached by being laterally stipitate, sessile or broad stalked; surface bright orange to burnt-orange; context pale yellow. **Pores** surface bright citron-yellow; 2-4 per mm, elongating in age to irregular/angular. **Basidiospores** 6.5-8 X 4-5 µm; pale brown in deposit.

Fig. 084a

Fig. 084b

HABITAT AND ROLE:
It is said to occur on mature and over-mature living and dead conifers (Burd-sall and Banik 2001), but we have seen it only on old hemlock stumps in Southeast Alaska and spruce logs in Southcentral Alaska.

EDIBILITY, TASTE, AND ODOR:
Delicious if prepared properly; lemony, with a crunchy texture; smells of lemon.

LOOK-ALIKES:
L. gilbertsonii (Western US oaks and eucalyptus), *L. huroniensis* (Great Lakes conifers), *L. sulphureus* (Eastern and Midwestern hardwoods).

COMMENTS:
There are seven groups of *Laetiporus* in North America, but only three others with yellow pore surfaces, two of which are found on conifers; *L. gilbertsonii* (Western US oaks and eucalyptus), *L. huroniensis* (Great Lakes conifers), *L. sulphureus* (Eastern and Midwestern hardwoods). None of these occur in Alaska.

Leathery, Corky, to Woody Bracket, or Conk Mushrooms: Polyporoid Fungi

FAMILY: Hymenochaetaceae
COMMON NAME: Flecked-Flesh False Tinder or Birch Polypore
GENUS AND SPECIES: *Phellinus igniarius* (L.) Quél. 1886

STRIKING FIELD CHARACTERS:
Heavy black conk with a brown pore surface.

MACRO- & MICRODESCRIPTION:
Fruit body perennial, single, usually sessile, hoof-shaped or flattened, upper surface usually black, becoming purple-brown. **Pores** circular, 5-6 per mm, interior dark reddish brown, zonate, woody, off-white and brown where the fungus is in contact with the wood. **Basidiospores** 5-6.5 X 4.5-6 µm; smooth, ovoid to subglobose; dull white in deposit.

HABITAT AND ROLE:
Phellinus igniarius is found on living hardwoods, where it causes a uniform white heart rot, surviving the death of the tree and causing decay of the deadwood.

EDIBILITY, TASTE, AND ODOR:
Because of its hard woody texture, *Phellinus igniarius* is not edible.

LOOK-ALIKES:
Unlike *Phellinus tremulae*, *P. igniarius* is restricted to birch, not aspen, where it causes white heart rot decay.

COMMENTS:
P. igniarius is collected, dried, and ashed (burned), and the ashes are sold and mixed with chewing tobacco by coastal Eskimo populations. Acting as a DMSO-like carrier of nicotine through mucus membranes, the bolus of nicotine provides one heck of a wallop, as explained to me by an elderly Iñupiat Eskimo woman who said it often caused one to "black out."

Fig. 085

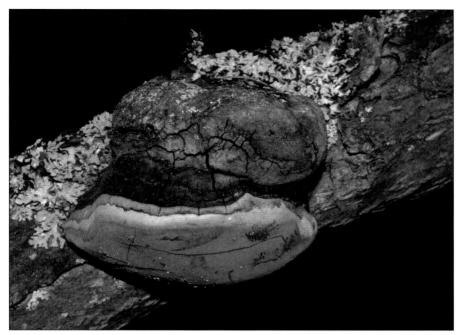

Fig. 086

FAMILY: Hymenochaetaceae
COMMON NAME: Aspen
Polypore or Conk
GENUS AND SPECIES: *Phellinus tremulae* (Bondartsev) Bondartsev and P.N. Borisov 1953

STRIKING FIELD CHARACTERS:
Black conk with brown pore surface, found on aspen.

MACRO- & MICRODESCRIPTION:
Fruit bodies perennial, single, sessile, at branch scars; triangular in longitudinal section; with white and brown mottled core of tissue at the decayed branch stub; upper surface black, crust-like, and cracked. **Pore** surface purple brown, the pores circular, 5-7 per mm; interior dark reddish-brown. **Basidiospores** 4.5-5 X 4-4.5 μm; smooth, subglobose, thick walled; white in deposit.

HABITAT AND ROLE:
This species is very similar to *P. igniarius*, but is restricted to aspen, where it causes white heart rot decay.

EDIBILITY, TASTE, AND ODOR:
As in the case for *P. igniarius*, this fungus is too hard and tough in texture to eat.

LOOK-ALIKES:
P. igniarius, which in Alaska grows on living birch; *B. neoalaskana* in the Interior.

COMMENTS:
P. tremulae, on quaking aspen, *Populus tremuloides*, and its close cousin, *P. igniarius*, are used as an additive in chewing tobacco (See Comments entry on Flecked-Flesh False Tinder or Birch on page 106.) It otherwise causes serious white heart rot in its host.

FAMILY: Fometopsidaceae
COMMON NAME: Birch Polypore
GENUS AND SPECIES: *Piptoporus betulinus* (Bull.) P. Karst. 1881

STRIKING FIELD CHARACTERS:

Whitish-cream to light tan, smooth leathery conk, on "topless" dead (widow-maker) birch.

MACRO- & MICRODESCRIPTION:

Fruit bodies are annual, semicircular, sessile, or stalked (stipitate) and if stalked, then with a short stalk; often pendant, solitary, cracks in age; margin white, usually rolled down over the edge of pore surface. **Pore** surface white, yellowish-brown in age, the pores circular to angular, 3-5 per mm, pore surface often appearing brush-like in old specimens; flesh white, tough when fresh. **Basidiospores** 5-6 X 1.5-2 µm; smooth, cylindric, slightly allantoid; white in deposit.

HABITAT AND ROLE:

This species causes a brown cubical rot of dead birch sapwood.

EDIBILITY, TASTE, AND ODOR:

The texture of *Piptoporus betulinus* is not undesirable in young specimens, but the taste is reported to be very bitter even though the odor is quite pleasant.

LOOK-ALIKES:

Distinctive as it is, we know of no look-alikes in Alaska.

COMMENTS:

This soft, pliant, tan to light brown annual bracket fungus grows only on dead birch (*B. neoalaskana*) in the Interior. It dies during winter, but may remain as a blackened "ghost," and like other birch polypores is known to be dried, ground up, then mixed with smoking tobacco by Native peoples for its analgesic properties.

Fig. 087

Fig. 088

FAMILY: Polyporaceae
COMMON NAME: Turkey Tail or Many-Colored Polypore
GENUS AND SPECIES: *Coriolus [Trametes] versicolor* (L.) Quél 1886

STRIKING FIELD CHARACTERS:
Fuzzy, thin, leathery, grayish to brownish, and concentrically ringed.

MACRO- & MICRODESCRIPTION:
Fruit body 4-10 X 3-5 cm, 1-3 mm thick; leathery, often overlapping; surface velvety; color variable (often green with algae) otherwise grayish-brown to rusty-brown with whitish margins; concentrically zoned. **Pores** 3-5 per mm, round to angular; whitish to yellowish-brown. **Basidiospores** 5.5-6 X 1.5-2 μm; straw-yellow in deposit.

HABITAT AND ROLE:
On hardwoods (alder, birch, willow, and aspen).

EDIBILITY, TASTE, AND ODOR:
Not edible, albeit, some make tea from it; the taste and smell are nondistinctive.

LOOK-ALIKES:
There are many smaller, annual bracket fungi that form dense, overlapping basidiomes on hardwoods. Some are zoned concentrically and/or are variously colored and could be confused with the one and only "Turkey Tail."

COMMENTS:
This is one of fourteen mushroom species or groups claimed to have anticancer properties, which is most likely why some prepare a drinkable infusion from it. Otherwise, the fungus itself is not considered edible.

Toothed, Spiny, or Hedgehog Mushrooms:
The Hydnoid Fungi

As the common name suggests, the fungi of this group feature a hymenium that is formed on the outside of pendant "teeth" or spines hanging down underneath the mushroom cap. The family Hydnaceae is represented by only a few genera, six of which (*Dentinum, Hericium, Hydnellum, Hydnum, Sarcodon,* and *Phellodon*) are commonly collected; *Sarcodon* and *Dentinum* are commonly seen when fruiting. The fruiting body of a tooth fungus is often mushroom-shaped (albeit, usually tougher) and has numerous small spines or teeth pointed downward. It is on these teeth (hymenophore) that the reproductive spores of the fungi (basidiospores) are borne and from which they are forcibly discharged.

Only the pinkish-orange *Dentinum* and white *Hericium* should be considered edible. All others are tough-fleshed, not palatable, bitter, or may produce gastrointestinal problems. It is simply best not to attempt eating members of this group.

Fig. 089

FAMILY: Hydnaceae
COMMON NAME: Hedgehog or Pig's Trotter Mushroom
GENUS AND SPECIES: *Dentinum repandum* (L.) Gray 1821

STRIKING FIELD CHARACTERS:
Small to medium-sized, pinkish to buff-brown, centrally stipitate tooth fungus.

MACRO- & MICRODESCRIPTION:
Cap 3-8cm; convex to broadly so in age, flesh-buff to orange-buff; margin often smooth-wavy; context yellowish-buff. **Teeth** 2-5 mm; creamy-buff. **Stalk** 3-8 X 0.5-1 cm, pale orange-buff, dry, smooth. **Basidiospores** 6.5-9 X 6.5-8 μm; subglobose; smooth, white in deposit.

HABITAT AND ROLE:
Grouped in deep mosses under black spruce and willow.

EDIBILITY, TASTE, AND ODOR:
Delicious, mild to fungoid.

LOOK-ALIKES:
H. umbilicatum of Southeast Alaska found in coastal *Pinus contorta v. contorta* muskeg.

COMMENTS:
This fungus is very common in the Interior of Alaska, and found in coastal Southcentral Alaska in late September or early October under spruce on well drained sites often with False Azalea, *Menziesia ferruginea.*

FAMILY: Hericiaceae
COMMON NAME: Comb-Toothed Hericium
GENUS AND SPECIES: *Hericium coralloides* (Scop.) Pers. 1794 =*Hericium ramosum* (Bull.) Letell. (1826)

STRIKING FIELD CHARACTERS:
Fruiting bodies white to yellowish-tan (in age), amorphous to somewhat globose, with pendant spines hanging from branching limbs, attached to log butts or standing trees.

MACRO- & MICRODESCRIPTION:
Caps of fruiting bodies are clusters of white branches up to 20 cm long and up to 20-30 cm in diameter. **Spines** (teeth) are white and hang from the undersides of the branches from base to tips. Texture of both branches and spines is soft at first with spines becoming brittle. **Stalk** arising from a basal stub. The stalk base is inconspicuous and the branches are up to 1 cm diam., and the teeth are up to 2 cm long. **Basidiospores** 3-5 X 3-4 µm; smooth to minutely roughened, subglobose, amyloid; white in deposit.

HABITAT AND ROLE:
Hericium coralloides is easily identified and occurs on (or in) the wood of mostly downed hardwood logs, but occasionally on standing trees and stumps, and occasionally from old limb wounds of living trees (especially birch).

EDIBILITY, TASTE, AND ODOR:
Hericium coralloides is an edible fungus that is quite good with a mild flavor and aroma.

LOOK-ALIKES:
H. abietis, predominantly on fir with branches arranged in clusters and longer spines.

COMMENTS:
This fungus often yields large multi-branched fruitings up to 30 cm across that are startlingly white when fresh, but they're always found on dead *Betula neoalaskana* in the Interior. In age, the pendant, spiny mass becomes droopy, soft, and often develop buff to brown stains on the white branches.

Fig. 090

Fig. 091

FAMILY: Bankeraceae
COMMON NAME: Blue-Gray Hydnellum
GENUS AND SPECIES: *Hydnellum caeruleum* (Hornem.) P. Karst. 1879

STRIKING FIELD CHARACTERS:
Bluish-purple cap context and brown stalk context.

MACRO- & MICRODESCRIPTION:
Cap 3-10 cm; single to fused with others, convex to depressed, velvety and white in youth, margin bluish becoming rusty-brown; context zoned, bluish. **Teeth** 1-3 mm; white to bluish in youth, aging to purple-brown. **Stalk** context brown. **Basidiospores** 5.5-6 X 3.5-4.5 μm; brown, irregularly lobed and warted.

HABITAT AND ROLE:
Mycorrhizal with our northern conifers. Common.

EDIBILITY, TASTE, AND ODOR:
Inedible; bitter, cucumber-like.

LOOK-ALIKES:
H. peckii, at least when young.

COMMENTS:
This fungus has a cucumber-like odor when cut in half, but is not an edible.

FAMILY: Bankeraceae

COMMON NAME: Strawberries and Cream or Bleeding Hydnellum

GENUS AND SPECIES: *Hydnellum peckii* Banker 1912

STRIKING FIELD CHARACTERS:
Irregular, white, red juice drops on top, farinaceous odor.

MACRO- & MICRODESCRIPTION:
Cap 3-7 cm; single to fused with others, convex to flattened, irregular, knobby, ± ridged or even pitted in age; velveteen and white in youth, with exuding red droplets, darkening in age to pinkish-brown, reddish-brown, to blackening. **Teeth** 3 mm. **Stalk** 2.5-5 X 1-3 cm; tapering; pinkish-flesh to concolorous with cap. **Basidiospores** 5-5.5 X 3.5-4 μm; brown in deposit, tuberculate.

HABITAT AND ROLE:
Mycorrhizal with our black spruce and larch and common in our Interior forests.

EDIBILITY, TASTE, AND ODOR:
Inedible; bitter, woody, mild odor.

LOOK-ALIKES:
H. diabolus with a sweet and pungent odor, unlike *H. peckii*.

COMMENTS:
We have received more calls by intrigued enthusiast about this fungus than any other, as to what it is, with its irregular shape, white surface, and contrasting red juice droplets on top. It may look inviting, but better left to the bugs and slugs.

Fig. 092

Fig. 093

FAMILY: Bankeraceae
COMMON NAME: Scaly Tooth Shingled Hedgehog
GENUS AND SPECIES: *Sarcodon imbricatus* (L.) P. Karst. 1881

STRIKING FIELD CHARACTERS:
Mushroom-like fruiting bodies, light to dark tan with large (and darker) scales all over cap and in concentric rings, spines white, tan, or brown.

MACRO- & MICRODESCRIPTION:
Cap of fruiting bodies up to 15 cm across, circular to lobed, convex to flattened, with depressed center or sometimes with a central hole; scaly from the beginning; scales in concentric rings, more or less dark brown on a tan background. **Stem** 5-12 by 0.7-2.0 cm, central to somewhat off-center, stocky to slender, equal or somewhat enlarged below, fibrillose, hairless (glabrescent). **Spines** are up to 9 mm long, extending down stem, crowded, nearly white at first but brown in age, flesh pale brown to tan in the cap, somewhat darker in the stem. **Basidiospores** 6-8 X 5-7 μm; subglobose, warted; brown in deposit.

HABITAT AND ROLE:
Sarcodon imbricatus occurs in spruce or in mixed forests.

EDIBILITY, TASTE, AND ODOR:
Sarcodon imbricatus is not recommended for eating because of its tough texture. Another look-alike, *S. fennicus* (P. Karst.) P. Karst. (1887), has a stipe base context tissue that is bluish (seen when the whole fruit body is cut in half) and with a bitter taste with a tendency to cause gastrointestinal upset.

LOOK-ALIKES:
H. scabrossum with its olive-green to bluish-green stalk base and less pronounced and lighter cap scales. It is reported by Arora (1986) to have an inedible bitterness to its taste.

COMMENTS:
This brown recurved (imbricate) scaly-capped tooth fungus is very common throughout Alaska's boreal forest because of its affinity and association with conifers (especially black, white, and Sitka spruce).

Toothed, Spiny, or Hedgehog Mushrooms: The Hydnoid Fungi

Single to Branched Coral Mushrooms:
Coralloid Fungi

The coral fungi that one is likely to encounter are dull tan to bright yellow in color. The fruiting bodies often project upward through the forest floor duff or from rotting wood and take the form of a single "club," a straight to branched, coral-like growth form, or a dense cauliflower-like structure resembling the underwater marine corals of the Caribbean or South Pacific. Here, their resemblance ends, because these fungi are soft, pliable, or brittle and fleshy to the touch. The hymenium, like that of the tooth fungi, consists of a thin layer over the surface of the upright branches.

These fungi could probably be eaten, but we caution against it, as some *Ramaria* species may cause gastrointestinal upset and/or diarrhea in some people. In general, only the larger coral-like clusters tend to cause the latter, but the smaller fungi are infrequently found, at least in great enough quantity to make a suitable meal.

FAMILY: Clavariadelphaceae
COMMON NAME: Hairy-Based Fairy Club Strap Coral
GENUS AND SPECIES: *Clavariadelphus ligula* (Schaeff.) Donk 1933

STRIKING FIELD CHARACTERS:
Simple small- to medium-sized clubs, yellow, with whitish hairy bases.

MACRO- & MICRODESCRIPTION:
Fruit body simple clavate clubs, erect and unbranched, but sometimes irregularly forked, terete (rounded cylindrical) to compressed (flattened along their length); dull yellow to yellowish-tan or with reddish to vinaceous (wine-red) tints; apex bluntly pointed; 3-8 cm by 3-12 mm broad, and mostly smooth to lightly wrinkled. **Basidiospores** 8-18 X 3-6 μm; smooth, elliptic to elongated; white to pale yellow in deposit.

HABITAT AND ROLE:
Clavariadelphus ligula, when fruiting, forms gregarious troops over the floor in mixed conifer-deciduous forests. These and other similar club fungi are thought to be decomposers, but some species are suspected to be mycorrhizal.

EDIBILITY, TASTE, AND ODOR:
The taste of this fungus is bland, and the odor mild, but it is edible. Once again, best left to the bugs and slugs.

LOOK-ALIKES:
Smaller and slimmer than *Clavariadelphus pistilaris*, without the blunted-flattened heads of more brightly colored *Clavariadelphus truncates*. *Clavariadelphus sachalinensis* differs only microscopically. *Clavariadelphus mucronatus* is a yellowish-white with nippled tips.

COMMENTS:
These fungi are often hard to see at first, but once seen will form massive gregarious troops over conifer duff.

Fig. 094

Fig. 095

FAMILY: Clavariadelphaceae
COMMON NAME: Strap-Like Coral
GENUS AND SPECIES: *Clavariadelphus sachalinensis* (S. Imai) Corner 1950

STRIKING FIELD CHARACTERS:
Looks amazingly like *Clavariadelphus ligula* with white spores, pale yellowish to pale brownish, club-shaped small cap, and stalk being one with slighter yellower spores in deposit.

MACRO- & MICRODESCRIPTION:
Fruit body 2-7 (-15) cm X 3-15 (-35) mm, simple to occasionally branched, cylindrical, sub-clavate to finally clavate to sub-ventricose; apex acute to obtuse, rugose to irregularly flattened, never depressed; pale yellow to yellow-buff, to dull yellow in age; smooth to rugulose; base becoming white-pruinose with abundant white basal mycelium; contextual flesh white to yellowish. **Basidiospores** (13-) 16-24 (-28) X 4-6 μm, narrow, ellipsoid; pale yellowish to yellowish-tan in deposit.

HABITAT AND ROLE:
Grows scattered or in groups, on mossy ground in well-drained conifer forests during late summer and fall.

EDIBILITY, TASTE, AND ODOR:
Not recommended for eating. Mild to slightly acrid to bitter.

LOOK-ALIKES:
Clavariadelphus ligula.

COMMENTS:
This, too, is best left to the slugs and bugs.

Fig. 096

FAMILY: Clavariadelphaceae
COMMON NAME: Truncate Club Coral
GENUS AND SPECIES: *Clavariadelphus truncatus* Donk 1933

STRIKING FIELD CHARACTERS:
A broad, golden, flattened apex and large size.

MACRO- & MICRODESCRIPTION:
Fruit body 5-15 (-18) cm X 2-6 cm at apex; simple, turbinate to clavate, erect, unbranched, but may fork, apex often depressed; smooth to rugulose; pinkish-brown, ochraceous to brownish-orange; context white, pale cream to buff. **Basidiospores** 9-13 X 5-8 μm; elliptic, smooth; pale yellow in deposit.

HABITAT AND ROLE:
Scattered to thinly gregarious on conifer duff.

EDIBILITY, TASTE, AND ODOR:
Reported to be edible and sweet.

LOOK-ALIKES:
Clavariadelphus borealis, having white, not yellowish spores in deposit, as does *C. truncatus*.

COMMENTS:
This is always a wonderful find and evokes the very essence of anything an all-out Easter egg hunt yields!

FAMILY: Clavulinaceae
COMMON NAME: Crested or
  Wrinkled Coral
GENUS AND SPECIES: *Clavulina*
  (coralloides) cristata (Holmsk.)
  J. Schröt. 1888

STRIKING FIELD CHARACTERS:
Generally small, thin, white, daintily branched coral with fine (cristate) tips.

MACRO- & MICRODESCRIPTION:
Fruit body 2-7 (12) X 5 cm, erect, variable, and generally branched; smooth; tips generally sharp, finely toothed; mostly white to slightly buff; context white, brittle. **Basidiospores** 7-11 (-14) μm; smooth, subglobose; white in deposit.

HABITAT AND ROLE:
Solitary, scattered to gregarious in open-wooded forest edges.

EDIBILITY, TASTE, AND ODOR:
With a pleasant odor, edibility and taste are rated highly by some.

LOOK-ALIKES:
Clavulina rugosa (unbranched to few branches, ± knobby form of *Clavulina cristata*) or *Ramariopsis kunzei* (white and branched). However, neither of these species is reported from Alaska at the time of this writing.

COMMENTS:
This white coral fungus with its sharp tips is easily discerned from other more robust *Ramaria* in Alaska.

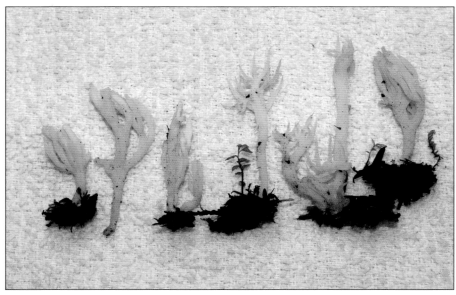

Fig. 097

Fig. 098

FAMILY: Gomphaceae
COMMON NAME: Handsome
Yellow-Tipped or Pinkish Coral
GENUS AND SPECIES: *Ramaria
formosa* (Pers.) Quél. 1888

STRIKING FIELD CHARACTERS:
Dense clusters of upright, crowded branches; 7-15 cm high; dull cream to tan to faintly pink.

MACRO- & MICRODESCRIPTION:
Fruit body profusely branched (see plate introducing the Coral Fungi (Fig. 007) from a large stalk, 7-15 cm high and as wide; hymenium (branches) smooth to gently grooved, erect to flaring (spreading out); dull yellow, cream colored below to pink or with vinaceous (wine-red) tinges above; stalk often massive in relation to branches, white fibrous and not gelatinous. **Basidiospores** 9-12.5 X 3.5-6 μm; ellipsoid, ± roughened; pale ochraceous in deposit.

HABITAT AND ROLE:
On rich forest floor humus, or duff of mixed deciduous and white spruce forests.

EDIBILITY, TASTE, AND ODOR:
The odor of this fungus is mild, and the taste bitter, but it should not be eaten due to its reputation for promoting gastrointestinal upset when consumed.

LOOK-ALIKES:
There may be several species of *Ramaria* in Alaska, but their differences lie predominantly in their staining/bruising reactions. Note and record these variances if seen.

COMMENTS:
The light pinkish, pinkish-orange, to pinkish-tan thick non-gelatinous branches distinguish this stately coral fungus.

Lichen-Coral Basidiolichen

FAMILY: Clavulinaceae
COMMON NAME: Scum Lover
GENUS AND SPECIES: *Multiclavula mucida* (Pers.) R.H. Petersen 1967

STRIKING FIELD CHARACTERS:
Massive troops over lignin-rich mossy peat or soil.

MACRO- & MICRODESCRIPTION:
Fruit body 0.5-1.5 cm X 1-2 mm, simple, unbranched (sometimes forking), long-clavate, smooth, buff to yellowish; context white. **Basidiospores** 4.5-7.5 X 2-3 μm; smooth, elliptic to oblong; white in deposit.

HABITAT AND ROLE:
Our Alaskan form grows where the lichen's algae component (algal phycobiont) lives abundantly, though I have never seen it on wood per se, only on lignin-rich and raised peaty soil.

EDIBILITY, TASTE, AND ODOR:
This fungus is of no consequence, as it is just too small to attempt collecting for the table.

LOOK-ALIKES:
Multiclavula vernalis, which is pale orange and grows on soil.

COMMENTS:
This always constitutes an exciting find and is easily identified in the field. It is first thought of as a coral fungus, but one needs to examine the base carefully with a hand lens to find its lichen counterpart, which is a small bluish-green, egg-shaped thallus.

Fig. 099

Blunt Ridged Chanterelle Mushrooms: Cantharelloid Fungi

Only a few members of the chanterelle family, the Cantharellaceae, are found with any regularity, and even then they can be rather inconspicuous. *Cantharellus [cibarius] formosis* is restricted to Southeast and perhaps Southcentral Alaska. *Craterellus tubaeformes* and *Gomphus clavatus* are the more ubiquitous species seen throughout Alaska. *Poloyzellus multiplex* has only been seen in Southeast.

Chanterelles, unlike agaric mushrooms, have thick, blunt ridged hymenia that often meander or interconnect to form a reticulum of sorts. These are not considered to be true gills (lamellae), thus placing them into their own distinct taxonomic group. All of these species are edible.

FAMILY: Cantharellaceae
COMMON NAME: Golden Chanterelle, Chanterelle, Girolle, Pfifferling
GENUS AND SPECIES: *Cantharellus (cibarius) formosis* Fr. 1821

STRIKING FIELD CHARACTERS:
Golden-yellow cap, gill-like blunt ridges and stalks, decurrent and forking ridges, compressed and tapering stipes, firm white context tissues and wavy cap margins.

MACRO- & MICRODESCRIPTION:
Fruit body (2-) 3-15 (-25) cm, broadly convex, plane to depressed; smooth, moist, but not viscid; yellow, yellow-orange to golden-orange; margin often lobed, undulating, eroded to split; context white to yellowish-white. **Ridges** thick, spaced, blunt ridged, shallow, decurrent, forking, concolorous with young caps, otherwise yellower. **Stalk** 2-10 X 0.5-3 (-5) cm; equal to most often tapering toward base, solid, dry, concolorous with cap. **Basidiospores** 7-11 X 4-6 μm; smooth, elliptical; cream to light yellow in deposit.

HABITAT AND ROLE:
Associated with Southeast Alaska conifers (spruce). We have never seen this species north of Anchorage.

EDIBILITY, TASTE, AND ODOR:
Edible and choice as reported by most; mild odor to mildly peppery to fruity taste.

LOOK-ALIKES:
Hygrophoropsis aurantiacus (poisonous), *C. cibarius* whitish to yellowish, robust *C. infundibuliformes* (also edible), and its whitish to violet tinted mountain cousin, *C. subalbidus*.

COMMENTS:
Once verified, this mushroom is seldom misidentified or confused with other Alaskan species. It is delicious, but needs tender loving cooking.

Fig. 100

FAMILY: Cantharellaceae
COMMON NAME: Funnel or
 Winter Chanterelle
GENUS AND SPECIES: *Craterellus
 tubaeformis* (Fr.) Quél. 1888
(= *Cantharellus infundibuliformis* Fr.,
 s.s. Smith and Morse 1947)

STRIKING FIELD CHARACTERS:
Grayish gill-like forked ridges. This long,
hollow-stemmed, pliant, darkly colored
chanterelle is often found in dense troops.

MACRO- & MICRODESCRIPTION:
Fruit body 6-11 cm, broadly convex-
depressed to broadly infundibuliform,
glabrous, moist, hygrophanous; margin
wavy to lobed; yellow- to blackish-brown,
fading to an ochraceous-gray; context
thin, tough, pliant. **Ridges** distant, narrow, forked, pale yellow, orange-yellow,
yellow-brown, brownish, violet tinted to
grayish and waxy looking. **Stalk** 2-8 (-10)
cm X 0.3-2 (-4) mm, tapering toward
base, flattened, hollow, context a whitish
pith, ± pallid basil mycelium. **Basidiospores** 9-12 X 6.5-8 µm; smooth, broadly
ovate to elliptic, ± subglobose; pale
"creamy-buff" to yellowish in deposit.

HABITAT AND ROLE:
Scattered to gregarious in understory
mosses of spruce forests.

EDIBILITY, TASTE, AND ODOR:
Alaskan material is reported to be edible,
and even good by some, but I would add,
"with a bit of caution," especially if you've
never eaten it before because the white,
rather than the typical yellow color, may
result in a less than accurate identification.

LOOK-ALIKES:
Cantharellus lutecens (smooth to slightly
veined hymenophore), *Craterellus tubaeformis* (a white-spored possible synonym), *Cantharellula umbonata* (a truly
gilled mushroom).

COMMENTS:
Try it carefully. You just might come to
like this little fella.

Fig. 101

Fig. 102

FAMILY: Gomphaceae
COMMON NAME: Pig's Ear
GENUS AND SPECIES: *Gomphus clavatus* (Pers.) Gray 1821

STRIKING FIELD CHARACTERS:
A meaty nature and fluted, often irregular mass with long decurrent ridges; red-wine (vinaceous)- to drab purple in color.

MACRO- & MICRODESCRIPTION:
Fruit body 3.5-10 (-15) cm; appearing undifferentiated from stipe in youth, margin flaring becoming lobed in age, yielding irregular, shallow to deep funnel; dry, unpolished-dull; dull vinaceous to purplish at first, fading to dark purple-drab to light russet-vinaceous, avellaneous to clay-color and finally dingy yellow-brown; context thick below, thin at margin, whitish to pale buff. Hymenophore of numerous low, crowded, and frequently forking and anastomosing, decurrent purple to purple-vinaceous ridges fading to vinaceous with age. **Stipe** 4-10 X 0.8-3 cm, frequently compound, expanding upward, often many fused at base (caespitose) into a fleshy mass; solid but may become somewhat hollow in age; concolorous with hymenophore. **Basidiospores** 10-13 X 5-6.5 µm; warty to rugulose, narrowly ellipsoid to ovoid; ochraceous in deposit.

HABITAT AND ROLE:
Scattered amongst mixed birch-spruce forest uplands.

EDIBILITY, TASTE, AND ODOR:
Reported to be a choice edible, but insects love them, too! Otherwise mild, non-distinctive, and pleasant.

LOOK-ALIKES:
Nothing else in our neck of the woods looks like this very easily recognizable mushroom.

COMMENTS:
When you first stumble across one of these, camouflaged by the understory, you'll be amazed that you haven't seen them sooner, as many can become very large.

FAMILY: Thelephoraceae
COMMON NAME: Blue Chanterelle
GENUS AND SPECIES: *Poloyzellus multiplex* (Underw.) Murrill 1910

STRIKING FIELD CHARACTERS:
Deep purple, grayish-purple to bluish-gray fruit body, hymenophore and stalk, a cornucopia-like appearance, and the often en masse growth habit are dead giveaways.

MACRO- & MICRODESCRIPTION:
Fruit body 2-10 cm, en masse (multiple caespitose-like fruit bodies) appearing undifferentiated from stipe in youth, margin flaring becoming lopsided in age yielding irregular, shallow to deep purplish funnels; dry, unpolished; color dull purple, purple-gray, bluish-purple, and/ or ± frosted; context bluish-black. **Hymenophore** nearly smooth to generally very wrinkled; concolorous with cap. **Stalk** 2-5 X 0.5-2 cm, most often short, off-center, and fused with others en masse; solid to hollow; concolorous with hymenophore. **Basidiospores** (4-) 6-8.5 X 5.5-8 µm; globose to broadly elliptical, warted; white in deposit.

HABITAT AND ROLE:
We have only found this species in Southeast Alaska in the coastal boreal forest associated with Sitka spruce and hemlock along cut banks and trails.

EDIBILITY, TASTE, AND ODOR:
Edible, and some say good, while others say inferior to other chanterelles.

LOOK-ALIKES:
Craterellus species, which have been reported in Alaska by Wells and Kempton.

COMMENTS:
This is such a unique fungus that we suspect it is hard to confuse with anything else you might see. For that reason, it should be easy to identify in the field.

Fig. 103

Vase, Thelephore Mushrooms: Thelephoroid Fungi

Members of the genus Thelephora are placed into its own family, the Thelephoraceae. They are often very common as dark purple brown "vases" 6-25 mm high, typically almost equally wide, and found on disturbed, thin, or sparsely moss-carpeted soils in close association with pioneering plants such as willows and alders along stream courses. The hymenium covers the outside of the vase above whatever stalk may be present. Most often the spore-bearing part of the fungus (*hymenophore*) is smooth to wrinkled, green-brown to red-brown, or sometimes deep chocolate brown.

These fungi are quite small and even though they often carpet the ground in places, we usually never think of them as a potential food source.

Fig. 104

FAMILY: Thelephoraceae
COMMON NAME: Common Earth Fan or Fiber Vase
GENUS AND SPECIES: *Thelephora terrestris* Ehrh. 1787

STRIKING FIELD CHARACTERS:
Small, tough, brown, stalked, vaselike mushrooms with a smooth, warted, or rippling, gray underside.

MACRO- & MICRODESCRIPTION:
Fruit bodies with a cap up to 6 cm in diam., circular to semicircular, stalk 1-3 cm long, cap hairy to scaly, reddish-brown to dark brown; margin rough and toothy, lower surface irregular, smooth to warted, pinkish-gray to reddish-brown, and quite variable in its habit. **Basidiospores** 8-12 X 6-9 μm; ellipsoid-angular and warted; purple-brown in deposit.

HABITAT AND ROLE:
This species is a mycorrhizal associate of spruce and many other "pioneering" plants, like willows, throughout Alaska. It is not uncommon on exposed soil beneath conifers.

EDIBILITY, TASTE, AND ODOR:
Thelephora terrestris is not considered edible.

LOOK-ALIKES:
Some species of *Sebacina*, which has white spores in deposit, in contrast to the purple-brown spores of *T. terrestris*.

COMMENTS:
This fungus is an important ectomycorrhizal species with pioneering higher plants in the disturbed environs that are so common throughout Alaska.

Puffball or Stomach Mushrooms:
Gasteroid Fungi

Most often referred to as Gasteromycetes, the stomach fungi abound throughout Alaska. Puffballs, the most commonly encountered members of the group, occur as single fruiting bodies or are gregarious to forming tufted masses on moss-covered soil, on woody debris or rotting logs, along the forest floor, and amongst disturbed camp sites.

If you are preparing puffballs for the table, cut them in half with a sharp knife to make sure the puffball you've collected is actually just that and not a very young, developing, and unexpanded agaric. If so, toss it! However, if white and undifferentiated throughout, then the puffball is generally considered edible. If the puffball interior (**gleba**) is changing color—from white to yellow, greenish-yellow, olive, rusty, olive-brown, or chocolate—then one should refrain from eating it. At full maturity, the interior will be dry, powdery, and impossible to eat without choking.

The outer wall (**peridium**) may have a hole-like opening (**ostiole**) on top, be deeply cracked, or simply badly weathered. This is necessary for spore dissemination, as the spores of these fungi, unlike those of agarics, boletes, polypores, tooth fungi, coral fungi, chanterelles, and many cup fungi, are not forcibly discharged. Therefore, spore distribution in the puffball is affected by animals stepping on fruiting bodies, small animals carrying away spores stuck to their fur, by the impact of raindrops, or by simple erosion of parts for eventual wind dissemination of spores. Children love to stomp puffballs but inhaling the spores is not good for anyone.

FAMILY: Agaricaceae (once Lycoperdaceae)
COMMON NAME: Tumbling Puffball, Tumble Ball, Smooth, or Stalked Puffball
GENUS AND SPECIES: *Bovista plumbea* Pers. 1795

STRIKING FIELD CHARACTERS:
The fruiting body is relatively large, smooth, cranium-like, white to pinkish-gray to light tan, becoming bluish-gray (steely) with an egg-shaped top above and distinct sterile base below and papery thin at maturity. These features set this puffball apart from all others one is likely to encounter.

MACRO- & MICRODESCRIPTION:
Fruit body 5-12 cm high and 4-7 cm broad, somewhat pear-shaped overall, but with a well-delimited and relatively thick sterile base and egg-shaped head; peridium smooth below to minutely warted

Fig. 105

with small spiny tufts and somewhat wavy, wrinkled on top, white to light pinkish-gray. **Gleba** white to yellow-green. **Sterile base** one-third to one-half the height of the entire puffball. **Basidiospores** 5-7 X 4-5 µm; smooth, ovoid, broad elliptic to round; olive- to deep chocolate brown in deposit.

HABITAT AND ROLE:

This fungus has been found in areas of grass-covered gravelly soil on a river "bench" along a river course—what one might think of as well-drained, dry to arid sites, given their surroundings. As a decomposer, it most probably breaks down dead grasses.

EDIBILITY, TASTE, AND ODOR:

As long as the gleba of this puffball is pure white and not discoloring, then it is safe and often good to eat. Cut this fungus open to make sure that it is indeed a puffball (it should be pure white throughout) before attempting to prepare it for the table.

LOOK-ALIKES:

Other small, round, smooth *Bovista*, *Calvatia*, and *Lycoperdon* species.

COMMENTS:

This is a decomposer mushroom feeding on bits of forest and path-side debris, such as dead grasses.

FAMILY: Agaricaceae (once Lycoperdaceae)
COMMON NAME: Western Giant Alpine Puffball, Western Giant Puffball
GENUS AND SPECIES: *Calvatia booniana* A.H. Sm. 1964

STRIKING FIELD CHARACTERS:

Large, egg-shaped, white to yellowish-brown, sessile fruiting body; outer surface warts patterned, flattened with tan to yellow-brown centers, and a convex sterile base rising up into a ball-like shape from an attachment point; found on meadow tundra.

MACRO- & MICRODESCRIPTION:

Fruit body large, 8-10 cm high, 15-18 cm long, flattened egg-shaped, upper half of surface covered with low, flattened scale-like warts, wrinkled to smooth below to point of ground attachment. Inner **gleba** white and firm in youth becoming soft to spongy with age, becoming olive yellow, olive-brown, and finally dark brown at maturity. **Sterile base** remains white, broadly lenticular (convex lens-shaped) ⅓ to ½ the total height. **Basidiospores** 4-6.5 X 3.5-5.5 μm; smooth to minutely ornamented, round to broadly elliptical; olive-brown in deposit.

HABITAT AND ROLE:

Calvatia booniana is a fungus that has been found twice at Sable Pass on a hillside ca. 100 m south of the road where it occurred in a mesic alpine tundra meadow herb field. This fungus is a decomposer of herbaceous detritus (dead plant remains).

EDIBILITY, TASTE, AND ODOR:

Both the taste and odor of *Calvatia booniana* are mild. It is edible and good if fresh and solid white. Once it begins turning greenish yellow, it also becomes waterlogged and therefore unappealing. At maturity you would never want to eat it, lest you choke to death trying!

LOOK-ALIKES:

No other this large; albeit, *C. cretacea* and *C. tatrensis* in the Arctic look like, but have, much smaller fruit bodies.

COMMENTS:

This is by far the largest puffball we have seen and collected in Alaska. More striking to us was its being found near Sable Pass, a high tundra environ, in association with *Betula nana*.

Fig. 106

Fig. 107

FAMILY: Geastraceae
COMMON NAME: Sessile Earth-star
GENUS AND SPECIES: *Geastrum saccatum* Fr. 1829

STRIKING FIELD CHARACTERS:
A nonpedicilate (stalked), buff to tan inner sac sitting on a stellate base.

MACRO- & MICRODESCRIPTION:
Fruit body spore (inner peridium) case 0.5-2 cm atop a 4-8 ray stellate base (outer peridium) (1.5-) 2-5 cm; inner surfaces fleshy, pallid, buff to pale tan or ochre-brown; rupturing via an apical raised and fibrillose pore. **Gleba** white in youth, becoming brown and powdery dry in age. **Sterile base** absent (i.e., sessile). **Basidiospores** 3.5-5 μm, globose and warted.

HABITAT AND ROLE:
Single to gregarious below understory plants of forest margins and precipitous south to southwestern-facing slopes.

EDIBILITY, TASTE, AND ODOR:
This is not a mushroom you'd want to try, because when most often found (or seen), it has opened up and become powdery dry inside.

LOOK-ALIKES:
There have been only a handful of *Geastrum* species seen in Alaska. The size and stature of *Geastrum saccatum* beats them all and looks quite different from the others.

COMMENTS:
It's a rare and unusual find to come across this delightfully recognizable species. As Alaska's climate warms, we will most likely see increased numbers of these and other gasteromycetes.

Fig. 108a

FAMILY: Agaricaceae (once Lycoperdaceae)
COMMON NAME: Common or Gemmed Puffball
GENUS AND SPECIES: *Lycoperdon perlatum* Pers. 1796

STRIKING FIELD CHARACTERS:
Stalked puffball with a sterile base, white to buff to pinkish buff, with deciduous, cone-shaped spines that leave scars; terrestrial.

MACRO- & MICRODESCRIPTION:
Fruit body 1-4 cm broad X 2-5 (-6) cm high, top-shaped with a stem-like base; outermost surface with slender, spatially arranged short cone-shaped spines and granules that leave scars or pockmarks when rubbed off. **Peridium** white to dull white, with a pinkish to brownish cast; spines white to gray to brown; inner layer of peridium darkening in age to tan, yellowish-brown, or dark brown when old; peridium ruptures by means of an ostiole (pore) at the top-center of the fruiting body. **Sterile base** well developed, minutely chambered below the glebal mass; white and spongy when young, then yellowing and finally turning brown. **Gleba** white at first, then yellow, olive, brown and powdery dry at maturity. **Basidiospores** 3.5 X 4.5 µm; ± round, smooth to ± spiny; dark olive- to chocolate brown in deposit.

HABITAT AND ROLE:
This terrestrial puffball may be solitary, gregarious, or (most often) clustered in white spruce forests, or along paths, trails, and disturbed roadbeds. It fruits in July and August and is most likely a humus decomposer (saprophyte).

EDIBILITY, TASTE, AND ODOR:

This is another fine edible puffball that needs only to be white throughout on the inside and devoid of creepy crawlers (see entry for *Bovista plumbea* on page 126). The taste is mild to bland and may even be bitter, while the odor is pleasant.

LOOK-ALIKES:

Several other puffballs that are ornamented with peridial warts and/or spines are common to Alaska, but none leave the telltale scars on the surface when warts are rubbed off. *L. umbrinum* is similar, but the mature gleba is differently colored (dark- to purple-brown) and no scars are left when warts are removed.

COMMENTS:

Be sure to section these fellas before attempting to fry them up for eating. They sometime prove to be young agaric buttons, which are mushrooms waiting only for a water source to induce expansion (with gills), not puffballs, and could be baby poisonous mushrooms.

Fig. 108b

Fig. 109

FAMILY: Agaricaceae (once Lycoperdaceae)
COMMON NAME: Pear-Shaped Puffball
GENUS AND SPECIES: *Lycoperdon pyriforme* Schaeff. 1774

STRIKING FIELD CHARACTERS:
Clustered on rotting wood, white to buff, apical pored and stalked, but without the prolific squamules (small scales or warts) seen in *L. perlatum*.

MACRO- & MICRODESCRIPTION:
Fruit body 1.5-5 cm X 2-4 cm; stalked puffball with a sterile base (cut it open to differentiate between the base and peridial spore sac and gleba); round to inverted pear-shaped; color white at first, becoming buff to light brown in age and cinnamon-brown and papery thin in old age; smooth to granulose; with an apical pore at maturity. **Gleba** white in youth, changing from olive-yellow to dark olive-brown in age. **Sterile base** spongy, seemingly well developed in that it is quite distinct from the glebal chamber above.

Basidiospores 3-4.5 µm; smooth, globose; olive brown in glebal mass (no deposit—no forcible spore discharge).

HABITAT AND ROLE:
We find these traditionally associated with old, rotting conifer wood—logs, branches, sticks, lignin-rich peaty soil, etc.—and often in dense clusters of 15-30 fruit bodies.

EDIBILITY, TASTE, AND ODOR:
Edible with the usual cautions, and worth collecting and eating if they are found en masse when young.

LOOK-ALIKES:
L. umbrinum (without spines) and *L. perlatum* (with spines).

COMMENTS:
I've had folks try a bit of this mushroom in the field when found young and fresh and have known it to cause anaphylactic-like allergenic reactions in at least one person. So to restate, one must be careful with eating any mushroom.

Bird's Nest Stomach Mushrooms: The Gasteroid Fungi

Bird's nest fungi are Gasteromycetes; hence, they are close relatives of the puffballs. In fact, they are puffballs, but with a slightly different mechanism for spore discharge. The puffballs contain a cinnamon brown, rusty brown to purple brown dry powdery spore mass (**gleba**) that puffs out through a hole (**ostiole**), through cracks, or directly from weathered fruiting bodies being eaten by insects and other small animals, or by being stepped on by big animals such as you, me, bears, moose, etc. Sometimes the name "booters" is applied to puffballs, especially those larger forms, since they "puff" when booted. Bird's nest fungi, however, rely mainly on big raindrops to disperse their small egg-like sacs of spores (**peridioles**).

Bird's nest fungi derive their name from the appearance of the fruiting bodies when the lid-like covering (**epiphragm**) over the natural opening weathers away to expose egg-like flattened sacs of spores. The resulting cup-shaped fruit bodies (basidiocarps) employ raindrops to splash the peridioles out of the cup. Peridioles catch onto or adhere to surrounding vegetation, where they hang or stick, dry out, and then ultimately crack open to release their spores, which are carried away by the wind. This mechanism is very effective, so if you find a few bird's nest fungi on sticks or wood chips, take a close look around and you're likely to see a whole lot more.

Fig. 110

FAMILY: Geastraceae
COMMON NAME: Cannon Fungus, Cannonball Blaster, or Sphere Thrower
GENUS AND SPECIES: *Sphaerobolus stellatus* Tode 1790

STRIKING FIELD CHARACTERS: Tiny, whitish-yellow, on woody (stick) debris in moist weather.

MACRO- & MICRODESCRIPTION: **Fruit body** 1-3 mm, globose to subglobose, white outer and yellow-orange center; peridial wall splitting into 3-7 earthstar-like rays. **Gleba** a single, forcibly ejected spore-containing sac (peridiole—as in the bird's nest fungi) leaves behind a clear to opaque gelatinous inner peridial wall. **Basidiospores** 6-10 X 4-6.5 μm; smooth, subglobose, borne inside the dark brown to olive-black peridiole that will adhere to any substrate for drying, cracking, and spore release.

HABITAT AND ROLE:
We see this fungus growing often in massive troops on rotting stems/sticks of alder, birch, and spruce.

EDIBILITY, TASTE, AND ODOR:
These qualities are all reported as unknown because they are so small and too much energy would be utilized to collect even a pauper's mouthful.

LOOK-ALIKES:
Other woody debris inhabiting mushrooms that initially look very much like *Sphaerobolus stellatus* are the tiny bird's nest fungi in the genera *Cyathus*, *Crucibulum*, *Nidula*, and *Nidularia* before their epiphrams (lids) erode away. But all of these have numerous peridioles in each cup; in two of them, *Cyathus* and *Crucibulum*, there is even a funicular cord connected to each peridiole, unlike *Sphaerobolus stellatus*.

COMMENTS:
When you encounter these elusive fungi, you'll be amazed that you found something so small. They are easy to identify using your trusty hand lens!

Fig. 111

FAMILY: Agaricaceae
COMMON NAME: Woodchip Loving Bird's Nest or Deep Splash Cup
GENUS AND SPECIES: *Cyathus olla* (Batsch) Pers. 1801

STRIKING FIELD CHARACTERS:

Troops in mass fruitings on wood chips; brown cup with little hairy plugs becoming smooth outside with whitish eggs inside at maturity.

MACRO- & MICRODESCRIPTION:

Fruit body 8-12 X 5-8 mm; sub-stipitate with a wide base; goblet-shaped in youth, expanding and flaring to recurved; light to medium brown outside, shaggy-fibrillose in youth to almost smooth in age; inner surface silvery-brown to gray-brown in age. **Gleba** of large disc-shaped dull-brown peridioles, 2-3 X 0.5 mm, attached by funicular cord. **Basidiospores** 8-12 (-14) X 8-12 μm, subglobose to ellipsoid, white in deposit.

HABITAT AND ROLE:

These tiny fungi grow profusely on chipped up woody substrates along paths, in gardens, etc.

EDIBILITY, TASTE, AND ODOR:

Don't even think about it, as they are too small to make even the smallest meal and like "puffball" fungi, are dry and powdery when mature.

LOOK-ALIKES:

C. stercoreus with a less flaring, but often shaggy-edged cup and black peridioles at maturity; found on dung and manured ground.

COMMENTS:

Where beauty bark and wood chips are used, you can expect to see large fruiting of this and other similar fungi.

Witch's Broom Mushrooms:
Conifer Rust Fungi

The "rusts" belong to a group of Basidiomycetes that are very different from and more primitive than traditional mushrooms. These rather distinctive fungi can be found everywhere in Alaskan forests. Many species are represented, but two will probably stand out most to the casual observer. Rust fungi often have complex life cycles involving plants other than the primary or economically important spruce trees upon which they live as parasites. Look carefully at the leaves of shrubby understory plants like Labrador tea and bearberry for black, blue, red, cinnamon, orange, or yellow spots. You're probably looking at another stage of the rust fungi on its alternate host. However, some of these spots may also be caused by viruses or insects, which are not of interest to us here.

FAMILY: Coleosporiaceae
COMMON NAME: Spruce or Witch's Broom Rust
GENUS AND SPECIES: *Chrysomyxa arctostaphyli* Dietel 1894

STRIKING FIELD CHARACTERS:
Look at the tops of white or black spruce for branch proliferations into large ball-like orange fungus colored witch's brooms, from which needles are shed after turning yellow, then orange, and finally rusty-orange. The fungus causes purple-brown leaf spot on its alternate host, kinnikinnick.

MACRO- & MICRODESCRIPTION:
Spores (teliospores) 13-18 X 23-64 µm, on spruce needles; (**basidiospores**) 8.5-9.5 X 7.5-8 µm.

HABITAT AND ROLE:
Chrysomyxa arctostaphyli infects an ericaceous ground cover plant, bearberry (*Arctostaphylos uva-ursi*), causing a purple-brown leaf spot on this alternate host. Spruce is the primary host, the one most affected. These "brooms" provide nest building sites and ultimately fungal

Fig. 112

basidiocarp caching sites for northern red and flying squirrels. Often, the fungi the squirrels pick up from the forest floor are epigeous (above ground) or hypogeous (below ground), or are ectomycorrhizal species of agaric and false truffle fungi. Once dried on the limbs of trees, fruiting bodies are stored by the rodents (flying squirrels, northern red squirrels, and red-backed voles) for winter food in the old nest sites. *Chrysomyxa arctostaphyli* may cause growth stunting (in height and diameter) of the tree at infection sites, bole (trunk) deformation, knots, and even mortality in the host trees.

EDIBILITY, TASTE, AND ODOR:
Edibility is unreported, but why would one want to eat it in the first place!

LOOK-ALIKES:
Nothing else in Alaska looks quite like the "brooms" stimulated by the auxin-producing rust fungus *Chrysomyxa arctostaphyli*. Dwarf mistletoe (parasites of higher plants), such as *Arceuthobium tsugense* do form "brooms" (called witch's or spruce brooms) of a sort in the western and mountain hemlocks of Southeast Alaska, which are not present in the Interior or further north (Hennon et al 2001). These mistletoe "brooms" look quite different, but could be confused with our northern spruce brooms from a general morphology point of view.

COMMENTS:
This "broom" (Fig. 152a-k) is most interesting in that it provides a protective site for northern flying and northern red squirrels as nest building sites. Once the young squirrels have been raised and leave the nest site, adults use the nests to store mushrooms dried on the tree's limbs. These are called "mushroom caches." We have seen some unusual fungi in caches not seen in our collecting.

Jelly Mushrooms: Gelatinous Fungi

The jelly fungi often abound in nature, but one really has to look carefully to find them, as they dry out quickly and shrink to mere films on woody substrates. Some live on hardwoods such as alder and birch, while others grow on dead branches of spruce and willow, particularly at higher elevations. The jelly fungi are an intriguing lot, and their fruiting bodies are most conspicuous right after a prolonged rainy, foggy, or wet period. Often found to exhibit bright colors such as black, red, orange, yellow, and buff to almost white, jelly fungi have amorphous shapes and look like globs of jelly on their selected substrates. Surprisingly, however, they do have integrity, in that they don't smear and stick to you like fresh plasmodium of a slime mold. When fresh, their texture is like that of an ear lobe. When dry, jelly fungi often turn black, shrivel to practically nothing, and appear as brown to blackened, dried glue-like blobs, crusts, or films.

These fungi are Basidiomycetes, but their microscopic architecture is different; hence, the taxonomic position and placement into their own separate group of fungi. Their role is no less important than some of the other Basidiomycetes. They are saprophytic fungi that decompose deadwood (sticks, branches, and fallen logs) and, with time, clean up the woody debris on the forest floor.

Fig. 113

FAMILY: Tremellaceae
COMMON NAME: Witch's Butter
GENUS AND SPECIES: *Tremella mesenterica* Retz. 1769

STRIKING FIELD CHARACTERS:
Yellow, jellylike (when fresh) blobs on alder.

MACRO- & MICRODESCRIPTION:
Fruit bodies 2.5-10.0 cm wide and 3-4 cm high, tough, jellylike, irregularly shaped globs or lobes; translucent pale yellow to yellow-orange, changing to orange red upon drying. **Basidiospores** 7-18 X 6-14 µm; smooth, globose to sub-globose, broadly elliptical; pallid to yellow in deposit.

HABITAT AND ROLE:
Tremella mesenterica is commonly found on small dead hardwood branches, especially those of alder.

EDIBILITY, TASTE, AND ODOR:
Tremella mesenterica is sometimes said to be edible, as an additive to soups, but it is not commonly eaten. Arora says they are "harmless but flavorless," due to their being mostly H_2O. Their cousin, *Auricularia*, is, however, served in many Chinese restaurants as an additive to chow mein.

LOOK-ALIKES:
Several other jelly fungi including *Excidia glandulosa* (black), *T. foliacea* (brown), *Guepiniopsis alpinus* (yellow "gumdrops"), and *Dacrymyces palmatus* (yellow) have similar morphologies, but differ in their colors and in other microscopic features.

COMMENTS:
In our area, you are most apt to see these, and rather abundantly, during wet weather. They otherwise shrivel to mere dark thin plaques on the deadwood they decompose.

Cup or Sac Mushrooms: Cupuloid Fungi

The cup fungi, unlike all other groups considered thus far, do not produce their spores on the outside of basidia. Instead, they produce their spores inside hollow, elongated, sausage-shaped cells (sacs) called **asci**, and are most often arranged into an organized hymenium (Fig. 153a-d); hence, the name ascomycete. These fungi are often small, fairly inconspicuous, or hidden from view, even though some are brightly colored. Many forcibly discharge their spores. When you find one, blow (breathe) very gently across the cup and watch for a light colored "smoke" that emanates from the colored hymenium that lines the cup. Unlike the Thelophores, which resemble some cup fungi, the spore-producing surface (hymenium) is found **inside** the vase or cup or these fungi. Of course, the spore-producing cells (asci) differ significantly too. Genera in as many families (Cudoniaceae, Dermatiaceae, Discinaceae, Helotiaceae, Helvellaceae, Hypocreaceae, Pezizaceae, and Pyronemataceae) are commonly found throughout Alaska. There are, however, a number of other genera and many more species known to occur here.

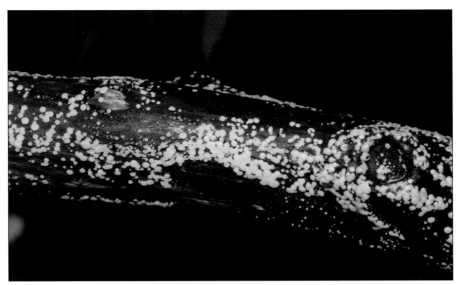

Fig. 114

FAMILY: Helotiaceae
COMMON NAME: Lemon Drops, Yellow Fairy Cup
GENUS AND SPECIES: *Bisporella citrina* (Batsch) Korf and S.E. Carp. 1974

STRIKING FIELD CHARACTERS:
Bright yellow, massive fruitings of tiny flattened fruit bodies on wet wood.

MACRO- & MICRODESCRIPTION:
Cap 1-3 (-4) mm; apothecia addressed, overlapping-crowded. **Stalk** ±, if present, then rudimentary. Smooth, bright yellow to golden yellow, pale yellow below. **Ascospores** 9-14 X 3-5 μm; elliptic ± septate, smooth, white in deposit.

HABITAT AND ROLE:
Groups or dense clusters on dead hardwoods.

EDIBILITY, TASTE, AND ODOR:
These are too small to scrape off the log and eat, if you haven't already stepped onto and slipped on them!

LOOK-ALIKES:
B. subpallida and *B. sulfurina* are only separated from *B. citrine* by spore size and shape.

COMMENTS:
These bright yellow-colored small to very small stalked flattened disc cup fungi are very often easily spotted against their often dark, wet, woody substrates.

FAMILY: Cudoniaceae
COMMON NAME: Common Cudonia
GENUS AND SPECIES: *Cudonia circinans* (Pers.) Fr. 1849

STRIKING FIELD CHARACTERS:
Small to medium-sized, rounded, creamy pink, pinkish tan to rosy tan, often with a split margin, cap folded down over an irregularly flattened, fluted, or ridged darker rosy tan to rosy brown stalk. Most often found in dense clusters or troops during summer and fall.

MACRO- & MICRODESCRIPTION:
Cap 0.5-2.0 cm broad, rounded, sometimes splitting over the often-incurving margin and indented on top, smooth to wrinkled, pinkish-tan. **Stalk** 3-8 cm long and 3-10 mm broad, darker wine-brown, smooth to scruffy, irregularly flattened, fluted or ridged. **Ascospores** 30-45 X 2.5 μm; needlelike, multiseptate, smooth, white in deposit.

HABITAT AND ROLE:
Cudonia circinans is a rather small- to medium-sized fungus that usually occurs in clusters in our conifer forest, especially the deep mosses under black spruce. These clusters may be scattered around, so if you find one, take a good look around at the deep moss-covered humus (soil or rotting wood) for others.

EDIBILITY, TASTE, AND ODOR:
Cudonia circinans is reported to be poisonous, as it contains monomethylhydrazine toxins.

LOOK-ALIKES:
Helvella spp. with much larger heads and stalks. *Leotia lubrica*, being much smaller and more brightly colored, is also similar, but generally grows in watercourses on wood and is, as its name implies, slimy. *C. grisea* is similar, but is a spring fruiter. Leave these for the slugs and bugs.

COMMENTS:
This is a commonly seen fall fungus and the largest *Cudonia* sp., which sometimes has rather long stipes irregularly entwined with its moss substrate. To extract them, grasp deeply in the dense moss.

Fig. 115

Cup or Sac Mushrooms

FAMILY: Pyronemataceae
COMMON NAME: Pixie Cup
GENUS AND SPECIES: *Geopyxis carbonaria* (Alb. and Schwein.) Sacc. 1889

STRIKING FIELD CHARACTERS:
Brown, deep, goblet cups with toothed yellow (cream) margin and slender, dull white to buff colored stalk on burned ground.

MACRO- & MICRODESCRIPTION:
Cup 0.5-1.5 cm broad, often as deep as wide; outer surface tan to light brown, becoming darker toward margin that is dissected, cream to yellow-brown and scaly-toothed; inner surface an orange-brown (darker). **Stalk** 0.5-1.5 cm long and 2-3 mm broad, dull white, smooth to wrinkled. **Ascopores** 11-17 X 6-9 μm; narrowly elliptical; white in deposit.

HABITAT AND ROLE:
After a forest fire, this gregarious cup fungus pops up everywhere on charred white and black spruce needles. This species is close to others in its genus (e.g., *Geopyxis vulcanalis*) and several species in other genera (*Tarzetta* and *Pustularia*) that may ultimately be found, but so far these other fungi have eluded us.

EDIBILITY, TASTE, AND ODOR:
The edibility of *Geopyxis carbonaria* is not reported one way or the other. They're so small that a mouthful would take hours to collect.

LOOK-ALIKES:
G. vulcanalis with a rounded, then deep, and finally flattened apothecium, *Tarzetta cupularis* (small stalk, grayish-tan, tan to light brown), and *T. rosea* (± stalk, pink to pinkish-red).

COMMENTS:
I have seen previous years' fire burns where this little stalked and fringed cup fungus blankets the burn site, especially where the fire was particularly hot and burned duff down to the soil. With recent summer fires, this little fungus will become omnipresent throughout Alaska with spring fruitings.

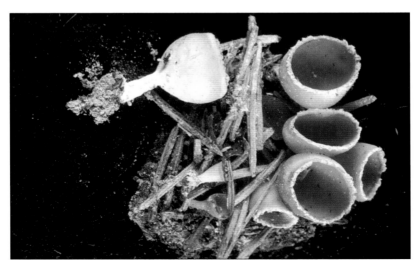

Fig. 116

FAMILY: Discinaceae
COMMON NAME: Brain False Morel
GENUS AND SPECIES: *Gyromitra esculenta* (Pers.) Fr. 1849

STRIKING FIELD CHARACTERS:
Wrinkled, more so than *G. infula*, reddish- to orange-brown saddle-like, lobed, very wrinkled, and brittle cap; a whitish to buff hollow stalk and growing on disturbed sites, trails, etc. and generally at higher altitudes in Alaska.

MACRO- & MICRODESCRIPTION:
Cap 4-10 cm; irregularly lobed, saddle-shaped, and most often very wrinkled; smooth to uneven, moist, thin, and brittle; orange- to reddish-brown or darker in age; margin free or ± attached in places. **Stalk** 2-6 X 1.5-3 cm; whitish to buff with reddish-brown flushes in age; hollow. **Ascospores** 15-25 X 8-14 µm, smooth, elliptical.

HABITAT AND ROLE:
A suspected mycorrhizal associate with pioneering plants, dwarf willows, dwarf birch, and alder, on disturbed sites such as trails.

EDIBILITY, TASTE, AND ODOR:
☠ This fungus is reported to be poisonous and should not be confused with *Gyromytra* (*Helvella*) *gigas*, an alpine species in Alaska that is quite delectable.

LOOK-ALIKES:
Gyromytra (*Helvella*) *gigas*, which is much lighter in color and often larger, but only found in our alpine and tundra zones. I have only eaten *G. gigas* that was collected in the alpine zone of Glacier National Park in Montana and it was good. *G. ambigua* is very similar, but it has violet to lavender tints and a darker red-brown disc.

COMMENTS:
Be cautious with this delightful group of false morels, almost all of which should be carefully avoided.

Fig. 117

FAMILY: Discinaceae
COMMON NAME: Saddle Shaped or Hooded False Morel
GENUS AND SPECIES: *Gyromitra infula* (Schaeff.) Quél. 1886

STRIKING FIELD CHARACTERS:
Tan to brown, smooth to wrinkled cap that does not attach to the white stalk.

MACRO- & MICRODESCRIPTION:
Cap yellow-brown, reddish-brown to dark brown (center-top), smooth to folded fertile surface (hymenium), 1.5-4.0 cm broad and high, lobed, saddle, or hoodlike to mostly irregularly lobed (not tightly wrinkled), with incurved margin, ± attached in a few places to stalk. **Stalk** hollow, somewhat irregular to flattened, but generally larger toward base, 1-4 cm long and 0.5-1.5 cm broad. **Ascospores** 18-23 X 7-10 μm; smooth, biseriate, narrowly elliptic; white in deposit.

HABITAT AND ROLE:
Solitary to ± gregarious on the moss-covered soil of previously burned spruce needle duff; this fungus is a saprophyte, and usually occurs on wood, but ours occurs on burned peat, conifer duff, and hard-packed trail soil substrates that are also high in cellulose content.

EDIBILITY, TASTE, AND ODOR:
The *Gyromitra infula* group is reported to be poisonous, as the fruiting bodies contain the carcinogen monomethylhydrazine (MMH), and other volatile and water-soluble substances that may cause serious health problems.

LOOK-ALIKES:
Possibly a less wrinkled *Gyromytra esculenta*, which is poisonous, or the lighter shaded tan to brown *Gyromytra gigas*, which is edible, while *G. infula* is not.

COMMENTS:
In late season, *G. infula* may become infected by a white sheathing fungus, *Sphaeronemella helvellae*, which is often confused for another ascomycete that commonly infects basidiomycete fruit bodies, *Hypomyces*.

Fig. 118

Fig. 119

FAMILY: Helvellaceae

COMMON NAME: Smooth-Stalked Helvella or Brown Elfin Saddle

GENUS AND SPECIES: *Helvella elastica* Bull. 1785

STRIKING FIELD CHARACTERS:
Tall, pliant white to buff stalk with a saddle-like folding and pendant apothecium.

MACRO- & MICRODESCRIPTION:
Cap 2-5 cm; saddle-like apothecium folding down over but free of the stalk; brown to sooty-brown fertile surface and gray-brown and smooth excipulum. **Stalk** 3-15 cm X 5-10 mm; smooth, wavy to flattened-grooved, pliant; white to buff. **Ascospores** 17-20 X 10-14 μm; elliptic to oblong, smooth, white in deposit.

HABITAT AND ROLE:
Most likely a decomposer of forest floor detritus.

EDIBILITY, TASTE, AND ODOR:
We have no knowledge of its edibility, but being a false morel, with this category's propensity toward being poisonous, this, too, is better left to the slugs and bugs.

LOOK-ALIKES:
H. albella (darker brown) and *H. compressa* with a furfuraceous (pubescent) excipulum.

COMMENTS:
In Alaska, these can become rather tall in amongst the forest floor grasses, mosses, and duff.

FAMILY: Hypocreaceae
COMMON NAME: Lobster Mushroom
GENUS AND SPECIES: *Hypomyces lactifluorum* (Schwein.) Tul. and C. Tul. 1860

STRIKING FIELD CHARACTERS:
Reddish-orange to orange pimpled covering layer (subiculum/stroma) having embedded flask-shaped ascocarps (perithecia) over gills of *Russula brevipes* and *Lactarius* spp. when mature, otherwise a weft of white ascome mycelium covering the basidiome.

MACRO- & MICRODESCRIPTION:
Cap lacking; instead a sterile subiculum harbors embedded perithecia; white at first then turning orange at maturity. **Ascospores** 30-50 X 4-8 µm; long fusiform.

HABITAT AND ROLE:
It is known as the lobster mushroom for a reason; it's edible. But I still can't get past the aversion that the peritheciate (flasked) Ascomycete (sac fungus) is parasitizing and decomposing the agaric/club Basidiomycete, which may be of unknown edibility itself.

EDIBILITY, TASTE, AND ODOR:
Reported as a good to excellent edible; mild taste and odor.

LOOK-ALIKES:
There are other *Hypomyces* species in Alaska, but none of which are the same color.

COMMENTS:
The other species of *Hypomyces* we see in Alaska are: *H. aurantius* (orange on polypores), *H. cervinigenus* (white, on false morels), *H. chrysospermum* (yellow, on boletes), and *H. hyalinus* (white, on Amanita), in addition to *Hypomyces luteovirens* (green, also on species of *Russula* and *Lactarius*).

Fig. 120

FAMILY: Morchellaceae
COMMON NAME: Black Morel
GENUS AND SPECIES: *Morchella elata* Fr. 1822

STRIKING FIELD CHARACTERS:
Sharp to ± rounded cone-shaped head with multiple dark to blackish-brown ridges and apothecia that are attached to the hollow white stalk. More often than not, it occurs on the ground in areas of recent and hot forest fires.

MACRO- & MICRODESCRIPTION:
Cap 2-12 X 1.5-4 cm; pits and ridges dark- to blackish brown; context hollow and whitish. **Stalk** 1.5-8 X 1-3 cm; white to buff; context concolorous. **Ascospores** 18-24 X 10-13 μm; smooth, elliptic, white in deposit.

HABITAT AND ROLE:
This fungus is a suspected mycorrhizal associate with our black spruce and black cottonwood.

Fig. 121

EDIBILITY, TASTE, AND ODOR:
This is the mushroom that pops up the first spring after the previous season's forest fires, sometimes in prolific fruitings. It all depends upon the heaviness of the spring rains. It is edible for most, but my major professor's wife finds the morel mushrooms very emetic! Be cautious, as the second year after our fires, the false morels take over and might be confused with our true morels.

LOOK-ALIKES:
Morchella angusticeps, *M. conica*, and *M. tomentosa*, a new species for Alaska that is easy to identify, in that it looks fuzzy with copious amounts of small projecting hairs.

COMMENTS:
If you don't get to it before the flies and other bugs, the hymenium within the many cups covering the head may be stripped, giving the fungus a gray to gray-tan rather than a dark brown to blackish-brown color. When morels are found, they are often found in prolific troops, especially the "black" morels *M. angusticeps*, *M. conica*, and/or *M. elata* (if in fact, these really are taxa different, as suspected, from those purported to fruit in the Lower 48).

Fig. 122

FAMILY: Pyronemataceae
COMMON NAME: Yellow Rabbit or Hare's Ear
GENUS AND SPECIES: *Otidea leporina* (Batsch) Fuckel 1870

STRIKING FIELD CHARACTERS:
Deeply cleft, ear-shaped, tan, brown, reddish-brown to purple-brown ascome with a smooth hymenium and excipulum.

MACRO- & MICRODESCRIPTION:
Cap 3-10 cm; split ear-shaped and smooth apothecium; reddish-brown to deep chestnut-brown; excipulum dark brown above, brown to tan below and finally buff to white at base; smooth. Margin often "fringed"; context tan. **Stalk** 1-3 cm; white, deeply buried in substrate. **Ascospores** 12-15 X 6-8 µm; elliptical; smooth; 2-celled; white in deposit.

HABITAT AND ROLE:
This fungus could very well be mycorrhizal with a number of tree species with which we've found it fruiting; e.g., *Picea glauca* predominantly, but also *Salix* sp., *Arctostphylos rubra* and even close to *Populus trichocarpa* in, of all places, the Great Kobuk River Sand Dunes of Kobuk Valley National Park above the Arctic Circle.

EDIBILITY, TASTE, AND ODOR:
We've not tried it. The taste and odor are mild, but its edibility is unknown.

LOOK-ALIKES:
Not known to Alaska, but Arora (1986) reports several in *O. abietina*, *O. bufonia* (dark brown), *O. concinna* (yellowish), *O. grandis*, *O. rainierensis*, and *O. smithii*, all of which may ultimately be found.

COMMENTS:
We find this fungus throughout Alaska and all of its six physiographic regions (Arctic, Interior, Southcentral, Northwest, Southwest, and Southeast).

Fig. 123

FAMILY: Pezizaceae
COMMON NAME: None (Blue Bottom)
GENUS AND SPECIES: *Peziza praetervisa* Bres. 1897

STRIKING FIELD CHARACTERS:
Large, smooth, deep tan to purple-brown inside and velveteen violet outside; sessile; associated with burn sites (pyrophilous).

MACRO- & MICRODESCRIPTION:
Cap 8-15 cm; grayish-tan, brown, reddish-brown to chestnut-brown apothecia; excipulum gray-brown, furfuraceous, violet-brown, violet to whitish-violet base near rudimentary stalk. **Stalk** absent to rudimentary, appearing sessile. **Ascospores** 11-15 X 6-8 μm, elliptic, minutely warted, 2-celled.

HABITAT AND ROLE:
A decomposer of lignin-rich substrates, e.g., spruce cones, wood chips, decaying plywood, etc.

EDIBILITY, TASTE, AND ODOR:
We have not tried it and we don't know if anyone has—with no ill effect, as its edibility is unreported.

LOOK-ALIKES:
P. arenaria, P. lobulata, P. repanda (on wood), *P. sublilicina* (with smooth spores and burn site associated), and *P. sylvestris* (on soil).

COMMENTS:
This has been, by far, the largest cup fungus we've found, but only in Southcentral Alaska's higher elevations around Homer.

Fig. 124

FAMILY: Pezizaceae
COMMON NAME: Boring Brown Cup Fungus or Fairy Tub
GENUS AND SPECIES: *Peziza [silvestris-sylvestris] arvernensis* Roze and Boud

STRIKING FIELD CHARACTERS:
Small to very large, expanded to irregularly flattened, smooth to wrinkled, and fragile-brittle apothecia (cups); yellow-tan, tan, brown to dull-brown; whitish and roughened excipulum.

MACRO- & MICRODESCRIPTION:
Cap 3-15 cm; cupulate, expanded to irregularly flattened, brittle; tan to brown. **Stalk** rudimentary if present at all. **Ascospores** 15-20 X 8-10 μm; smooth, elliptical.

HABITAT AND ROLE:
A decomposer of lignin-rich detritus (leaves, needles, small branches, sticks, and stems) and found in disturbed sites seemingly always on soil.

EDIBILITY, TASTE, AND ODOR:
We've never tried it and probably wouldn't risk it, because of its unknown edibility.

LOOK-ALIKES:
Peziza repanda on wood; *P. badia* and *P. badioconfusa*, both smaller and with deeper brown apothecia, but also on the ground, not manure, like a smaller look-alike *P. vesiculosa*.

COMMENTS:
We have seen large fruitings of this fungus throughout the boreal forest, but almost always on recently disturbed soils.

FAMILY: Morchellaceae
COMMON NAME: Wrinkled Thimble Cap
GENUS AND SPECIES: *Verpa bohemica* var. *bohemica* (Krombh.) J. Schröt. 1893

STRIKING FIELD CHARACTERS:
Resembles a tall, thin morel with a stunted, but detached cap.

MACRO- & MICRODESCRIPTION:
Cap conic to elongated campanulate, often flaring in age, not attached to stalk except at very apex, 2-5 cm X 2-4 cm; light to dark brown with olive tints, convoluted and almost plicate-ridged; trama concolorous with cap, 0.5-2 mm thick, pallid grayish-brown, and often brittle. **Stalk** 5-15 cm X 1-2 cm, dry, brittle, equal, dirty-white to yellowish, often smooth above and granulose below; trama whitish, stuffed to ± hollow. **Ascospores** 55-85 X 17-22 μm; ellipsoid to sub-allantoid, smooth with granular contents; white in deposit.

HABITAT AND ROLE:
Found scattered to gregariously distributed in disturbed gardens and rockeries and under deciduous trees.

EDIBILITY, TASTE, AND ODOR:
Edible, with caution. Odor and taste are mild fungoid.

LOOK-ALIKES:
Morchella punctipes, M. semilebra, although more robust, might easily be confused with *V. bohemica*.

COMMENTS:
Like its cousins, the true morels, this false morel is eaten by many. However, in a few instances (Wells and Kempton 1967), this morel may cause gastrointestinal upset, vomiting, and diarrhea in the unsuspecting. It's best to remember this caveat: If you have never eaten this fungus before, try just a little bit the first time.

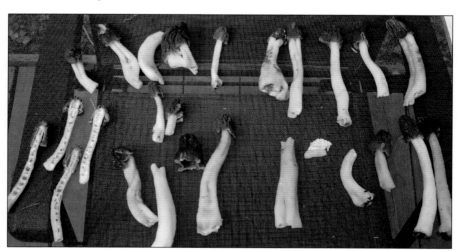

Fig. 125

Cup or Sac Mushrooms: Earth Tongue Fungi

The earth tongues are relatively small Ascomycetes in which the spore-producing surface is similar to the basidiomycetous coral fungi, occurring around the outside of the often flattened, spade-like fruiting bodies that typically project out of mossy substrates. Unlike cup fungi, their microscopic asci (sacs) have no "lid-covered" opening. Instead, there exists a pore through which spores are forcibly ejected. The earth tongues common to Alaska are stalked, yellowish tan to black, and generally conspicuous when fruiting against a bright green moss background. Members of the group are saprophytes on plant detritus. The more colorful earth tongues belong to the genera *Spathularia* (buff to yellow-brown) and *Mitrula* (yellow), whereas the darker (green and black) forms belong to the genus *Geoglossum*.

FAMILY: Neolectaceae
COMMON NAME: Irregular
  Yellow Earth Tongue
GENUS AND SPECIES: *Neolecta irregularis* (Peck) Korf and J.K. Rogers 1971

STRIKING FIELD CHARACTERS:
What appears to be a dainty, twisted, irregular, bright to dull-yellow, unbranched coral-like fungus with a white stalk buried amongst deep mosses.

MACRO- & MICRODESCRIPTION:
Cap 1-5 cm; round in cross section to flattened, irregularly grooved, yellowish-white (cream) to deep yellow. **Stalk** 1.5-3 cm X 2-10 mm; white. **Ascospores** 5-9 X 3-5 μm; short elliptical to subglobose; smooth; white in deposit.

HABITAT AND ROLE:
A suspected decomposer of leaf and needle detritus in deep mosses under white spruce.

EDIBILITY, TASTE, AND ODOR:
Reported to be edible, but we've never found enough of it to try eating. Otherwise it has a mild taste, albeit watery, and mild odor.

LOOK-ALIKES:
This dainty fungus may be reminiscent of several basidiomycetous *Clavariadelphus* species, particularly *C. ligula*, *C. pistillaris*, and *C. sachalinensis*, all having straw-yellow to yellow-buff stalks, rather than the white ones we see in *N. irregularis*, and the much smaller ascomycetous *Mitrula borealis*.

COMMENTS:
It's always exciting to run across this infrequently seen fungus, which we find at first confusing, then exhilarating.

Fig. 126

Fig. 127

FAMILY: Cudoniaceae
COMMON NAME: Yellow Paddle Earth Tongue, Fairy Fan
GENUS AND SPECIES: *Spathularia flavida* Pers. 1794

STRIKING FIELD CHARACTERS:
Flattened, spathulate, smooth to wrinkled, light yellow, fan-shaped head straddling a darker swollen stalk.

MACRO- & MICRODESCRIPTION:
Cap compressed to flattened, spathulate or fanlike, smooth to wrinkled (sometimes contorted), pale yellow, yellow-tan to brown. **Stalk** is often darker colored and smooth. **Ascospores** yellow-brown in deposit, (hyaline *sub lenta*) needlelike, cylindric-clavate, smooth, one to many septate, 30-75 (-95) X 1.5-3 µm.

HABITAT AND ROLE:
Widely to closely scattered on mosses under white and black spruce and larch.

EDIBILITY, TASTE, AND ODOR:
We are unaware of any reports relating to the edibility of the fungus. Mild and fungoid, often smelling like a semiaquatic environ of wet mosses and algae.

LOOK-ALIKES:
There are other Alaskan species of "earth tongues" like *Geoglossum*, *Mitrula*, and *Neolecta* (this volume) and possibly *Trichoglossum*, but none appear as *Spathularia flavida*.

COMMENTS:
This earth tongue is variable in color—from a bright yellow to yellow-buff head with a buff, dirty buff, to light tan stalk. It is always found in clusters in deep mosses, principally *Pleurozium schreberi* and, to a lesser extent, *Hylocomium splendens*.

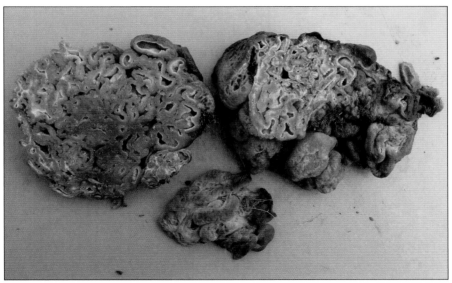

Fig. 128

FAMILY: Discinaceae
COMMON NAME: "Brain Truffle"
GENUS AND SPECIES: *Hydnotrya tulasnei* (Berk.) Berk. & Broome 1846

STRIKING FIELD CHARACTERS:
Brown to reddish-brown amorphous ± lobed mass with exposed heavily to tightly folded and convoluted hymenial elements.

MACRO- & MICRODESCRIPTION:
Fruit body 3-8 cm; reddish-brown to brown outer surface; hymenial folds within ± tight. **Ascospores** globose to subglobose, knobby.

HABITAT AND ROLE:
White spruce and birch with an understory of prickly rose, alder, and willows; mycorrhizal.

EDIBILITY, TASTE, AND ODOR:
Truffles are so rarely found in Alaska that they always end up in our collections rather than on our tables, so we do not know if our species is edible. Neither taste nor smell was recorded.

LOOK-ALIKES:
Nothing else we've seen in Alaska; albeit, *H. cerebriformis* (with spiny rather than tuberculate spores) and *H. variiformis* are said to be very similar (Arora 1986), but it is unknown whether or not these species exist in the state.

COMMENTS:
Our specimens were found by Lisa and Shon Jodwallis in Fairbanks in lawn grass on top of loess mixed with organic matter very near a chokecherry tree and two very large white spruce trees during mid August to early September 2012.

Fig. 129a

FAMILY: Pyronemataceae
COMMON NAME: Fuzzy True Truffle
GENUS AND SPECIES: *Geopora cooperi* Harkn. 1885

STRIKING FIELD CHARACTERS:
Small to medium sized, hypogeous to erumpent, irregular, tan to brown ball whose "skin" wears away to yield a maze of folded tissue and vugs (open spaces).

MACRO- & MICRODESCRIPTION:
Fruit body 3-10 cm; hypogeous to erumpent; globose to subglobose, velveteen, cranioid (lightly furrowed), dirty tan with light- to dark-brown fuzz. **Gleba** densely convoluted, creamy-white to yellowish-buff. **Ascospores** 18-28 X 12-20 µm; elliptical, smooth.

HABITAT AND ROLE:
Thought to be an important mycorrhizal associate of colonizing willow and aspen, even though it has been reported with white spruce in mixed woods in the Interior.

EDIBILITY, TASTE, AND ODOR:
Edible, mild, and mild-fungoid. Our sciurid rodents really love these fungi, and collect, dry, and stash them in their winter caches.

LOOK-ALIKES:
Nothing else in Alaska is quite like this truffle champion.

COMMENTS:
We have seen this medium to large (for a truffle) species on a few occasions, but always associated with old outhouse wells.

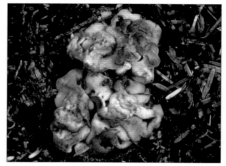

Fig. 129b

FAMILY: Elaphomycetaceae
COMMON NAME: Marbled Deer Truffle
GENUS AND SPECIES: *Elaphomyces muricatus* Fr. 1829

Fig. 130a

STRIKING FIELD CHARACTERS:
Ovoid, brown, roughened balls under *Alnus* found on disturbed sites, e.g., lake margins, river benches, road cuts, etc.

MACRO- & MICRODESCRIPTION:
Fruit body 1-3 (-4) cm, hypogeous, ovoid to almost spherical, tough; yellow-brown to dull-brown; peridium warted, thick, 1-2 mm, almost walnut shell-like toughness ("sclerenchyma-like" in plants), often encrusted with ectomycorrhizal root associates. **Gleba** stuffed with a cottony pinkish-beige hyphal mass, chambered, dark brown to blackish-brown, and powdery dry at maturity. **Ascospores** 18-30 μm; globose to subglobose, warted, dark- to blackish-brown.

HABITAT AND ROLE:
We find this rather common true truffle associated only with our alders along erosion cut banks. It is an important ectomycorrhizal associate. If you find one, keep looking, as there will be others.

EDIBILITY, TASTE, AND ODOR:
Squirrels love these and they are possibly edible for us, but we do not see the utility in doing so. One student in a field class put a mature, dry, gleba specimen to his mouth and claimed it produced a lip- and tongue-numbing sensation, which may have been an allergenic reaction to this mushroom.

LOOK-ALIKES:
Elaphomyces grannulatus, also found in Alaska.

COMMENTS:
There are at least seven other Alaskan true truffles (*E. grannulatus, Geopora cooperi, G. arenicola, G. arenosa, Hydnotrya cerebriformis, Tuber californicum, T. rufum*).

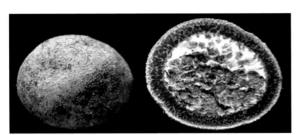

Fig. 130b

LICHENIZED
ASCOMYCOTA FUNGI:

The Lichens

Lichens are very common throughout Alaska, as are other Ascomycetes fungi. In fact, the lichen body, the **thallus**, is composed mostly of fungal hyphae interspersed with photosynthetic green algae (in 7 of 8 Lichen Orders) or cyanobacteria (in 1 of 8 Lichen Orders, the Peltigerales) or rarely both. Thus, the lichen is what might be termed a "composite" organism, since it consists of two (or even three) entirely different organisms in a close symbiotic or mutually beneficial relationship. The photosynthetic algal or cyanobacterium partners forming these associations are **photobionts**, while the fungal partner is referred to as the **mycobiont**. The photobionts are members of two entirely different kingdoms; the green algae belong to the phototrophic eukaryotic Protista (Protoctista) and the cyanobacteria to the phototrophic prokaryotic Monera. As noted in the introduction, fungi belong to the Kingdom Fungi (or Myceteae), as do the lichens.

The association between the photobiont and mycobiont is beneficial to both; the fungus captures water, essential minerals, and some vitamins for the photobiont, while the photobiont provides photosynthetic products to the fungus. The fungus provides structural support for the photobiont and a favorable microclimatic and chemical environment in which the photobiont can grow and flourish. The fungus also serves as an effective filter of excess photosynthetically active and ultraviolet radiation.

The vast majority of lichenized fungi produce ascospores; hence, they are **ascolichens** (ca. 99 percent + of all lichens) and typically have disc-shaped spore-producing surfaces. The group includes crustose, foliose, and fruticose forms. The remaining examples of lichenized fungi produce basidiospores and thus are **basidiolichens** (less than 0.5 percent of all lichens). The basidiospores emanate from upright and clubbed coral fungi or gilled agaric fungi. In each instance, the fungus partner determines the shape of the lichen thallus. However, the free-living fungus does not assume the morphological form expressed in the lichen unless combined with its photosynthetic partner.

Lichens generally fall into three categories—crustose, foliose, and fruticose. **Crustose lichens**, as their name implies, grow very closely attached to their substrate. Structurally, they consist of an upper differentiated cortex layer that is usually pigmented; an algal layer seen as a green or bluish-green layer just below the cortex; and a medulla, composed of loosely arranged fungal hyphae that also serve to attach the lichen to the substrate. **Foliose lichens**, as their name suggests, are flattened with often leaflike lobes. Structurally, they have an upper cortex, an algal layer immediately below, a medulla of loosely arranged fungal hyphae, and a differentiated lower cortex. Foliose lichens may be closely attached to the substrate by wrinkles or folds in the lower cortex, by special hair or fingerlike projections or rhizines on the lower surface or, as found in *Umbilicaria* species, by a central umbilicus. Some lichens, such as the reindeer antler lichen *Masonhalea*, are not attached to the substrate and can be blown around freely by wind. **Fruticose lichens** often grow erect on their substrate or, if growing on twigs and branches, can form pendent masses. Structurally, they have an outer cortical layer, an algal layer below this, and an inner medullary layer. Some fruticose lichens, such as *Usnea*, have a differentiated stiff central strand, which gives the lichen considerable strength and flexibility.

Cold-tolerant lichens often dominate the higher subarctic and alpine environments. Competition from higher plants is significantly reduced in these cold-stressed regions and lichens are able to spread luxuriously over organic and mineral soils—found most often among mosses, on rocks, bark, and wood, on old antlers and bones, and under intermittent snowbanks and sometimes in quite wet environments, although lichens generally don't care for extremely wet habitats.

Ascolichen: Crustose

FAMILY: Icmadophilaceae
COMMON NAME: Candy, Spray-Paint, Fairy, or Peppermint Drop Lichen
GENUS AND SPECIES:
Icmadophila ericetorum (L.) Zahlbr. 1895

STRIKING FIELD CHARACTERS:
Thallus mint-green, consisting of rounded pink to grayish pink discs (apothecia) on a smooth to granular crustose bed that is off-white to pale green and on old conifer logs, stumps, or on barren soil.

Fig. 131

MACRO- & MICRODESCRIPTION:
Thallus granular; apothecia pale red, margin thick but becoming excluded when older. Thallus K+ yellow, apothecia K+ orange, C+ orange.* **Ascospores** 15-27 X 4-6 μm; fusiform, 2-4-celled; white in deposit.

HABITAT AND ROLE:
Common and widespread, occurring on shaded rotting spruce logs, soil, humus, and mosses, especially some species of *Sphagnum*. In more southern parts of Alaska, *Icmadophila ericetorum* is also found on tree trunks over bark or wood. Sometimes also found on old compact *Sphagnum* hummocks or cushion-forming plants.

EDIBILITY, TASTE, AND ODOR:
Not poisonous, but of no known culinary value.

LOOK-ALIKES:
Even though there are six species of *Icmadophila*, only *I. ericetorum* is found throughout North America, and rather commonly, too, but generally on rotting wood in Alaska.

COMMENTS:
It's always a surprise to come upon this striking crustose lichen with its pink apothecia set against the mint-green background.

Common chemicals are used to test differences and separate lichen and some mushroom species where morphological differences cannot. Lichen and mushroom tissues are fresh/ tested for differences using chemicals. For lichens, they are noted as 10 percent K— potassium hydroxide, C—calcium hypochlorite or bleach (as in Milton Sterilizing Fluid), I—1.5 percent iodine potassium iodide (I2KI—Lugol's or Melzer's solutions), 1 percent Pd—para-phenylenediamine (Steiner's solution), and a weak acid (lemon juice). Melzer's solution, 3-5 percent KOH, distilled water, 95 percent ethanol, and others are also used in distinguishing mushrooms.

Ascolichens: Foliose

FAMILY: Peltigeraceae
COMMON NAME: Studded Vein Lichen
GENUS AND SPECIES: *Peltigera aphthosa* (L.) Willd. 1787

STRIKING FIELD CHARACTERS:
Thallus large, leafy green with thin, black, irregularly shaped warts (cephalodia) containing cyanobacteria on the upper surface.

MACRO- & MICRODESCRIPTION:
K-, C-, KC-, P-. Amyloid asci. **Ascospores** 48-70 X 4-7 µm; acicular, 4-10-celled; white in deposit.

HABITAT AND ROLE:
Peltigera aphthosa is ubiquitous throughout Alaska. It is found in willow (*Salix alaxensis*) thickets, near moss-covered stream margins, in spruce forests, and even in dryer, colder heath thickets at or above tree line. *Peltigera aphthosa* is usually found on moss-covered humic soil or on decaying wood. *Peltigera leucophlebia* (Nul.) Gyeln. is a similar species found in habitats that overlap with those occupied by *P. aphthosa*. *Peltigera leucophlebia* is clearly veined on the lower surface and the undersides of the fertile lobe tips have a patchy green cortex. In contrast, typical specimens of *P. aphthosa* lack veins and have a continuous green cortex on the underside of each fertile lobe tip. However, the two species do intergrade in appearance. This is especially true for specimens of *P. aphthosa* that occur in habitats with a heavy snow cover. Such specimens are often difficult to distinguish from *P. leucophlebia*.

Fig. 132

EDIBILITY, TASTE, AND ODOR:

Even though *Peltigera* species are known to contain antibacterial and antioxidant agents, and have been used by people over the millennia for medicinal purposes to treat wounds, urinary disorders, thrush, tuberculosis, and even rabies, it is perhaps best left to our four-legged friends and the slugs when considering its "edibility."

LOOK-ALIKES:

There are several look-alike species of *Peltigera*: *P. didactyla, P. latiloba, P. leucophlebia, P. membranaceae, P. venosa.* All resemble *P. apthosa.*

COMMENTS:

This lichen is an important nitrogen producer in our nutrient-poor forest soils. The blue-green to blackish raised papillae, cephalodia, contain the blue-green cyanobacteria, *Nostoc commune*, that fixes atmospheric N_2 with O_2 to form NO_2 and NO_3, nitrites and nitrates, needed by plants for healthy growth.

Ascolichens: Fruticose

FAMILY: Cladoniaceae
COMMON NAME: Gray or True Caribou and/or Reindeer Lichen
GENUS AND SPECIES: *Cladina (Cladonia) rangiferina* (L.) Nyl. 1866

STRIKING FIELD CHARACTERS:
Thallus gray-green, ashy gray, pale green to almost white (but never yellow-green), forming ground cover cushions or tufts, and sometimes forming extensive mats. The thallus is highly branched with terminal branches in whorls of 2-3 around a hollow main axis, usually curved in one direction, which gives the lichen a windswept appearance.

MACRO- & MICRODESCRIPTION:
K+ yellow, KC-, P+ red, UV+. **Ascospores** dimensions are rarely, if ever, published.

HABITAT AND ROLE:
Cladina rangiferina occurs on humic soils and is a source of food for the woodland caribou. The thallus is fast growing and can form large, dense, and deep mats. *Cladina mitis* (Sandst.) Hustich and *C. arbuscula* (Warr.) Hale and Culb. are similar in appearance, but differ in having a yellow-green color and not appearing windswept.

EDIBILITY, TASTE, AND ODOR:
It is an important food for our northern caribou (reindeer), a consumer of this lichen as a food source, and therein lies its economic importance, but it is also known to have some antibacterial properties.

LOOK-ALIKES:
Cladonia portentosa.

COMMENTS:
This fruticose species is found throughout northern boreal forests, and especially in alpine zones within. Its photobiont is the blue-green cyanobacterium, *Trebouxia irregularis.*

Fig. 133

PREPARING WILD
MUSHROOMS FOR USE

After you've gathered edible wild mushrooms, it's time to put them to use in the kitchen. Here's an informal look at how some Alaskans like to prepare them. Mushrooms collected in the wild look a lot less clean and tidy on the cutting board than they do in the heat of the chase. First, make sure the shrooms you're about to prepare are all the same species and that the species is indeed the edible one that you had in mind.

Next, carefully remove any mud, sand, spruce needles, strands of moss, and cowering insects. Most debris is more easily removed when dry rather than when wet. You can buy special brushes for this purpose, but we improvise. A small paintbrush or a sturdy feather works well.

Finally, cut off and discard any portions of mushrooms that are discolored, infested with maggots, or otherwise suspect. Maggots are fond of many of our edible favorites, particularly the stalk and portions of the cap. While one or two of the little wrigglers doesn't hurt the flavor, they're not appealing to eat, and large numbers of maggots cause foul odors and major decomposition of the mushroom.

Refrigerating. Depending on the species, mushrooms will keep from one to three days in the refrigerator stored in a paper bag or waxed paper. Do not store mushrooms in plastic bags because they need air circulation or they will putrify. I advise cooking all mushrooms before refrigerating to slow their decomposition. Inky Caps and Shaggy Manes must be cooked immediately after collecting, unless you're trying to make ink the old-fashioned way. These fungi will autodigest (deliquesce) themselves through paper wrapping in cool temperatures, and the refrigerator temperature is ideal for full-blown autodigestion, which results in black "ink" dripping onto everything.

Freezing. Be sure to sauté or cook mushrooms before freezing. Let the cooked mushrooms cool, then transfer to small zip-sealing freezer bags, being careful to squeeze out all of the air before sealing. Label each bag clearly noting the species and date on a length of freezer tape wrapped all the way around the bag (you want to be sure the tape stays on). Use the mushrooms within six months of freezing them. Frozen mushrooms are usually best added to recipes without thawing them first. Species we freeze are Hedgehogs, Orange Delicious, and Meadow Mushrooms.

Drying. Some mushrooms are excellent dried, and tend to be even more flavorful than when they are fresh. Species we especially like dried are morels and the King Bolete. They keep very well.

To dry mushrooms, prepare them as described above (clean, dry, and section). Thinly slice the mushrooms into ⅛-inch-thick slices and place these onto screened shelving of a vegetable dehydrator.

Few of us own commercially made food dehydrators, so we have devised our own drying methods. Mushroom slices can be placed onto window screen–like racks. With the exception of stainless steel, metal is a less desirable surface for drying. Use the "plastic" window screen material. Some people dry mushrooms in the oven at the lowest setting, with the door propped slightly open. You can use plastic window screens placed in the house where air circulation is good (e.g., above a heated woodstove), but where they are out of the sun's light. Later in the season, you can hang the screens above the heating toyo, monitor, or woodstove. It's important that mushrooms dry fairly promptly, without overheating or becoming damp or dirty.

Mushroom slices should be dried until brittle (or in some cases slightly leathery), shrunken, and virtually weightless. They can then be stored in tightly sealed glass jars, awaiting the cook's desire.

To reconstitute dried mushrooms, soak them briefly in a minimal amount of water. If they are to be simmered in soup or sauce, you can skip the reconstitution step.

Be sure to carefully clean the mushroom drying screens and racks, as mushrooms leave a film that may mold before the next season.

MUSHROOM FIELD and
REFERENCE GUIDES

Alexopoulos, C.J. and C.W. Mims. 1979. *Introductory Mycology*. John Wiley and Sons, New York. 632 pp.

Ammirati, J.F., J.A. Traquair and P.A. Horgen. 1985. *Poisonous Mushrooms of Canada: Including other inedible fungi*. Fitzhenry and Whiteside Ltd. (Canada) and Univ. of Minnesota Press (US). 396 pp.

Arora, D. 1986. *Mushrooms Demystified: A Comprehensive Guide to the Fleshy Fungi*, 2nd Ed. Ten Speed Press, Berkeley, CA. 959 pp.

Arora, D. 1991. *All That the Rain Promises and More: A Hip Pocket Guide to Western Mushrooms*. Ten Speed Press, Berkeley, CA. 263 pp.

Atkinson, G.F. 1900. *Studies of American Fungi, Mushrooms Edible, Poisonous, Etc.* Andrus and Church, Ithaca, NY. 275 pp.

Bandoni, R.J. and A.F. Szczawinski. 1964. *Guide to Common Mushrooms of British Columbia*. A. Sutton, Victoria. 179 pp.

Barron, G.. 1999. *Mushrooms of Northeast North America*. Lone Pine Publishing, Auburn, WA. 336 pp.

Barron, G. 2005. *Mushrooms of Northeast North America: Midwest to New England*. Lone Pine Publishing, Auburn, WA. 336 pp.

Beneke, E.S. 1979. *Human Mycoses*. Upjohn, MI. 64 pp.

Benjamin, D.R. 1995. *Mushrooms: Poisons and Panaceas. A Handbook for Naturalists, Mycologists, and Physicians*. W.H. Freeman and Co., NY. 422 pp.

Bessette, A.E., A.R. Bessette and D.W. Fischer. 1997. *Mushrooms of Northeastern North America*. Syracuse University Press, Syracuse, NY. 336 pp.

Bessette, A.E., D.W. Fischer (Contributor) and A.R. Bessette. 2005. *Mushrooms of Northeastern North America*. Syracuse Univ. Press, Syracuse, NY. 336 pp.

Bessette, A.E., O.K. Miller, Jr., A.R. Bessette, and H.H. Miller. 1995. *Mushrooms of North America in Color: A Field Guide Companion to Seldom-Illustrated Fungi*. Syracuse Univ. Press, Syracuse, NY. 172 pp.

Bessette, A.E., W.C. Roody and A.R. Bessette. 1999. *North American Boletes: A Guide to the Fleshy Pored Mushrooms*. Syracuse Univ. Press, Syracuse, NY. 400 pp.

Bessette, A.E. and W.J. Sundberg. 1987. *Mushrooms, A Quick Reference Guide to Mushrooms of North America*. MacMillan, New York, NY.

Beug, M.W, A.E. Bessette and A.R. Bessette. 2014. *Ascomycetes Fungi of North America; A Mushroom Reference Guide*. Univ. of Texas Press, Austin. 488 pp.

Bigelow, H.E. 1974. *Mushroom Pocket Field Guide*. Macmillan, New York, NY. 117 pp.

Binion, D.E., S.L. Stephenson, W.C. Roody, H.H. Burdsall, Jr., O.K. Miller, Jr. and L.N. Vasilyeva. 2008. *Macrofungi Associated with Oaks of Eastern North America*. West Virginia Univ. Press, Morgantown. 467 pp.

Boertmann, D. 1995. *The Genus Hygrocybe*. Low Budget Publishing, Denmark. 184 pp.

Brandrud, T.E., H. Lindström, H. Marklund, J. Melot and S. Muskos. 1992. *Cortinarius Flora Photographica, Vol. 2*. Cortinarius HB. 40 pp.

Brandrud, T.E., H. Lindström, H. Marklund, J. Melot and S. Muskos. 1994. *Cortinarius Flora Photographica, Vol. 3*. Cortinarius HB. 35 pp.

Brandrud, T.E., H. Lindström, H. Marklund, J. Melot and S. Muskos. 1998. *Cortinarius Flora Photographica, Vol. 4*. Cortinarius HB. 31 pp.

Bresinsky, A. and H. Besl. 1990. *A Color Atlas of Poisonous Fungi: A Handbook for Pharmacists, Doctors and Biologists*. Wolfe Publishing, Ltd., London. 295 pp.

Brodie, H.J. 1975. *The Bird's Nest Fungi*. Univ. of Toronto Press, Toronto. 199 pp.

Cash, E.K. 1953. *A Checklist of Alaskan Fungi*. The Plant Disease Survey Division of Mycology and Disease Survey. Plant Disease Reporter Supp. #19. 70 pp.

Charles, V.K. 1974. *Introduction to Mushroom Hunting*. Dover Publishing Inc., New York. 58 pp.

Christensen, C.M. 1943. *Common Edible Mushrooms*. Univ. of Minnesota Press, Minneapolis. 124 pp.

Christensen, C.M. 1965. *Common Fleshy Fungi*. Burgess Publishing Co., Minneapolis, MN. 237 p.

Coffin, G. and M. Lewis. 1965. *Twenty Common Mushrooms and How to Cook Them*. International Pocket Library, Boston, MA. 96 pp.

Cripps, C.L., ed. 2004. *Fungi in Forest Ecosystems: Systematics, Diversity and Ecology. Volume 89*, Memoirs of the New York Botanical Garden, NYBG, New York.

Cummins, G.B. and Y. Hiratsuka. 1983. *Illustrated Genera of Rust Fungi* Revised Ed. APS Press, St. Paul, MN. 152 pp.

Davis, R.M., R. Sommer and J.A. Menge. 2012. *California Natural History Guides: Field Guide to Mushrooms of Western North America*. Univ. of California Press, Oakland. 459 pp.

Denis, R.W.G. 1968. *British Ascomycetes. Revised and Enlarged Edition of "British Cup Fungi."* Verlag von J. Cramer. 455 pp. and 40 Color Plates.

Faubion, N.L. 1964. *Some Edible Mushrooms and How to Cook Them*. Binfords and Mort, Portland, OR. 198 pp.

Farr, M.L. 1981. *How to Know the True Slime Molds.* Wm. C. Brown Co. Pub., Dubuque, IA. 132 pp.

Fischer, D.W. and A.E. Bessette. 2006. *Edible Wild Mushrooms of North America A Field-to-kitchen Guide.* Univ. of Texas Press, Austin.

Foster, M., G. Bills and G. Mueller Eds. 2004. *Biodiversity of Fungi.* Elsevier Academic Press, Burlington, MA. 760+ pp.

Freedman, L. 1987. *Wild About Mushrooms.* Aris, Berkeley, CA. 239pp.

Funk, A. 1981. *Parasitic Microfungi of Western Trees.* Can. For. Serv. BC-X-222. 190 pp.

Funk, A. 1985. *Foliar Fungi of Western Trees.* Can. For. Serv. BC-X-265. 159 pp.

Gamundi, I.J. and E. Horak. 1995. *Fungi of the Andean-Patagonian Forests: Field Guide to the Identification of the Most Common and Attractive Fungi.* Vazquez Mazzini Editores, Buenos Aires. 141 pp.

Garnweidner, E. 1996. *Mushrooms and Toadstools of Britain and Europe.* Harper Collins Publishers, London. 253 pp.

Gilbertson, R.L. and L. Ryvarden. 1986. *North American Polypores; Volume 1.* Fungiflora A/S. 433 pp.

Gilbertson, R.L. and L. Ryvarden. 1987. *North American Polypores; Volume 2.* Fungiflora A/S. 450 pp.

Glick, P.G. 1979. *The Mushroom Trail Guide.* Holt, Rinehart and Winston, NY. 247 pp.

Graham, V.O. 1944. *Mushrooms of the Great Lakes Region.* Spec. Pub. No. 5, The Chicago Academy of Sciences, Chicago, IL. 390 p.

Groves, J.W. 1962. *Edible and Poisonous Mushrooms of Canada.* Publication 1112, Research Branch, Canada Dept. of Agriculture, Ottawa. 298 pp.

Guba, E.F. 1970. *Wild Mushrooms Food and Poison.* Published by the Author, 36 Marianne Road, Waltham, MA. 118 pp.

Guild, B. 1977. *The Alaskan Mushroom Hunter's Guide.* Alaska Northwest Publishing, Portland, OR. 286 pp.

Güssow, H.T. and W.S. Odell. 1927. *Mushrooms and Toadstools.* F.A. Acland, Ottawa, Canada. 274 pp.

Hanlin, R.T. and M. Ulloa. 1988. *Atlas of Introductory Mycology.* Hunter Textbooks, Inc., Winston-Salem, NC. 196 pp.

Hard, M.E. 1908. *The Mushroom Edible and Otherwise.* The New Franklin Printing Co., Columbus, OH. 609 pp.

Hawksworth, D.L., P.M. Kirk, B.C. Sutton, and D.N. Pegler. 1995. *Ainsworth and Bisby's Dictionary of the Fungi.* CAB International, UK. 616 pp.

Hesler, L.R. 1960. *Mushrooms of the Great Smokies.* Univ. of Tennessee Press, Knoxville. 289 pp.

Hesler, L.R. and A.H. Smith. 1963. *North American Species of Hygrophorus.* Univ. of Tennessee Press, Knoxville. 416 pp.

Hesler, L.R. and A.H. Smith. 1979. *North American Species of Lactarius*. Univ. of Michigan Press, Ann Arbor. 841 pp.

Holsten, E.H., P.E. Hennon and R.A. Werner. 1985. *Insects and Disease of Alaskan Forests*. USDA-FS AK. Reg. Rpt. # 181. 217 pp.

Hudler, G.W. 1998. *Magical Mushrooms, Mischievous Molds*. Princeton Univ. Press, Princeton, NJ. 248 pp.

Huffman, D.M., L.H. Tiffany and G. Knaphus. 1989. *Mushrooms and Other Fungi of the Mid Continental U.S.* Iowa State Univ. Press, Iowa City. 326 pp.

Jenkins, D.T. 1986. *Amanita of North America*. Mad River Press, Eureka, CA. 197 pp.

Katsaros, P. 1989. *Illustrated Guide to Common Slime Molds*. Mad River Press, Eureka, CA. 66 pp.

Katsaros, P. 1990. *Familiar Mushrooms [of] North America*. The Audubon Society Pocket Guides, Alfred A. Knopf, Inc., New York, NY. 191 pp.

Katsaros, P. 1984. *Illustrated Guide to Common Slime Molds*. Mad River Press, Eureka, CA.

Katz, A. 1986. *Naturewatch*. Addison-Wesley, Boston. 128 pp.

Kendrick, B. 1985. *The Fifth Kingdom*. Mycologue Publications. Waterloo, Ontario, Canada. 406 pp.

Kibby, G. 1993. *An Illustrated Guide to Mushrooms and Other Fungi of North America*. Dragons' World Ltd., London. 192 pp.

Krieger, L.C.C. 1936. *The Mushroom Handbook*. Macmillan, New York, NY. 560 pp.

Krieger, L.C.C. 1967. *The Mushroom Handbook*. Dover, Mineola, NY. 560 pp.

Kuo, M. 2005. *Morels*. Univ. of Michigan Press, Ann Arbor, MI. 216 pp.

Kuo, M. 2007. *100 Edible Mushrooms; With Tested Recipes*. Univ. of Michigan Press, Ann Arbor. 329 pp.

Laessoe, T., A. Del Conte and G. Lincoff. 1996. *The Mushroom Book*. DK Publishing. 256 pp.

Laessoe, T. and G. Lincoff. 1998. *Eyewitness Handbooks/Mushrooms*. DK Publishing, Inc., New York, NY. 304 pp.

Lange, M. and F.B. Hora. 1963. *A Guide to Mushrooms and Toadstools*. E. P. Dutton and Co., Inc.

Largent, D.L. 1986. *How to Identify Mushrooms to Genus I: Macroscopic Features*. Mad River Press, Eureka, CA. 166 pp.

Laursen, G.A. and J.F. Ammirati. 1982. *Arctic and Alpine Mycology: The First International Symposium in Arcto-Alpine Mycology*. Univ. of Washington Press, Seattle. 559 pp.

Laursen, G.A., J.F. Ammirati, and S.A. Redhead. *Arctic and Alpine Mycology II*. Plenum Press, New York. 364 pp.

Laursen, G.A. and R.D. Seppelt. 2009. *Common Interior Alaska Cryptogams: Fungi, Lichenicolous Fungi, Lichenized Fungi, Slime Molds, and Mosses and Liverworts*. Univ. of Alaska Press, Fairbanks. 218 pp.

Laursen, G.A., H.H. Burdsall and R.D. Seppelt. 2005. *Wood Inhabiting Fungi: Their*

Diversity, Roles and Uses. IN Alaska Park Science: Connection to Natural and Cultural Resource Studies in Alaska's National Parks. Spring 2005. Pp. 18-25.

Laursen, G.A., R.D. Seppelt, and M. Hallam. 2003a. *Cycles in the Forest: Mammals, Mushrooms, Mycophagy, Mycoses and Mycorrhizae.* Alaska Park Science: Connection to Natural and Cultural Resource Studies in Alaska's National Parks. Winter 2003, Pp. 13-19.

Laursen, G.A., R.D. Seppelt and M. Hallam. 2003b. *Cycles in the Forest: Mammals, Mycophagy, and Mycorrhizae.* Pp.111-112. USDA Forest Service General Technical Report 579, 150pp. IN Proceedings: Hidden Forest Values. The First Alaskanwide Non-Timber Forest Products Conf. and Tour. 8-11 Nov. 2001.

Lincoff, G. 1981. *Simon and Schuster's Guide to Mushrooms.* Simon and Schuster, New York. 510+ pp.

Lincoff, G. and A.A. Knopf. 1981. *The Audubon Society Field Guide to Mushrooms.* Chanticleer Press, New York. 926 pp.

Lincoff, G.H. and Nehring. 1984. *The Audubon Society Field Guide to North American C. Mushrooms,* 2nd Printing. Alfred A. Knopf, NY. Chanticleer Press Ed. 928 pp.

Lockwood, T.F. 2006. *Treasures from the Kingdom of Fungi.* 127 pp.

Mad River Press Series. *How to Identify Mushrooms to Genus,* Volumes 1-6, Eureka, CA. 166 pp.

Marshall, N.L. 1905. *The Mushroom Book.* Doubleday, Page and Co., NY. 170 pp.

McCune, B. and L. Geiser. 1997. *Macrolichens of the Pacific Northwest.* Oregon State Univ. Press, Corvallis. 386 pp.

McDougall, W.B. 1925. *Mushrooms.* The Riverside Press, Cambridge. 151 pp.

McIlvaine, C. and R.K. Macadam. 1902. *One Thousand American Fungi.* Revised Ed. 729 pp.

McKenny, M. 1971. *The Savory Wild Mushroom* (Rev. by Daniel E. Stuntz). Univ. of Washington Press, Seattle. 242 pp.

McKenny, M. and D.E. Stuntz, revised by J.F. Ammirati. 1987. *The New Savory Wild Mushroom.* Univ. of Washington Press, Seattle.

McKnight, K.H., and V.B. McKnight. 1987. *A Field Guide to Mushrooms of North America.* Peterson Field Guide Series. Houghton Mifflin, Boston. 429 pp.

McKnight, K.H. and V.B. McKnight. 1996. *Mushrooms Flash Guide.* Houghton Mifflin, Boston.

Metzler, S. and V. Metzler. 1992. *Texas Mushrooms: A Field Guide.* Univ. of Texas Press, Austin. 48 pp.

Miller, O.K., Jr. 1972. *Mushrooms of North America.* E. P. Dutton and Co., Inc., New York. 360 pp.

Miller, O.K., Jr. and D. Farr. 1975. *An Index of the Common Fungi of North America (Synonymy and common names).* Band 44. 206 pp.

Miller, O.K., Jr. and H. Miller. 2006. *North American Mushroom: A Field Guide to Edible and Inedible Fungi.* Globe Pequot Press, Guilford, CT. 584 pp.

Morgan, A. 1994. *Toads and Toadstools*. Celestial Arts Publishing, Berkeley, CA. 224 pp.

Orr, R.T. and D.B. Orr. 1968. *Mushrooms and Other Common Fungi of Southern California*. Univ. of California Press, Berkeley. 91 pp.

Overholts, L.O. 1967. *The Polyporaceae of the United States, Alaska and Canada*. Univ. of Michgan Press, Ann Arbor. 465 pp.

Parker, H. 1994. *Alaska's Mushrooms: A Practical Guide*. Alaska Northwest Books, Portland, OR. 92 pp.

Pearson, L.C. 1987. *The Mushroom Manual*. Naturegraph Publishers, Happy Camp, CA. 224 pp.

Peck, Charles H. 1897. *Mushroom and Their Use*. Cambridge Botanical Supply Co., Cambridge. 80 pp.

Pegler, D. 1999. *The Easy Edible Mushroom Guide*. Aurum Press Limited, London. 256 pp.

Petrini, O. and G.A. Laursen. 1993. *Arctic and Alpine Mycology 3. Proceedings of the Third and Fourth International Symposium on Arcto-Alpine Mycology*. Bibliotheca Mycologica Bd. 150. J. Cramer, Berlin Stuttgart. ISBN 3-443-59051-9, Pp. i-xi, 1-169.

Phillips, R. 1981. *Mushrooms and Other Fungi of Great Britain and Europe: The Most Comprehensively Illustrated Book on the Subject This Century*. Macmillan, London. 288 pp.

Phillips, R. 1991. *Mushrooms of North America*. Little Brown and Co., Boston. 384 pp.

Pilz, D.L. Norvell, E. Danell and R. Molina. 2003. *Ecology and Management of Commercially Harvested Chanterelle Mushrooms*. USDA-FS, PNW Station General Technical Rpt. 576. 83 pp.

Pomerleau, R. 1951. *Mushrooms of Eastern Canada and the United States: How to Recognize and Prepare the Edible Varieties*. In cooperation with H.A.C. Jackson. Chanticleer, New York. 302 pp.

Pray, L.L. 1936. *Common Mushrooms*. Botany Leaflet 18. Field Museum of Natural History, Chicago. 68 pp.

Rice, M. and D. Beebee. 1980. *Mushrooms for Color*. Mad River Press, Eureka, CA.

Roody, W.C. 2003. *Mushrooms of West Virginia and the Central Appalachians*. Univ. Press of Kentucky, Lexington. 507+ pp.

Russell, B. 2006. *A Field Guide to Wild Mushrooms of Pennsylvania and the Mid-Atlantic*. Penn State Univ. Press, University Park, PA. 231+ pp.

Savonius, M. 1973. *All Color Book of Mushrooms and Fungi*. Mandarin Publishers Limited, Hong Kong. 72 pp.

Schaechter, E.1997. *In the Company of Mushrooms*. Harvard University Press, Boston, MA. 275+ pp.

Schalkwijk-Barendsen, H.M.E. 1991. *Mushrooms of Northwest North America*. Lone Pine Publishing, Auburn, WA. 414 pp.

Seaver, F.J. 1951. *The North American Cup-fungi (Inoperculates)*. NY Author Published. 428 pp.

Seymor, J. 1978. *A Color Nature Library: Mushrooms and Toadstools.* Crown Publ., New York. 320 pp.

Sisson, E.H. 1982. *Nature With Children of All Ages.* Prentice Hall Press, New York.

Smith, A.H. 1949. *Mushrooms in Their Natural Habitat. Vol. I.* Sawyer's Inc., Portland, OR. 626 pp.

Smith, A.H. 1951. *Puffballs and their Allies in Michigan.* Univ. of Michigan Press, Ann Arbor. 131 pp.

Smith, A.H. 1963. *The Mushroom Hunter's Field Guide.* Univ. of Michigan Press, Ann Arbor. 264 pp.

Smith, A.H. 1971. *The Mushroom Hunter's Field Guide: Revised and Enlarged.* Univ. of Michigan Press, Ann Arbor. 264 pp.

Smith, A.H. 1975. *A Field Guide to Western Mushrooms.* Univ. of Michigan Press, Ann Arbor. 288 pp.

Smith, H.V. and A.H. Smith. 1973. *How to Know the Non-gilled Fleshy Fungi.* Wm. C. Brown Co., Dubuque, IA. 402 pp.

Smith, A.H., H.V. Smith, and N.S. Weber. 1979. *How to Know the Gilled Mushrooms.* Wm. C. Brown Co. Pub., Dubuque, IA. 334 pp.

Smith, A.H. and N.S. Weber. 1980. *The Mushroom Hunter's Field Guide.* Univ. of Michigan Press, Ann Arbor. 324 pp.

Smith, A.H. and N.S. Weber. 1985. *A Field Guide to Southern Mushrooms.* Univ. of Michigan Press, Ann Arbor. 280 pp.

Smith, A.H. and N. Smith-Weber. 1988. *The Mushroom Hunter's Field Guide: All Color and Enlarged.* Univ. of Michigan Press, Ann Arbor.

Smith, A.H. and H.D. Thiers. 1971. *The Boletes of Michigan.* Univ. of Michigan Press, Ann Arbor. 428 pp.

Staments, P. and J.S. Chilton. 1983. *The Mushroom Cultivator: A Practical Guide to Growing Mushrooms at Home.* Agarikon Press, Olympia, WA. 415 pp.

Steinbeck, M. 1984. *Mushrooms in the Garden.* Mad River Press, Eureka, CA. 152 pp.

Stephenson, S.L. and M. Stempen. 1994. *Myxomycetes: A Handbook of Slime Molds.* Timber Press, Portland, OR. 183 pp.

Stubbs, A.H. 1971. *Wild Mushrooms of the Central Midwest.* Univ. of Kansas Press, Lawrence. 135 pp.

Stuntz, D.E. 1977. *How to Identify Mushrooms to Genus IV: Keys to Families and Genera.* Mad River Press, Eureka, CA. 94 pp.

Sundberg, W.J. and J.A. Richardson. 1980. *Mushrooms and Other Fungi of Land between the Lakes.* Tennessee Valley Authority. 39 pp.

Tekiela, S. and K. Shanberg. 1993. *Start Mushrooming: The Easiest Way to Start Collecting 6 Edible Wild Mushrooms.* Adventure Publications, Cambridge, MN. 128 pp.

Thomas, W.S. 1948. *Field Book of Common Mushrooms.* G. P. Putnam's Sons, New York. 369 pp.

Thomson, J.W. 1979. *Lichens of the Alaskan Arctic Slope*. Univ. of Toronto Press, Toronto. 314 pp.

Thomson, J.W. 1984. *American Arctic Lichens 1. The Macrolichens*. Columbia Univ. Press, New York. 504 pp.

Thomson, J.W. 1997. *American Arctic Lichens 2. The Microlichens*. Univ. of Wisconsin Press, Madison. 675 pp.

Tosco, U. and A. Fanelli. 1967. *Mushrooms and Toadstools: How to Find and Identify Them*. Orbis Publishing Limited, London. 102 pp.

Trudel, S. and J.F. Ammirati. 2009. *Mushrooms of the Pacific Northwest*. Timber Press, Portland, OR. 351 pp.

Turner, N.J. and A.F. Szczawinski. 1991. *Common Poisonous Plants and Mushrooms of North America*. Timber Press, Portland, OR. 311 pp.

Tylutki, E.E. 1987. *Mushrooms of Idaho and the Pacific Northwest: Vol. II Non-Gilled Hymenomycetes*. Univ. of Idaho Press, Moscow. 232 pp.

Vitt, D.H., J.E. Marsh, and R.B. Bovey. 1988. *Mosses, Lichen, and Ferns of Northwest North America*. Lone Pine Publishing, Auburn, WA. 296 pp.

Watling, R. 1978. *How to Identify Mushrooms to Genus V: Cultural and Developmental Features*. Mad River Press, Eureka, CA. 169 pp.

Watling, R. 2003. *Fungi*. Smithsonian Institution Press, Washington, D.C. 96 pp.

Watling, R. and A.E. Watling. 1980. *A Literature Guide for Identifying Mushrooms*. Mad River Press, Eureka, CA. 121 pp.

Wells, M.H. and D.H. Mitchell. 1966. *Mushrooms of Colorado and Adjacent Areas*. Museum Pictorial #17. Denver Museum of Natural History. Denver, CO. 81 pp.

Ziller, W.C. 1974. *The Tree Rusts of Western Canada*. Can. For. Serv. Pub. No. 1329. Dept. of the Environment. 272 pp.

LITERATURE CITATIONS

Ammirati, J.F., J.A. Traquair and P.A. Horgen. 1985. *Poisonous Mushrooms of the Northern United States and Canada*. Univ. of Minnesota Press, Minneapolis. 383+ pp.

Arora, D. 1986. *Mushrooms Demystified*. Ten Speed Press,Berkeley, CA. 959 pp.

Arora, D. 1991. *All That the Rain Promises, and More*. Berkeley, Calif. Ten Speed Press, Berkley, CA. 959 pp.

Beug, M.W, A.E. Bessette and A.R. Bessette. 2014. *Ascomycetes Fungi of North America; A Mushroom Reference Guide*. Univ. of Texas Press, Austin. 488 pp.

Binion, D.E., S.L. Stephenson, W.C. Roody, H.H. Burdsall, Jr., O.K. Miller, Jr., and L.N. Vasilyeva. 2008. *Macrofungi Associated with Oaks of Eastern North America*. West Virginia Univ. Press, Morgantown. 467 pp.

Blanchette, R.A., C.C. Renner, B.W. Held, C. Enoch and S. Angstman. 2002. "The Current Use of *Phellinus igniarius* by the Eskimos of Western Alaska." *Mycologist*, 16(4): 142-145.

Bresinsky, A. and H. Besl. 1990. *A Color Atlas of Poisonous Fungi: A Handbook for Pharmacists, Doctors and Biologists*. Wolfe Publishing, Ltd. 295 pp.

Brodie, H.J. 1975. *The Bird's Nest Fungi*. Univ. of Toronto Press, Toronto. 199 pp.

Brunner, I., F. Brunner and G.A. Laursen. 1992. "Characterization and comparison of macrofungal communities in Alnus tenuifolia and A. crispa forests in Alaska." *Can. J. Bot.*, 70: 1247-1258.

Burdsall, H.H. Jr. and Banik, M.T. 2001. "The genus *Laetiporus* in North America." *Harvard Papers in Botany* 6:43-55.

Cascio, J. and M. Johnson. 2011. *Morel Mushrooms; A Guide for Selection and Use*. Cooperative Extension Service, UAF. FNH-00020.

Cash, E.K. 1953. "A Checklist of Alaskan Fungi." The Plant Disease Survey Division of Mycology and Disease Survey. *Plant Disease Reporter* Supp. #19. 70 pp.

Fischer, D.W. and A.E. Bessette. 1992. *Edible Wild Mushrooms of North America*. Univ. of Texas Press, Austin. 248+ pp.

Freedman, L. 1987. *Wild About Mushrooms*. Aris, Berkeley, CA. 239 pp.

Geml, J., G.A. Laursen, K. O'Neill, H.C. Nusbaum and D.L. Taylor. 2006. "Beringian origins and cryptic speciation events in the fly agaric (*Amanita muscaria*)." *Molecular Ecology*, 15(1): 225–239.

Geml, J., G.A. Laursen, I.C. Herriott, J.M. McFarland, M.G. Booth, N. Lennon, H.C. Nusbaum, and D.L. Taylor. 2008. "Ecological partitioning of phylogenetic diversity of the ectomycorrhizal *Russula* (Russulales; Basidiomycota) among different boreal forest types." *New Phytologist*.

Geml J, Tulloss RE, Laursen GA, Sazanova NA, Taylor DL. 2008. "Evidence for strong inter- and intracontinental phylogeographic structure in *Amanita muscaria*, a wind-dispersed ectomycorrhizal basidiomycete." *Molecular Phylogenetics and Evolution*.

Geml J, Tulloss RE, Laursen GA, Sazanova NA, Taylor DL. 2008. "Phylogeographic analyses of a boreal-temperate ectomycorrhizal basidiomycete, *Amanita muscaria*, suggest forest refugia in Alaska during the Last Glacial Maximum." IN: Surviving on Changing Climate—Phylogeography and Conservation of Postglacial Relicts. Springer.

Geml, J., Rodham E. Tulloss, G.A. Laursen, Nina A. Sazanova, D.L. Taylor. 2008. "Strong biogeographic structure in a eukaryotic microbe: Evidence for provincial speciation in a cosmopolitan, wind-dispersed fungus." Submitted to *Molecular Phylogenetics and Evolution*. (manuscript tracking number 2007-10176).

Geml, J., Laursen GA., Timling, I., McFarland, J.M., Booth, M.G., Lennon N., Nusbaum, C. and Taylor, D.L 2009. "Molecular phylogenetic biodiversity assessment of arctic and boreal *Lactarius* Pers. (Russulales; Basidiomycota) in Alaska based on soil and sporocarp DNA." *Molecular Ecology*, 18: 2213-2227.

Geml, J., G.A. Laursen, I.C. Herriott, J.M. McFarland, M.G. Booth, N. Lennon, H.C. Nusbaum and D.L. Taylor. 2009. "Molecular phylogenetic biodiversity assessment of boreal ectomycorrhizal Russulaceae, with particular attention to the genus *Lactarius* Pers. (Russulales; Basidiomycota), based on soil and sporocarp DNA." *Molecular Ecology*, 18: 2213-2227.

Geml, J., G.A. Laursen, and D.L. Taylor. 2008. "Molecular diversity assessment of Arctic and boreal *Agaricus* taxa." *Mycologia*, 100: 577–589.

Geml, J., F. Kauff, G.A. Laursen and D.L. Taylor. 2010. "Genetic Studies Point to Beringia as a Biodiversity Hotspot for High-Latitude Fungi." *Alaska Park Science*, 8(2): 37-41.

Geml, József, Tulloss, R.E., G.A. Laursen, N.A. Sazanova and D.L. Taylor, 2010. "Phylogeographic Analyses of a Boreal-Temperate Ectomycorrhizal Basidiomycete, *Amanita muscaria*, Suggest Forest Refugia in Alaska during the Last Glacial Maximum." *Relict Species: Phylogeography and Conservation Biology* [IAB 3360].

Geml, J., G.A. Laursen, I.C. Herriott, Jack M. McFarland, M.G. Booth, N. Lennon, H.C. Nusbaum and D.L. Taylor, 2010. "Phylogenetic and ecological analyses of soil and sporocarp DNA sequences reveal high diversity and strong habitat partitioning in the boreal ectomycorrhizal genus *Russula* (Russulales; Basidiomycota)." *New Phytologist* 187: 494-507 [IAB 3359].

Geml, J., G.A. Laursen, I.C. Herriott, J.M. McFarland, M.G. Booth, N. Lennon, H.C.

Nusbaum and D.L. Taylor. 2010. "Phylogenetic and ecological analyses of soil and sporocarp DNA sequences reveal high diversity and strong habitat partitioning in the boreal ectomycorrhizal genus *Russula* Pers. (Russulales; Basidiomycota)." *New Phytologist*, 186(3): 1-14.

Geml, J., F. Kauff, C. Brochmann, F. Lutzoni, G.A. Laursen, S.A. Redhead, D.L. Taylor. 2012. "Frequent Circumarctic and rare Transequatorial dispersals in the lichenized agaric genus *Lichenomphalia* (Hygrophoraceae, Basidiomycota)." *Fungal Biol.* 116: 388-400.

Gilbertson, R.L. and L. Ryvarden. 1986. *North American Polypores; Volume 1*. Fungiflora A/S. 433 pp.

Gilbertson, R.L. and L. Ryvarden. 1987. *North American Polypores; Volume 2*. Fungiflora A/S. 448 pp.

Glawe, D.A. and G.A. Laursen. 2005. "First Report of powdery mildew on *Caragana arborescens* and *Caragana grandiflora* in Alaska caused by *Microsphaera* (*Erysiphe*) *palczewskii*." Online. *Plant Health Progress* DOI: 10.1094/PHP-2005-1017-01-BR.

Haight, J-E., G.A. Laursen, J. Glaeser and D.L. Taylor. (In press, 2015). "Phylogeny of *Fomitopsis pinicola*: A Species Complex." Submitted to *Mycologia*.

Hennon P.E., J.S. Beatty, and D. Hildebrand. 2001. *Hemlock Dwarf Mistletoe*. US Department of Agriculture Forest Service and Disease Leaflet 135. Revised January 2001.

Holsten, Edward H., Paul E. Hennon, and Richard A. Werner. 1985. *Insects and Diseases of Alaskan Forests*. USDA Forest Service, Alaska Region, Report No. 181.

Horak, E. and O.K. Miller, Jr. 1991."Phaeogalera and *Galerina* in Arctic-Sub Arctic Alaska (USA) and the Yukon Territory (Canada)." *Can. J. Bot.* 70: 414-433.

Krieger, L.C.C. 1967. *The Mushroom Handbook*. Dover, New York. 560 pp.

Kuo, M. 2007. *100 Edible Mushrooms*. Univ. of Michigan Press, Ann Arbor. 329 pp.

Largent, D.L. 1986. *How to Identify Mushrooms to Genus I: Macroscopic Features*. Mad River Press, Eureka, CA. 166 pp.

Laursen, G.A. and R.D. Seppelt. (2009). *Common Interior Alaska Cryptogams: Fungi, Lichenicolous Fungi, Lichenized Fungi, Slime Molds, and Mosses and Liverworts*. Univ. of Alaska Press, Fairbanks. 218 pp.

Laursen, G.A., H.H. Burdsall and R.D. Seppelt. 2005. *Wood Inhabiting Fungi: Their Diversity, Roles and Uses*. IN *Alaska Park Science: Connection to Natural and Cultural Resource Studies in Alaska's National Parks*. Spring 2005. pp. 18-25.

Laursen, G.A., R.D. Seppelt, and M. Hallam. 2003a. "Cycles in the Forest: Mammals, Mushrooms, Mycophagy, Mycoses and Mycorrhizae." *Alaska Park Science: Connection to Natural and Cultural Resource Studies in Alaska's National Parks*. Winter 2003, pp. 13-19.

Laursen, G.A., R.D. Seppelt and M. Hallam. 2003b. "Cycles in the Forest: Mammals, Mycophagy, and Mycorrhizae." Pp.111-112. USDA Forest Service General Technical Report 579, 150pp. IN *Proceedings: Hidden Forest Values*. The First Alaskanwide Non-Timber Forest Products Conf. and Tour. 8-11 Nov. 2001.

Laursen, G.A. and J.F. Ammirati. 1990. *Arctic and Alpine Mycology: The Third International Symposium on Arctic and Alpine Mycology Abstracts*. Biology and Wildlife Misc. Pub. #90-1, July.

Laursen, G.A., J.F. Ammirati and D.F. Farr. 1987. "Hygrophoraceae From Arctic and Alpine Tundra in Alaska." IN: *Arctic and Alpine Mycology II*. G.A. Laursen, J.F. Ammirati and S.A. Redhead (Eds.). Plenum Press, New York.

Laursen, G.A., J.F. Ammirati and S.A. Redhead. 1987. *Arctic and Alpine Mycology II*. Plenum Press, New York. 540 pp.

Laursen, G.A. 1985. "Mycorrhizae: A review of the importance of fungi from high latitude forests of Alaska." *Agroborealis*, 17(2): 58-66.

Laursen, G.A., R.A. Mowry and J.F. Ammirati. 1985. "Subarctic Truffles: Speciation, Range Extension, Associations and Spore Vectors." P. 268. IN *Proceedings of the 6th North American Conference on Mycorrhizae*. R. Molina (Ed.).

Laursen, G.A. and J.F. Ammirati. 1982a. *Arctic and Alpine Mycology. The First International Symposium on Arcto-Alpine Mycology*. 580 pp. Univ. of Washington Press, Seattle. G.A. Laursen and J.F. Ammirati (Eds.).

Laursen, G.A. and J.F. Ammirati. 1982b. "Lactarii from Alaskan Arctic Tundra." IN *Arctic and Alpine Mycology. The First International Symposium on Arcto-Alpine Mycology*. Barrow, AK. G.A. Laursen and J.F. Ammirati (Eds.). Pp. 245-281.

Laursen, G.A. and J.F. Ammirati. 1982c. "The FISAM in Retrospect." IN *Arctic and Alpine Mycology. The First International Symposium on Arcto-Alpine Mycology*. Barrow, AK. G.A. Laursen and J.F. Ammirati (Eds.). Pp. 532-544.

Laursen, G.A. and M. Chmielewski. 1982. The Ecological Significance of Soil Fungi in Arctic Tundra. *Arctic and Alpine Mycology. The First International Symposium on Arcto-Alpine Mycology*. Barrow, AK. G.A. Laursen and J.F. Ammirati (Eds.). Pp. 432-492.

Laursen, G.A., O.K. Miller, Jr. and H.B. Bigelow. 1976. "A New *Clitocybe* from the Alaskan Arctic." *Can. J. Bot.*, 54: 979-980.

Laursen, G.A. and H.H. Burdsall, Jr. 1976. "Notes concerning a new distribution record for *Geopora* (Pezizales) from Alaskan tundra." *Mycotaxon*, 4(2): 329-330.

Lincoff, G.H. 1981. *The Audubon Society Field Guide to North American Mushrooms*. Alfred Knopf, New York. 926 pp.

McCune, B. and L. Geiser. 1997. *Macrolichens of the Pacific Northwest*. Oregon State Univ. Press, Corvallis. 386 pp.

Miller, O.K., Jr., G.A. Laursen and B.M. Murray. 1974. Arctic and Alpine Agarics from Alaska and Canada. Ice-Field Ranges. Research Project, Sci. Results, *Geographical Review*, 4: 365-369.

Miller, O.K., Jr., G.A. Laursen and B.M. Murray. 1973. "Arctic and Alpine Agarics from Alaska and Canada." *Can. J. Bot.* 51: 43-49.

Miller, O.K., G.A. Laursen and D.F. Farr. 1982. "Notes on Agaricales from Arctic Tundra in Alaska." *Mycologia* 74(4): 576-591.

Miller, O.K., Jr., H.H. Burdsall, Jr., G.A. Laursen and I. Sachs. 1980. "The Status of

Calvatia cretacea (Berk.) Lloyd in Arctic and Alpine Tundra." *Can. J. Bot.*, 58(24): 2533-2542.

Miller, O.K., Jr. and H. Miller. 2006. *North American Mushroom: A Field Guide to Edible and Inedible Fungi*. Globe Pequot Press, Guilford, CT. 584 pp.

McKenny, M. and D.E. Stuntz, revised by J.F. Ammirati. 1987. *The New Savory Wild Mushroom*. Univ. of Washington Press, Seattle. 264 pp.

McKnight, K.H., and V.B. McKnight. 1987. *A Field Guide to Mushrooms of North America*. Peterson Field Guide Series. Houghton Mifflin, Boston. 448 pp.

Mushrooms, *The Journal of Wild Mushrooming*, 861 Harold Street, Moscow, ID 83843.

Mycological Society of San Francisco, P.O. Box 882163, San Francisco, CA 94188.

North American Mycological Association, 3556 Oakwood, Ann Arbor, MI 48104.

Orr, R.T., and D.B. Orr. 1979. *Mushrooms of Western North America*. Univ. of California Press, Berkeley. 293 pp.

Petrini, O. and G.A. Laursen. 1993. *Arctic and Alpine Mycology 3. Proceedings of the Third and Fourth International Symposium on Arcto-Alpine Mycology*. Bibliotheca Mycologica Bd. 150. J. Cramer, Berlin Stuttgart. ISBN 3-443-59051-9, Pp. i-xi, 1-169.

Phillips, R. 1981. *Mushrooms and Other Fungi of Great Britain and Europe: The Most Comprehensively Illustrated Book on the Subject This Century*. Macmillan, London. 288 pp.

Pilz, D. L., E.D. Norvell and R. Molina. 2003. *Ecology and Management of Commercially Harvested Chanterelle Mushrooms*. USDA-FS, PNW Station Gen. Tech. Rpt. 576. 83 pp.

Puget Sound Mycological Association, Center for Urban Horticulture, GF-15, Univ. of Washington, Seattle, 98195.

Saccardo, P.A., C.H. Peck and W. Trelease. 1904. *The Fungi of Alaska*. Harriman Alaska Expedition. 5:13-64, pl. 2-7. Missouri Botanical Garden.

Schalkwijk-Barendsen, H.M.E. 1991. *Mushrooms of Northwest North America*. Lone Pine Publishing, Auburn, WA. 414 pp.

Smith, A.H., H.D. Thiers and O.K. Miller, Jr. 1965. "The Species of *Suillus* and *Fuscoboletinus* of the Priest River Experimental Forest and Vicinity, Priest River, Idaho." *Lloydia*, 28(2): 120-138.

Smith, A.H., H.D. Thiers and R. Watling. 1967. "A Preliminary Account of the North American Species of *Leccinum*, Sections Luteoscabra and Scabra." *The Michigan Botanist*, 6(3A): 107-154.

Smith, A.H. 1951. *Puffballs and their Allies in Michigan*. Univ. of Michigan Press, Ann Arbor. 131 Pp.

Smith, A.H. 1968. "The Cantharellaceae of Michigan." *The Michigan Botanist*, 7: 143-183.

Smith, A.H., H.D. Thiers and R. Watling. 1968. "Notes on Species of *Leccinum*. I. Additions to Section Leccinum." *Lloydia*, 31(3): 252-267.

Smith, A.H. 1973. "Notes on Michigan Boletaceae." *Persoonia*, 7(2): 321-331.

Smith, A.H. 1975. *A Field Guide to Western Mushrooms*. Univ. of Michigan Press, Ann Arbor. 288 pp.

Thomson, J.W. 1984. *American Arctic Lichens 1. The Macrolichens*. Columbia Univ. Press, New York. 504 pp.

Thomson, J.W. 1997. *American Arctic Lichens 2. The Microlichens*. Univ. of Wisconsin Press, Madison. 675 pp.

Treu, R., G.A. Laursen, S.L. Stephenson, J.C. Landolt and R. Densmore. 1996. "Vascular plant-fungal symbioses (Mycorrhizae), from Denali National Park and Preserve." Springer-Verlag, *Mycorrhiza*, 6: 21-29.

United States Department of Agriculture. 2008. *Mosses and Liverworts of the National Forests In Alaska*. Forest Service Alaska Region, R10-RG-179.

Zhurbenko, M.P., G.A. Laursen and D.A. Walker. 2005. "New and rare lichenicolous fungi and lichens from the North American Arctic." *Mycotaxon*, 92: 201-212.

Ziller, W.C. 1974. *The Tree Rusts of Western Canada*. Can. For. Serv. Pub. No. 1329. Dept. of the Environment. 272 pp.

PICTORIAL GLOSSARY OF TERMS

BASIDIOMYCETES (CLUB FUNGI) AND
ASCOMYCETES (SAC FUNGI)

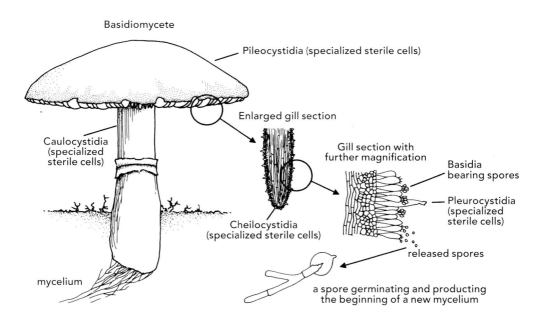

Basidiomycete

Pileocystidia (specialized sterile cells)

Caulocystidia
(specialized
sterile cells)

Enlarged gill section

Gill section with
further magnification

Basidia
bearing spores

Pleurocystidia
(specialized
sterile cells)

Cheilocystidia
(specialized sterile cells)

released spores

mycelium

a spore germinating and producing
the beginning of a new mycelium

Fig. 134a-d. MUSHROOM REPRODUCTION

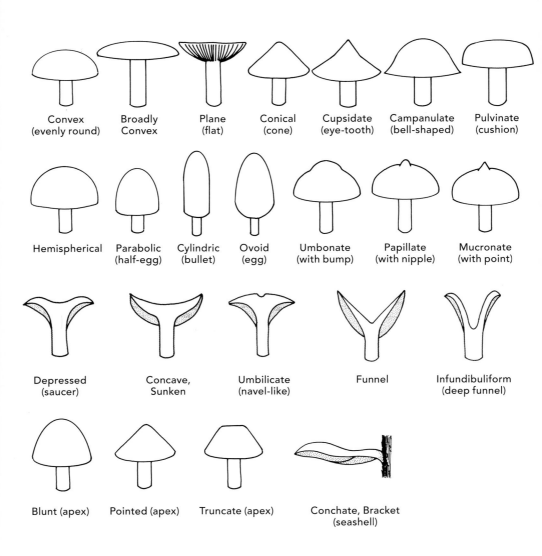

Fig. 135a–w. Cap Morphology

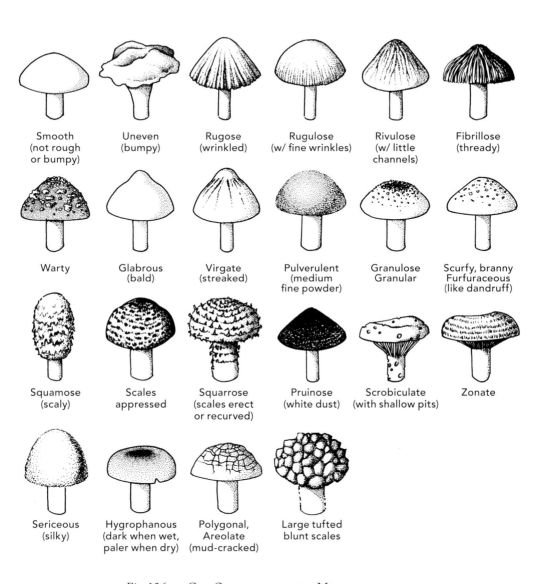

Smooth
(not rough
or bumpy)

Uneven
(bumpy)

Rugose
(wrinkled)

Rugulose
(w/ fine wrinkles)

Rivulose
(w/ little
channels)

Fibrillose
(thready)

Warty

Glabrous
(bald)

Virgate
(streaked)

Pulverulent
(medium
fine powder)

Granulose
Granular

Scurfy, branny
Furfuraceous
(like dandruff)

Squamose
(scaly)

Scales
appressed

Squarrose
(scales erect
or recurved)

Pruinose
(white dust)

Scrobiculate
(with shallow pits)

Zonate

Sericeous
(silky)

Hygrophanous
(dark when wet,
paler when dry)

Polygonal,
Areolate
(mud-cracked)

Large tufted
blunt scales

Fig. 136a-v. CAP ORNAMENTATION MORPHOLOGY

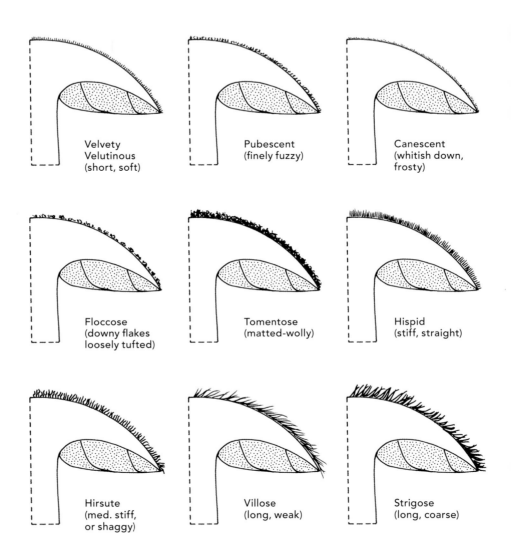

Velvety
Velutinous
(short, soft)

Pubescent
(finely fuzzy)

Canescent
(whitish down,
frosty)

Floccose
(downy flakes
loosely tufted)

Tomentose
(matted-wolly)

Hispid
(stiff, straight)

Hirsute
(med. stiff,
or shaggy)

Villose
(long, weak)

Strigose
(long, coarse)

Fig. 137a-i. CAP SURFACE HAIRINESS

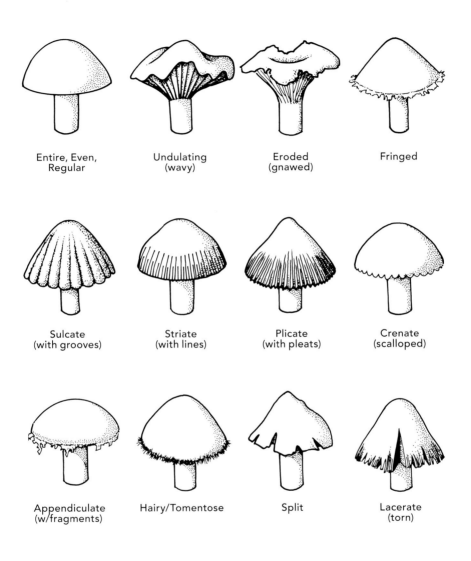

Entire, Even, Regular	Undulating (wavy)	Eroded (gnawed)	Fringed
Sulcate (with grooves)	Striate (with lines)	Plicate (with pleats)	Crenate (scalloped)
Appendiculate (w/fragments)	Hairy/Tomentose	Split	Lacerate (torn)

Fig. 138a-l. CAP MARGIN MORPHOLOGY

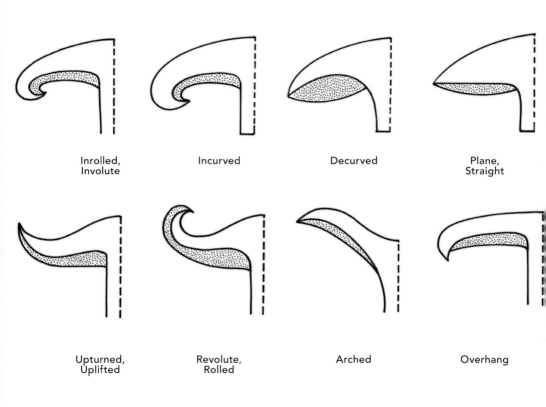

Fig. 139a-h. PILEUS MARGIN ARRANGEMENTS

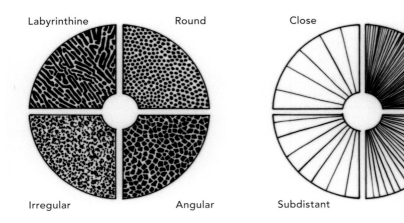

Labyrinthine   Round

Irregular   Angular

Close   Crowded

Subdistant   Distant

HYMENOPHORE VIEWED FROM BELOW

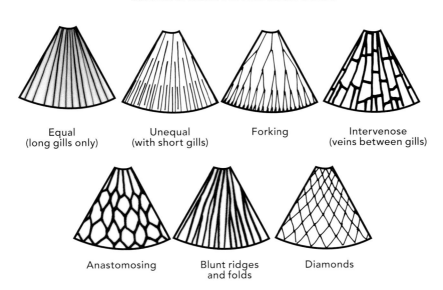

Equal
(long gills only)

Unequal
(with short gills)

Forking

Intervenose
(veins between gills)

Anastomosing

Blunt ridges
and folds

Diamonds

Fig. 140a-o. HYMENOPHORE (SPORE-PRODUCING SURFACE) MORPHOLOGY

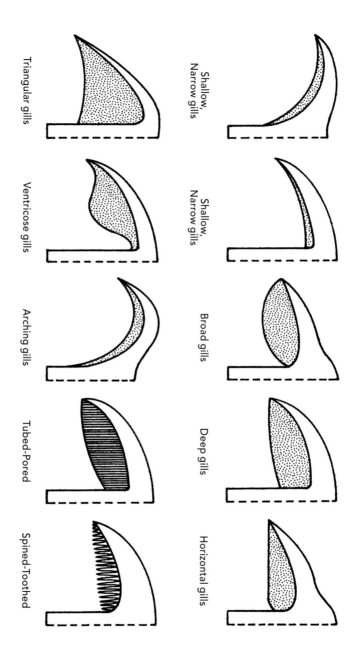

Fig. 141a-j. Hymenophore Morphology: Gill Breadth and Shape

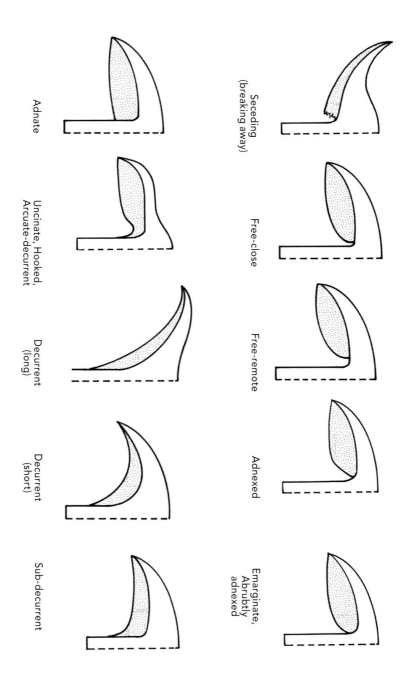

Fig. 142a-j. GILL ATTACHMENT MORPHOLOGY

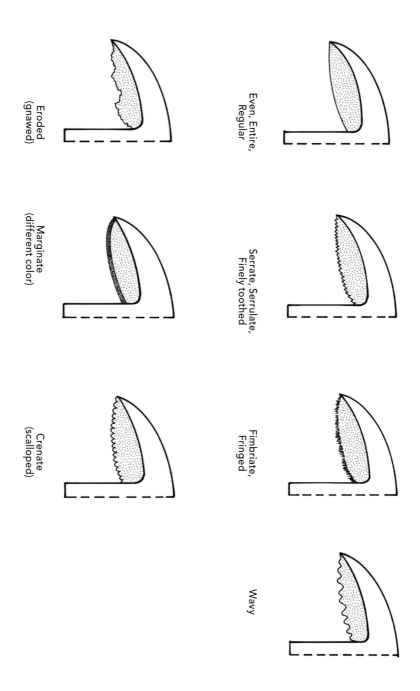

Fig. 143a-g. Gill Edge Morphology

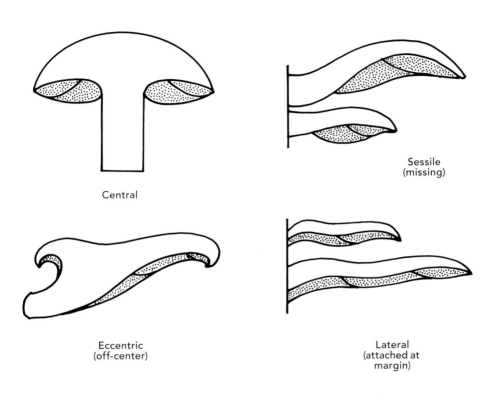

Central

Sessile
(missing)

Eccentric
(off-center)

Lateral
(attached at
margin)

Fig. 144a-d. STIPE PLACEMENT

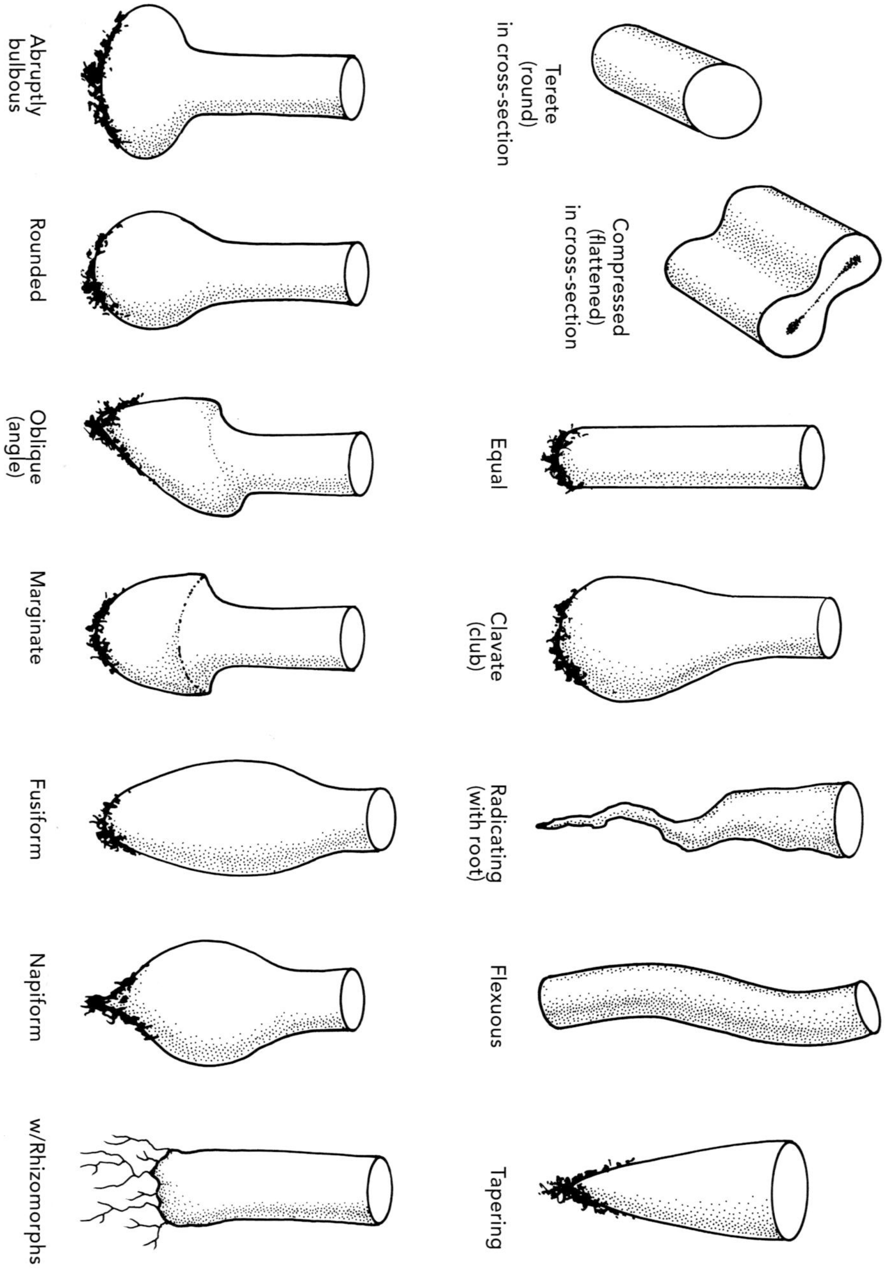
Terete (round) in cross-section
Compressed (flattened) in cross-section
Equal
Clavate (club)
Radicating (with root)
Flexuous
Tapering
Abruptly bulbous
Rounded
Oblique (angle)
Marginate
Fusiform
Napiform
w/Rhizomorphs

Fig. 145a-n. Stipe and Base Shapes

Punctate (w/ small dots)

Reticulate (fishnet)

Scaly

Scrobiculate (w/ shallow pits)

Banded

Glandular-dotted (dark sticky dots) to Scabrous

Costate/ Ribbed

Fibrous

Longitudinally striate (lines)

Lacunose (deep grooves)

Lightly scaly

Heavily scaly

Fig. 146a-l. STIPE ORNAMENTATION

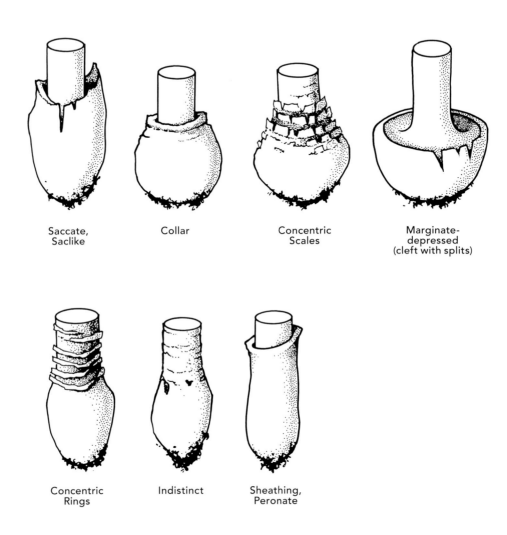

| Saccate, Saclike | Collar | Concentric Scales | Marginate-depressed (cleft with splits) |

| Concentric Rings | Indistinct | Sheathing, Peronate |

Fig. 147a-g. Stipe Base (volva) Morphology

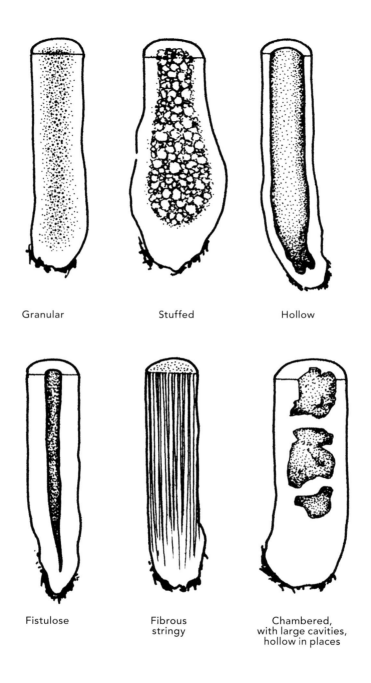

Granular   Stuffed   Hollow

Fistulose   Fibrous   Chambered,
                   stringy   with large cavities,
                                    hollow in places

Fig. 148a-f. STIPE INTERIOR MORPHOLOGY

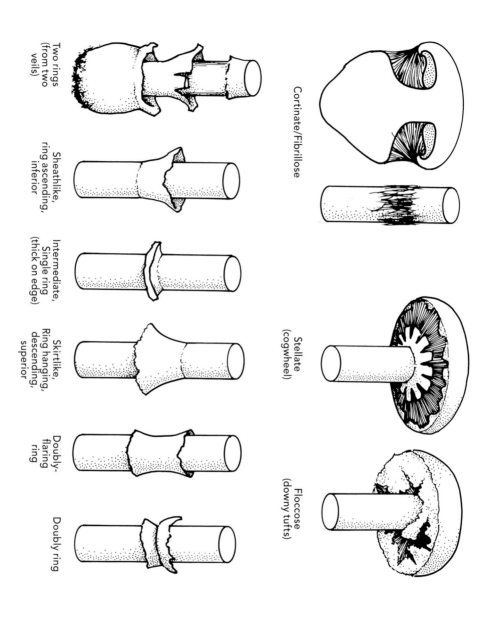

Two rings
(from two
veils)

Sheathlike,
ring ascending,
inferior

Intermediate,
Single ring
(thick on edge)

Skirtlike,
Ring hanging,
descending,
superior

Doubly-
flaring
ring

Doubly ring

Cortinate/Fibrillose

Stellate
(cogwheel)

Floccose
(downy tufts)

Fig. 149a-j. PARTIAL VEIL ARRANGEMENTS AND REMNANTS

Fig. 150a-f. Fungal Spore Morphology: Basidiospores

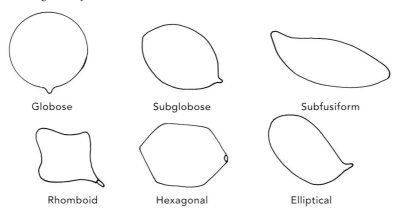

Globose

Subglobose

Subfusiform

Rhomboid

Hexagonal

Elliptical

Fig. 150g-k. Fungal Spore Morphology: Ascopores

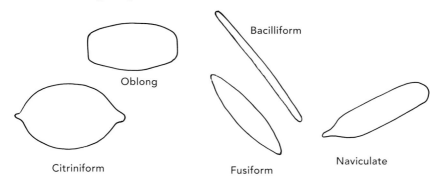

Oblong

Bacilliform

Citriniform

Fusiform

Naviculate

Fig. 150l-p. Fungal Spore Morphology: Ornamentation

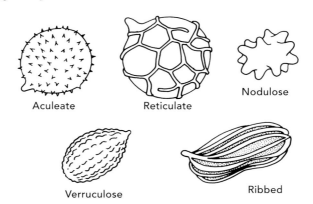

Aculeate

Reticulate

Nodulose

Verruculose

Ribbed

Fig. 150a-p. Fungal Spore Morphology and Ornamentation

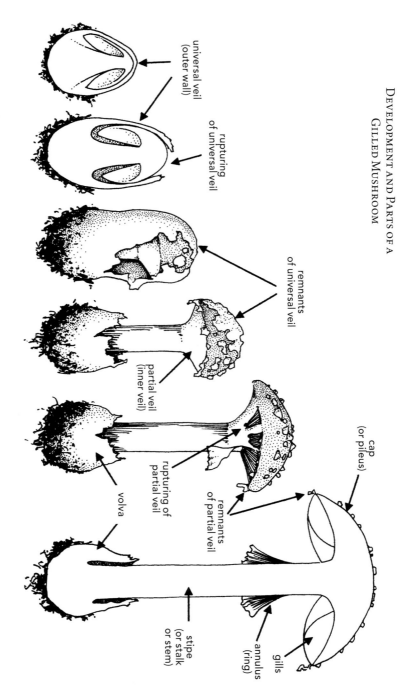

universal veil
(outer wall)

rupturing
of universal veil

remnants
of universal veil

partial veil
(inner veil)

rupturing of
partial veil

volva

remnants
of partial veil

cap
(or pileus)

stipe
(or stalk
or stem)

annulus
(ring)

gills

Fig. 151a-f. Basidiomycete (Agaric) Maturation Sequence

Interactions of the
Mammal Mycophagy and Mycorrhizae Cycle

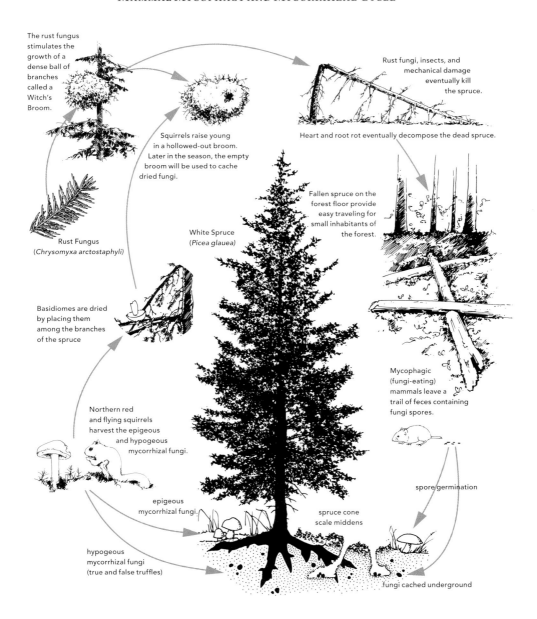

The rust fungus stimulates the growth of a dense ball of branches called a Witch's Broom.

Rust fungi, insects, and mechanical damage eventually kill the spruce.

Squirrels raise young in a hollowed-out broom. Later in the season, the empty broom will be used to cache dried fungi.

Heart and root rot eventually decompose the dead spruce.

Fallen spruce on the forest floor provide easy traveling for small inhabitants of the forest.

Rust Fungus
(*Chrysomyxa arctostaphyli*)

White Spruce
(*Picea glauea*)

Basidiomes are dried by placing them among the branches of the spruce

Mycophagic (fungi-eating) mammals leave a trail of feces containing fungi spores.

Northern red and flying squirrels harvest the epigeous and hypogeous mycorrhizal fungi.

epigeous mycorrhizal fungi.

spore germination

spruce cone scale middens

hypogeous mycorrhizal fungi (true and false truffles)

fungi cached underground

Fig. 152a-k. Cycles in the Forest:
Mycorrhizae, Mycophagy, and Mineralization

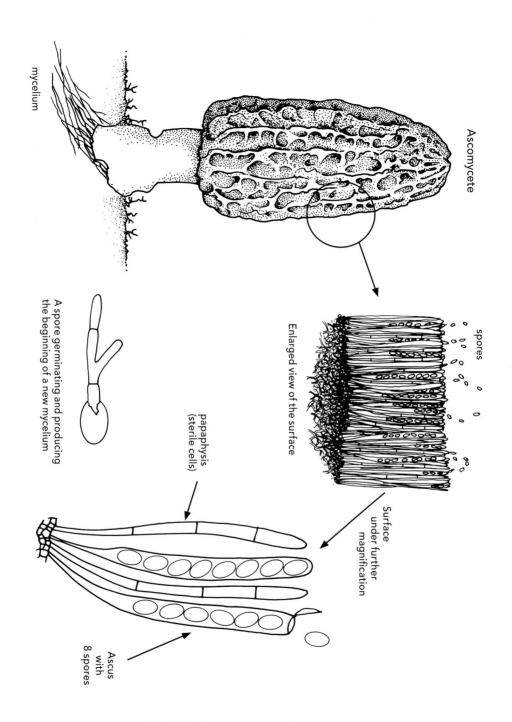

mycelium

Ascomycete

A spore germinating and producing the beginning of a new mycelium

spores

Enlarged view of the surface

Surface under further magnification

papaphysis (sterile cells)

Ascus with 8 spores

Fig. 153a-d. ASCOMYCETE REPRODUCTION

GLOSSARY OF TERMS

Abruptly bulbous: An "equal" (cylindrical) stipe (stalk) giving rise to an abrupt differentiated and swollen bulbous base

Acrid: Having a burning or peppery taste

Aculeate: Having narrow spines

Adnate: Of gills, broadly joining the stipe ± at right angles or "just" ascending

Adnexed: Gills just barely joining the stipe, without a "notch"

Annular zone: An often "collapsed" or evanescent partial veil or spore deposit band on the stipe

Agaric: A term applied to those Basidiomycetes that have gills

Alutaceous: A light leather to pale tan color

Amyloid: Staining blue with Meltzer's or Lugol's iodine

Anamorphic fungi: Fungi producing spores (conidia) by mitosis

Anastomose (-ing): Interconnecting or running together to form an irregular network

Annulus: The ring or skirt-like structure found on the stipe of some agarics and boletes; it represents a remnant of the partial veil

Apex: Where stipe (stalk) joins the cap

Apothecium (pl.: apothecia): The cuplike or saucer-shaped fruiting body with open hymenium produced by some ascomycetes

Appendiculate: Condition in which pieces of the partial veil remain attached to the margin of the cap after the latter has expanded

Applanate: Flattened or expanded horizontally

Appressed: With the leaves lying close to the stem

Arched: Cap with down-curved margins and a depressed center (disc)

Areolate: Cracked, lightly or deeply so as in drying mud

Ascocarp: Another term for the fruiting body of an ascomycete

Ascolichen: A lichen having asci and ascospores

Ascomata: Fruit bodies of Ascomycetes, ascomes

Asci: Spore-producing "sacs" that also support meiosis

Ascomycetes: Fungi whose meiotic products are spores enclosed in an ascus

Ascospore: The sexual spore produced within asci by fungi that are members of the ascomycetes

Ascus (pl.: asci): The saclike cell in which ascospores (usually eight) are formed: characteristic of the ascomycetes

Avellaneous: Pale gray tinged with pink

Bacilliform: Bacillus or rod shaped

Banded: Multiple flattened or raised "rings" on the stipe (stalk)

Basidiocarp: The fruit body of a club (Basidiomycete) fungus

Basidiolichen: A lichen that produces basidiospores on basidia, rather than ascospores in asci

Basidioles: Young or immature spore-producing basidia

Basidiome: Any fruit body or fructification of a Basidiomycete fungus

Basidiomycetes: Fungi whose meiotic products are spores produced on a basidium

Basidiospore: The sexual spore produced by fungi that are members of the basidiomycetes

Basidium (pl.: basidia): The club-shaped cell upon which basidiospores (usually four) are formed; characteristic of the Basidiomycetes

Boreal: Referring to the high-latitude regions of the northern hemisphere dominated by coniferous forests

Broad: Of gill "depth"

Bulbous: Of mushroom stalks, rounded, swollen or bulb-like

Bullate: Having blister-like swellings

Button: A very young mushroom initial

Caespitose: Aggregated or clustered; fruiting bodies occurring in groups

Calcareous: Containing lime

Campanulate: Bell-shaped, as in the cap of some agarics

Canescent: Having a "whitish downy" appearance

Cap: See pileus

Capillitium (pl.: capillitia): A system of sterile threadlike elements found with the spore mass of many slime molds

Capitate: With tip swollen into a head

Cartilagenous: Being tough pliant to tough brittle (of stipe or stalk)

Cavernous: Having hollow chambers inside the stipe (stalk)

Cephalodia: Small gall-like structures found in some lichen species and containing cyanobacterial photobionts

Chalky: Brittle, breaking easily, "snapping" in half

Cinereous: Bluish gray; the color of ashes

Citriniform: Lemon-like in shape

Clavate: Club-shaped

Cleft: Of a bulbous base with a recessed sharp walled well around the bulb top

Close: Of gills, spacing and proximity to stipe (stalk), if free

Clustered: Occurring close together in the same small area of the substrate

Collar(ed): A blunt "cleft"

Compressed: Flattened

Concave: Curved inwards, like the interior of a circle

Concentric: Of rings or scaly zones arranged in circles around a common center

Conchate: Shell or conch-like, bracketed, shelved, bivalved-shaped

Concolorous: Having the same color; of one color throughout

Conic: Cone-shaped, conical

Conidiophore: A hyphae on which conidia are produced

Conidium (pl.: conidia): Asexual spore of anamorphic fungi

Conk: Another name for a polypore; often applied to those species that occur on woody substrates

Connate: Connected stems growing together, a variant of caespitose

Context: The tissue that makes up the cap of a fruiting body

Contorted: Irregularly curved or twisted

Convex: Curved outward or rounded outward, like the exterior of a circle

Coprophilous: Dung-inhabiting; occurring on dung

Cortex: The thick covering over the spore mass in some slime molds that produce relatively large fruiting bodies; the outer part of a stem

Cortina (-te): The weblike strands that make up the partial veil of some agarics; characteristic of many members of the Cortinariaceae

Cottony: With long, soft, white hairs

Cranioid: Having the shape of a cranium or skull

Crenate: Scalloped (cap margin or gill edges); with the margin edged with notches

Crisped: Wavy, variously curved, twisted or contorted

Crowded: Of gills, with very little space between

Cuboid: Being cube-like in shape

Cup: A saclike, volvate stipe (stem) base

Cuspidate: Eye-toothed, broadly pointed

Crateriform: Like a crater

Crustose: A type of lichen in which the thallus is crust-like and so closely attached to the substrate as to be virtually inseparable from it, and lacking a lower cortex layer

Cuticle: The pilipellis (skin) of the cap or of the stipe (stalk); of plants, a non-cellular coating on the outer surface of cells in contact with the environment

Cyanobacterium: A blue-green alga or bacterium; in lichens, the "photobiont"

Cylindric (-al): Elongate, parallel sided, and circular in transverse section

Cystidium (pl.: cystidia): Any number of sterile cells found in the hymenium of many Basidiomycetes; such cells usually project beyond the basidia

Decurrent: With the basal margins of the leaf extending down the stem beyond the leaf insertion or attachments to the stem; of an agaric, when the attachment of the gills extends down the stipe (stalk)

Decurved: Cap margins "bent" downward

Deliquescent: Term applied to gills that dissolve into an "inky" liquid upon becoming mature; characteristic of many members of the genus *Coprinus*

Depressed: Of a fungal fruiting body, where the central part of the disc is "welled" or concave

Detritus: Dead organic matter

Dichotomous: Type of branching in which the main axis gives rise to two more or less equal secondary axes

Dimidiate: Globular half circle

Disc: The central portion of a lichen apothecium, as seen from above

Diploid: A cell, individual or generation with two sets of chromosomes (2n); the typical chromosome set of the sporophyte generation

Distal: Away from the base or point of attachment; toward the apex of a leaf or stem

Distant: Well-spaced

Doliiform: Barrel-formed

Dorsal: Of leaves, the abaxial or lower surface: of stems or thallus, the upper surface away from the substrate

Double Ring: Of a "thickened" partial veil

Eccentric: Of the stipe (stalk) being non-central, off-center

Ectomycorrhiza: A type of mycorrhizal association in which the fungus forms a covering (called a mantle or sheath) on the outside of small roots of the host green plant

Ellipsoid: Having the shape of an oval/ellipse, elliptic

Elongate: Stretched out, linear

Emarginate: Of gills, with a poorly defined notch or groove; lacking a margin

Entire/Even: Without teeth, more or less smooth on the margin

Epigeous: Occurring above the ground

Epihymenium: Upper layer of apothecium formed by apices of paraphyses over the top of the asci.

Epiphragm: The covering over the upper portion of the fruiting body of a bird's nest fungus; it detaches to expose the peridioles when the fruiting body is mature

Equal: Straight stemmed or gills extending from stipe (stalk) to cap margin

Eroded: Gnawed gill edges or cap margin

Erose: Irregularly notched or eroded

Erumpent: Bursting through the surface

Eukaryotic: A type of cell that has a membrane-enclosed nucleus and other membrane-enclosed organelles

Evanescent: Disappearing quickly

Excurrent: Extending beyond the apical margin

Exerted: Projecting beyond and exposed

Excipulum: Outer and often "fussy" cup skin

Fabaceous: With the smell of green beans/pea pods

Fairy Ring: An arching or circled growth pattern

Farinaceous: Smell of ground meal or cucumber

Ferruginous: Rusty-orange to red color

Fellfield: An area of tundra that is characterized by numerous rocks and sparse vegetation

Fibril: Fine, fiber-like wall thickenings

Fibrillose: Covered with small fibers

Fibrous: Of cap or stipe (stalk) surface, composed of tough stringy tissue; of lichens, with the hyphae of the outer cortex lying parallel with the thallus axis

Filamentous: Threadlike

Filiform: Slender and elongate, filamentous, threadlike

Fimbriate: Fringed

Fistulose: Hollow, pipelike, fistular

Flabelliform: Fan-shaped

Flesh: Interior tissue of the fruiting body of a fungus

Flexuose: Slightly and irregularly bent, or wavy

Floccose: Woolly or cottony; dry and loosely arranged

Flocculent: Having small tufts of fibers present

Foliose: Leafy or leaflike

Forked: Of gills, branching into two more or less equal arms

Free: Of gills, not adjoining the stipe (stem)

Friable: Breaking up, exfoliating, soon disappearing

Fruit (-ing) body: General term for the spore-producing structure produced during the reproductive stage in the life cycle of a fungus, lichen or slime mold

Fruticose: A type of lichen in which the thallus is club-like, shrub-like or more or less branched; a thallus attached to the substrate by a single point and which often develops erect branches, becoming shrub-like

Fugacious: Disappearing or fading early in development

Fulvous: Cinnamon to reddish-brown

Fungoid: Earthy odor or taste

Furfuraceous: Dandruff-like, flaky, scurfy

Fuscous: A darkened smoky to purplish-brown

Fusiform: Spindle-shaped; tapering at both ends

Gamete: A reproductive cell

Genus (pl.: genera): A group of closely related species

Glabrescent: Smooth; having the appearance of being smooth

Glabrous: Smooth, bald

Glandular: Dotted or punctate, spotted

Glaucous: Easily rubbed off fine white powdery "bloom"; bluish-green in color or with a grayish or whitish bloom

Gleba: Spore mass of a puffball and certain other related fungi

Globose: Spherical; having the general form or shape of a ball

Glutinous: Sticky; having the consistency of wet glue or jelly

Graminoids: Grasses of sedges

Granular: Composed of small grains, granulose

Gregarious: Occurring relatively close together in the same general area of the substrate but not clustered

Gyrose: Marked with wavy lines

Habit: The general appearance

Habitat: The local environment

Hairy: Tomentose to woolly

Haploid: A cell, structure or organism having a single set of chromosomes (n); the normal chromosome level of the gametophyte generation

Hemispherical: Half round

Heterotrophic: Term used for an organism that is incapable of making its own organic food molecules and, as a result, must obtain them from other organisms

Hispid: Stiff, straight hairs

Hirsute: Shaggy with medium stiff hairs

Hoary: Having a dense whitish to graying silky down

Humic: Containing high levels of organic material derived from the partial decay of plant and animal matter, growing on humus

Hyaline: Colorless or transparent

Hymenium: The ascospore-bearing layer of a fruiting body

Hygrophanous: Term that refers to a cap that undergoes a marked change in color as it dries out; as a result, the edge and middle of the same cap may appear very different in color

Hymenium: The spore-bearing surface of a fruiting body

Hymenophore: The portion of a fruiting body that bears the hymenium

Hypha (pl.: hyphae): One of the individual strands or threadlike elements that make up the fruiting body or mycelium of a fungus

Hyphomycetes: Group of anamorphic fungi producing conidia not within a fruiting body.

Hypogeous: Occurring or growing below ground

Hypophysis: A strongly differentiated neck between the apex of the seta and the base of the urn of the capsule of mosses (cf. apophysis, neck)

Hypothecium: Layer of a fruiting body below hymenium

Imbricate: Closely appressed and overlapping

Immarginate: Without a margin

Immersed: Enclosed

Inclined: Bent down; of mosses—capsules that are between the erect and the horizontal positions

Incurved: Curved upward (adaxially) and inward

Inferior: Toward the base; an annulus located below stipe (stalk) middle or downward hanging

Inflated: Swollen, puffed up; having a somewhat rounded or swollen shape

Inflexed: Bent upwards (adaxially) and weakly inwards

Infundibuliform: Having a depression in the center of the cap and thus resembling a funnel

Inrolled: Rolled upwards (adaxially) and tightly inwards, applied to the leaf margins

Interascal: Between asci

Intercollary: In between, middle, separating

Interveinose: Veins running between the gills

Labyrinthine: Mazelike pored

Lacerate: Appearing as if torn or roughly cut

Lacriform: Tear shaped

Lacunose: With holes, shallow to deep pits or deeply striated grooves

Lamella (pl.: lamellae): Of a gill, one of the platelike structures upon which the hymenium occurs in agaric fungi; Of mosses, parallel photosynthetic ridges or plates along a leaf blade or costa

Lamellula (pl.: lamellulae): Short gills that extend only part way to the stipe (stalk)

Lanceolate: Lance shaped; narrow and tapered from near the base to a long point; narrowly ovate-acuminate

Lateral: At the sides

Latex: Clear, wheylike, milky or colored (yellow, orange to violet) juice

Lenticular: Lens-shaped; convex on both sides and more or less circular in outline

Lignicolous: High lignin content duff or wood decomposing

Lobe: One of the divided distal segments or an appendage or thallus

Lubricous: Moist, slippery, soapy to greasy feeling

Macroscopic: Being of sufficient size to be observed with the naked eye

Marginate: Fringed

Mazaedium: Dry loose powdery mass of free ascospores and sterile hyphae on the surface of fruiting body (characteristic of Caliciales)

Mealy: Taste or smell of freshly ground flour

Membranous: Thin, having the appearance of a thin layer

Meristem: A localized region of growth or potential growth by cell division

Mesic: Moderately moist

Morphology: Form or shape

Mucronate: Sharply nippled at mushroom cap center

Multistratose: Of tissue, consisting of several to many layers of cells

Mycelium: System of hyphae that make up the vegetative portion of a fungus

Mycobiont: The fungal component of the lichen; usually an Ascomycete (rarely a Basidiomycete)

Mycology: The formal study of fungi

Mycorrhiza (pl.: mycorrhizae): A symbiotic association between a fungus and a green plant

Napiform: Turnip-like stipe (stalk) base; swollen or bulbous at the top and tapering abruptly toward the base

Narrow: Of gills, having a thin breadth

Naviculate: Boat shaped, cymbiform

Node: An expanded junction in the capillitium of a myxomycete

Nodulose: Spores with broad-based, blunt warts

Oblique: Slanted, angled

Oblong: Rectangular with rounded corners or ends

Obovate: Egg-shaped, with the apex broader than the base

Obovoid: An ovoid solid with apex broader than the base

Obpyriform: the reverse of pear-shaped

Obtuse: Broadly pointed, more than 90°; sometimes referring to blunt or rounded

Ochraceous: Dingy yellow to dull-brownish yellow

Opaque: Dense, impervious to light

Operculum: Of mosses, a lid covering the mouth of most moss capsules

Ornamentation: Any "raised" wall configuration

Ostiole (-ate): A pore that develops at the apex of a perithecium or a puffball

Ovate/ovoid: Egg-shaped, with the base broader than the apex

Ostiole (-ate): A pore that develops at the apex of some puffballs

Ovate: Egg-shaped, with the base broader than the apex

Ovoid: An egg-shaped solid

Pallid: Pale, indefinite colors

Papilla (pl.: papillae): Of cell ornamentation, a solid microscopic protuberance (cf. mamillae)

Papillose (-ate): Having papillae, papillate

Parabolic: Having the form or shape of a parabola

Paraphysis (pl.: paraphyses): Sterile hyphae growing upwards from the base of the hymenium among the asci

Parasite: An organism that lives on or within another organism (the host), from which it obtains nutrients

Parasymbiotic: Causing no visible damage to their hosts

Parenchymatous: Of or having large thin-walled cells

Parmelioid: Resembling lobed lichens of the genus *Parmelia*

Partial veil: A layer of tissue that covers the immature spore-bearing surface of some fungi

Pellucid: See-through, translucent

Pellucid-striate: Gill attachments from beneath seen through a translucent cap

Pendant: Hanging downward

Pendulous: Pendant or hanging

Peridiole: One of the egg-shaped structures that contain basidia and basidiospores in the bird's nest fungi

Peridium (pl.: peridia): The wall of a fruiting body

Perithecium (pl.: perithecia): Sac-shaped fruiting body opening by an ostiole produced by some ascomycetes

Persistent: Not falling, or not deciduous; remaining for a long time

Petaloid: Petallike

Photobiont: The photosynthetic component of lichens; either a green or blue-green alga

Phototrophic: An organism that is capable of using light energy to make its own food molecules

Phyllocladia: Of *Stereocaulon* spp., leaflike parts of a thallus growing on stem

Pileus: Another name for the cap; the upper expanded portion of the fruiting body of agarics and boletes

Pit: A small depression or cavity in a cell wall

Pith: Central stipe (stalk) stuffing

Plane: Flat, not curved or wavy, referring to the leaf margin or leaf blade or to a mushroom cap

Planoconvex: Term applied to a cap of a fungus that is convex but somewhat flat

Plasmodium (pl.: plasmodia): The acellular, multinucleate mass of protoplasm representing the main trophic stage in the life cycle of a slime mold

Plicate: With longitudinal furrows or pleats

Podetium (pl.: podetia): A hollow, upright, ascocarp-bearing structure that forms a portion of the thallus in some lichens

Polymorphic: Variable, of more than one form

Pore: A small aperture; in *Sphagnum*, a round or oval opening in the outer wall of the stem cortical cells or of a hyaline leaf cell; of liverworts, a small aperture in the dorsal epidermis of a thallus surrounded by specialized cells

Porose: Having pores

Prokaryotic: A type of cell lacking a membrane-enclosed nucleus and other membrane-enclosed organelles

Proliferations: Of *Cladonia* spp., successively developing new parts of thallus

Propagule: A bud, branch, or leaf serving in vegetative reproduction

Proximal: Near the base or point of attachment; the internal face of a spore (as opposed to distal)

Pruina (pruinose): A thin frosting of minute crystals covering surfaces of lichens and fruit bodies

Pseudocapillitium (pl.: pseudocapillitia): A system of irregular plates, tubes, or threadlike elements occurring within the spore mass of some slime molds

Pseudorhiza: Rootlike extensions

Pubescent: Fine fuzzy, downy

Pulverulent: Powdered; appearing as if powdered over

Pulvinate: Cushion-shaped; having the general shape of a small cushion

Punctate: Dotted

Pycnidium (pl.: pycnidia): A saclike body containing conidia

Pyriform: Pear-shaped

Raphanoid: Having the odor of radish

Radicate (-ing): Ramifying off into substrate, long penetrating stipe (stalk)

Rectangular: Shortly elongated cells with parallel sides and square-ended

Reticulate: Having or forming a fish netlike or ridged pattern

Revolute: Rolled downwards (abaxially) and backwards, referring to a leaf margin (opposite to involute)

Rhizines: Lower thallus hairlike growths that anchor thalli to substrates

Rhizoid: Hairlike structure that functions in water absorption and anchorage

Rhizomorph: Bundled mycelial strands or cords

Ribbed: Of spores, longitudinally striated

Rimose: Cracked, as in the cap of some agarics and boletes

Rivulose: With wavy channels

Rufus: Dull brick red

Rugose (rugulose): Wrinkled to finely so

Saprotrophic: Saprophytic, the "eating" of dead plant and animal remains

Scabers: Tufts of brown to blackish brown hyphae that occur on the stalk of some fungi, especially members of the genus *Leccinium*

Scabrous: Having a rough surface, especially one with minute projections present

Scrobiculate: Having gland-like shallow "pits"

Scurfy: Furfuraceous, dandruff-like

Seceding: Condition in which the gills pull or break away from the stipe of an agaric after being attached initially

Sericeous: Silky

Sessile: Lacking a stalk; attached directly to the substrate

Simple: Unbranched

Sinuate: Wavy, undulating or with indentations or furrows, sinusoidal

Sinuose: Wavy

Sinus: A notch or indentation between two lobes

Soleiform: Of spores, sole- or slipper-shaped

Sporangium (pl.: sporangia): A type of fruiting body formed when a myxomycete plasmodium breaks up into a number of small portions, each of which develops into a single stalked or sessile unit; of bryophytes, the spore-bearing structure

Spore: A general term for a reproductive unit in fungi, bacteria, and cryptogamic plants. Commonly 1-celled, but often in Fungi (and in a few bryophytes) multi-celled. Usually minute, and on germination giving rise to hyphae (in fungi)

Spore print: Deposit of spores found beneath the severed cap of an agaric or bolete; used in mass to determine the spore color of a particular fungus

Sporodochium (pl.: sporodochia): Cushion-shaped mass of conidia bearing and supporting hyphae, characteristic of anamorphic fungi

Squamose: Having squamules

Squamules: Small, rounded and somewhat leaflike lobes that form a covering over portions of the thallus in some lichens

Stalk: See stipe

Stellate: Star-shaped

Stipe: Stalk; the structure supporting the upper part of the fruiting body such as the cap of many agarics and boletes

Stipitate: Stalked; having a stalk

Striate: Marked with fine ridges or lines

Strigose: Long, coarse to hairy, ± matted

Stroma: The mass of vegetative hyphae from which the fruiting body develops in some ascomycetes

Stuffed: Full, loose, cotton candy-like

Sub-: A prefix meaning nearly or almost; frequently used in the sense of approaching but not quite achieving the condition in question

Subdistant: Of gill spacing, separated but not widely so

Subglobose: Off round

Subhygrophanous: Undergoes subtle changes in color as it dries out

Subperonate: A ringed swelling at the base of the stipe (stalk) in some agarics

Subumbonate: Having a low raised central disc

Subzonate: Concentric rings on cap not always pronounced or continuous

Sulcate: Grooved, deeply striate

Symbiosis: A situation in which two dissimilar organisms live together in an intimate association

Tawny: Dull yellow-brown

Terete: More or less round in cross section (xsect.); cylindrical

Terricolous/Terrestrial: Growing on the ground

Thallus (pl.: thalli): The vegetative body of lichens or thallose and thalloid liverworts

Tomentose: Woolly, with a tomentum

Tomentum: A feltlike mat of fungal hyphae that covers the surface of the thallus in some lichens; the mass of hairlike filaments covering the stems of some mosses

Tooth: A small, unicellular or composed of several cells, more or less triangular projection on the margin or apex

Truncate: Chopped off

Tuberculate: Warty or knobby

Umbilicus (umbilicate): A centrally positioned point of attachment for the thallus that is characteristic of some rock-inhabiting lichens

Umbonate: Having a central bump or raised area at the center of the cap

Uncinate: Hook-notched gill attachment with a short decurrent "tooth"

Undulate: Of a surface or margin, wavy alternately up and down

Unipapillose: With single papilla per cell

Universal veil: A layer of tissue that completely encloses the entire immature fruiting body of some fungi

Urn: The spore-bearing portion of the capsule (as distinct from the neck)

Variegate: Differently colored streaks of fibrils

Veil: That which initially covers the hymenium, remaining in marginal patches or stipe fragments, the partial veil

Velutinous: Velvety

Venose: Having veins, veined

Ventricose: Swollen or enlarged in the middle for gill depth and/or stipe (stalk)

Verrucose: Having small rounded wart-like bumps

Verruculose: Delicately verrucose, having low rounded bumps

Villose: Long, fine hairy

Vinaceous: Red wine color

Viscid: Sticky to the touch; usually referring to the surface of the cap

Volva: A cuplike structure found at the base of the stipe (stalk) in some fungi; it represents the basal portion of the universal veil

Volvate: Having a volva

Warty: With small irregular surface ornamentations

Waxy: Of gills belonging to *Hygrophorus*

Wide-spreading: Spreading at a wide angle but less than 90

Zoned (-ate): Concentrically ringed

SUBJECT INDEX

Page locators in *italics* indicate
photographs and illustrations.

PHOTO and FIGURE CREDITS

Alaska Map of Six Physiograpghic Regions: Gray Mouse Graphics and Vicki Knapton.

Aguilar-Islas, Ana: Fig. 125 Verpa bohemica v. bohemica.

Babacock, Pat: Fig. 076 Suillus grevillei.

Brown, Neal: Fig. 030 Hypsizygus tessulatus.

Geml, Jozsef: Figs. 060 Agaricus sylvicola and 118 Gyromytra infula.

Jodwalis, Lisa and Shon: Fig. 128a Hydnotrya tulasnei.

Laursen, Gary: All other 109 fungal figures and 154 Bio.

McArthur, Neil: Figs. 066 Boletus edulis, 095 Clavariadelphus sachalinensis, 053b Cortinarius ominosus, 081a Ganoderma applanatum, Hygrophorus (olivaceoalbus) persoonii, 032 Lactarius deterrimus, 071 Leccinum atrostipitatum, 039 Panellus serotinus, 051 Paxillus involutus, 044 Russula emetic, 155 Bio.

Morrison, Richard: Figs. 100 Cantherellis (cibarius) formosis, 117 Gyromitra esculenta.

Northwest Mushroomers Association: Fig. 083 *Inonotus obliquus.*

Rhodes, Fred: Fig 119 Ramaria formosa.

Richardson, Angela: Fig. 121 Morchella elata.

Artistic Line Drawing Figure Credits: 252 prepared by Ms. Maggie Hallam.

NUMERICAL LISTING OF FIGURES

Fig. 033 Lactarius pubescens var. betulae. GAL-BEST.JPG

Fig. 034 Lactarius repraesentaneus.GAL-BEST.jpg

Fig. 035 Lactarius rufus.GAL-BEST.JPG

Fig. 036 Lactarius torminosus.GAL-BEST.jpg

Fig. 037 Lentinellus cochleatus.GAL-BEST.jpg

Fig. 038 Lyophyllum decastes.GAL-BEST.jpg

Fig. 039 Panellus serotinus.C.N.McA-BEST.tif

Fig. 040 Phyllotopsis nidulans.GAL-BEST.jpg

Fig. 041 Pleurocybella porrigens.GAL-BEST.jpg

Fig. 042a Russula aeruginea.GAL-BEST.JPG

Fig. 042b Russula aeruginea.GAL-COLOR-VARIATIONS.jpg

Fig. 043 Russula brevipes.GAL-BEST.jpg

Fig. 044 Russula emetica.C.N.McA-BEST.tif

Fig. 045 Russula lutea.GAL-BEST.jpg

Fig. 046 Russula xerampelina.GAL-BEST.jpg

Fig. 047 Lichenomphalia umbellifera.GAL-BEST.JPG

Fig. 048 Pluteus cervinus.GAL-BEST.JPG

Fig. 049 Bolbitius vitellinus.GAL-BEST.jpg

Fig. 050 Phaeolepiota aurea.GAL-BEST.tiff

Fig. 051 Paxillus involutus.C.N.McA-BEST.tif

Fig. 052 Cortinarius [collinitus] trivialis. GAL-BEST.jpg

Fig. 053a Cortinarius ominosus.GAL-BEST.JPG

Fig. 053b Cortinarius ominosus.C.N.McA-BEST.tif

Fig. 054 Cortinarius traganus.GAL-BEST.jpg

Fig. 055 Cortinarius violaceus.GAL-BEST.tif

Fig. 056 Rozites caperatus.GAL-BEST.jpg

Fig. 057 Agaricus arvensis.GAL-BEST.jpg

Fig. 058 Agaricus augustus.GAL-BEST.JPG

Fig. 059 Agaricus campestris.GAL-BEST.jpg

Fig. 060 Agaricus silvicola/sylvicola.J.Geml-BEST.jpg

Fig. 061 Stropharia semiglobata.GAL-BEST.jpg

Fig. 062 Coprinus [Coprinopsis] atramentarius. GAL-BEST.JPG

Fig. 063 Coprinus comatus.GAL-BEST.jpg

Fig. 064 Alpova diplophloeus.GAL-BEST.jpg

Fig. 065 Gautieria graveolens.GAL-BEST.jpg

Fig. 066 Boletus edulis.C.N.McA-BEST.tif

Fig. 067 Boletus mirabilis.GAL-BEST.jpg

Fig. 068 Chalciporus piperatus.GAL-BEST.JPG

Fig. 069 Leccinum scabrum.GAL-BEST.JPG

Fig. 070 Leccinum alaskanum.GAL-BEST.JPG

Fig. 071 Leccinum atrostipitatum.C.N.McA-BEST.tif

Fig. 072 Leccinum aurantiacum.Rogers-BEST.JPG

Fig. 073a Leccinum testaceoscabrum.GAL-BEST. JPG

Fig. 073b Leccinum testaceoscabrum.GAL-SCAB-ERS-PORES-FLAP.JPG

Fig. 073c Leccinum testaceoscabrum.GAL-XSECT. JPG

Fig. 074 Suillus brevipes.GAL-BEST.tif

Fig. 075 Suillus cavipes.GAL-BEST.jpg

Fig. 076 Suillus grevillei.P.Babcock-BEST.JPG

Fig. 077 Xerocomus subtomentosus.GAL-BEST. JPG

Fig. 078 Albatrellus ovinus.GAL-BEST.jpg

Fig. 079 Fomes fomentarius.GAL-BEST.jpg

Fig. 080 Fomitopsis pinicola.GAL-BEST.JPG

Fig. 081a Ganoderma applanatum hymen.C.N.McA-BEST.tif

Fig. 081b Ganoderma applanatum pileus.GAL-BEST.jpg

Fig. 082a Ganoderma tsugae pileus.GAL-BEST1. jpg

Fig. 082b Ganoderma tsugae hymenium. GAL-BEST2.jpg

Fig. 083 004 Inonotus obliquus.jpg

Fig. 084a Laetiporus conifericola.GAL-BEST.JPG

Fig. 084b Laetiporus conifericola.GAL-HABIT.JPG

Fig. 085 Phellinus igniarius.GAL-BEST.jpg

Fig. 086 Phellinus tremulae.GAL-BEST.jpg

Fig. 087 Piptoporus betulinus.GAL-BEST.jpg

Fig. 088 Coriolus [Trametes] versicolor.GAL-BEST.jpg

Fig. 089 Dentinum repandum.GAL-BEST.JPG

Fig. 090 Hericium (ramosum) coralloides. GAL-BEST.JPG

Fig. 091 Hydnellum caeruleum.GAL-BEST.JPG

Fig. 092 Hydnellum peckii.GAL-BEST.tif

Fig. 093 Sarcodon imbricatus.GAL-BEST.jpg

Fig. 094 Clavariadelphus ligula.GAL-BEST.JPG

Fig. 095 Clavariadelphus cf. sachalinensis. C.N.McA-BEST.tif

Fig. 096 Clavariadelphus truncatus.GAL-BEST.JPG

Fig. 097 Clavulina [corralloides] cristata wMycena. GAL-BEST.jpg

Fig. 098 Ramaria formosa.GAL-BEST.jpg

Fig. 099 Multiclavula mucida.GAL-BEST.jpg

Fig. 100 Cantharellus (cibarius) formosis. GAL-BEST.jpg

Fig. 101 Craterellus tubaeformis.GAL-BEST.JPG

Fig. 102 Gomphus clavatus.GAL-BEST.jpg

Fig. 103 Poloyzellus multiplex.GAL-BEST.jpg

Fig. 104 Thelephora terrestris.GAL-BEST.jpg

Fig. 105 Bovista plumbea.GAL-BEST.JPG

Fig. 106 Calvatia booniana.GAL-BEST.jpg

Fig. 107 Geastrum saccatum.GAL-BEST.jpg

Fig. 108a Lycoperdon perlatum.GAL-BEST.JPG

Fig. 108b Lycoperdon perlatum.GAL-MATURE. jpg

Fig. 109 Lycoperdon pyriforme.GAL23572d-BEST.JPG

Fig. 110 Sphaerobolus stellatus.GAL4717-BEST. jpg

Fig. 111 Cyathus olla.GAL-BEST.JPG

Fig. 112 Chrysomyxa arctostaphyli.GAL-BEST.jpg

Fig. 113 Tremella mesenterica.GAL-BEST.jpg

Fig. 114 Bisporella citrina.GAL-BEST.jpg

Fig. 115 Cudonia circinans.GAL-BEST.jpg

Fig. 116 Geopyxis carbonaria.GAL-BEST.jpg

Fig. 117 Gyromytra esculenta.GAL-BEST.jpg

Fig. 118 Gyromytra infula.J.Geml-BEST.jpg

Fig. 119 Helvella elastica.GAL-BEST.jpg

Fig. 120 Hypomyces lactifluorum.GAL-BEST.jpg

Fig. 121 Morchella elata.A. Richardson-BEST.JPG

Fig. 122 Otidea leporina.GAL-BEST.jpg

Fig. 123 Peziza praetervisa.GAL-BEST.jpg

Fig. 124 Peziza [silvestris-sylvestris] arvernensis. GAL-BEST.JPG

Fig. 125 Verpa bohemica v. bohemica.Ana Aguilar-Islas-BEST.jpg

Fig. 126 Neolecta irregularis.GAL-BEST.jpg

Fig. 127 Spathularia flavida.GAL-BEST.jpg

Fig. 128 Hydnotrya tulasnei.GAL-BEST2.JPG

Fig. 129a Geopora cooperi31.jpg

Fig. 129b Geopora cooperi25.jpg

Fig. 130 Elaphomyces muricatus.GAL-BEST.jpg

Fig. 131 Icmadophila ericetorum3.GAL-BEST.jpg

Fig. 132 Peltigera aphthosa1.GAL-BEST.JPG

Fig. 133 Cladina rangiferina.GAL-BEST.jpg

20 Line Drawing Pictorial Glossary Plates in 214 psds & jpgs Figures

Fig. 134a-d Mushroom Reproduction.psd

Fig. 135a-w Cap Morphology.psd

Fig. 136a-v Cap Ornamentation Morphology.psd

Fig. 137a-i Cap Surface Hairiness.psd

Fig. 138a-l Cap Margin Morphology.psd

Fig. 139a-h Pileus Margin Arrangements.psd

Fig. 140a-o Hymenophore (spore-producing surface) Morphology.psd

Fig. 141a-j Hymenophore Morphology: Gill Breadth and Shape.psd

Fig. 142a-j Gill Attachment Morphology.psd

Fig. 143a-g Gill Edge Morphology.psd

Fig. 144a-d Stipe Placement.psd

Fig. 145a-n Stipe and Base Shapes.psd

Fig. 146a-l Stipe Ornamentation.psd

Fig. 147a-g Stipe Bases (volva) Morphology.psd

Fig. 148a-f Stipe Interior Morphology.psd

Fig. 149a-j Partial Veil Arrangements and Remnants.psd

Fig. 150a-p Fungal Spore Morphology and Ornamentation.psd

Fig. 151a-f Basidiomycete (Agaric) Maturation Sequence.psd

Fig. 152a-k Cycles in the Forest: Mycorrhizae, Mycophagy, and Mineralization.jpg

Fig. 153a-d Ascomycete Reproduction.psd

2 Bio/Author Figure jpgs

Fig. 154 GAL-Bio Photo w/Boletus edulis jpg

Fig. 155 NMcA-Bio Photo

AUTHOR BIOGRAPHIES

GARY A. LAURSEN, Ph.D.
Director, High Latitude Mycological Research Institute
Sr. Research Scientist and Adjunct Professor of Biology

Dr. Laursen was trained in the biological sciences at Western Washington University (B.A.-Science, B.A.-Education), University of Montana (M.S.-Botany), and classical taxonomic Mycology at Virginia Tech (Ph.D. at VPI and SU now VT) under the direction of Dr. Orson K. Miller Jr. before coming to Alaska to begin graduate work in 1971 on the higher fungi of high latitude environs. He joined the University of Alaska Fairbanks in 1976 and currently is a Sr. Research Scientist and an Adjunct Professor of Biology. His affliction for mushroom studies have taken him throughout Alaska, the circumpolar Arctic, the circumpolar Subarctic, and the Circumsubpolar Sub-Antarctic Island archipelago. He now directs the High Latitude Mycological Research Institute out of Fairbanks, Alaska, and Anacortes, Washington.

NEIL MCARTHUR grew up in Scotland, Quebec, and western New York, earned a B.Sc. in forestry from Syracuse in 1962, and ran away to Alaska. He worked as naturalist, forester, game biologist, cartographer, greenhouseman, carpenter, and museum facility manager. Neil helped his wife, Harriette Parker, author the 1994 edition of *Alaska's Mushrooms*, and provided most of its photos.